# Children in the Global Sex Trade

# Children in the Global Sex Trade

*Julia O'Connell Davidson*

polity

First published in 2005 by Polity Press Ltd.

Polity Press
65 Bridge Street
Cambridge CB2 1UR, UK.

Polity Press
350 Main Street
Malden, MA 02148, USA

ISBN 0 7456 2927 X
ISBN 0 7456 2928 8 (pb)

A catalogue record for this book is available from the British Library and has been applied for from the Library of Congress.

The publisher has used its best endeavours to ensure that the URLs for external websites referred to in this book are correct and active at the time of going to press. However, the publisher has no responsibility for the websites and can make no guarantee that a site will remain live or that the content is or will remain appropriate.

Typeset in 10.75 on 11 pt Times New Roman
by TechBooks
Printed and bound in Great Britain by MPG Books, Bodmin, Cornwall.

For further information on Polity, visit our website: www.polity.co.uk

# Contents

# Acknowledgements

I have accumulated many debts in the course of researching and writing this book. I am grateful to ECPAT International for funding research that I undertook between 1995 and 1996, with Jacqueline Sánchez Taylor, on the identity, attitudes and motivations of tourists who bought sex from child prostitutes in Latin America, the Caribbean, South Africa and India; to Save the Children Sweden and the NGO Group on the Convention on the Rights of the Child for funding research in 2001 for a theme paper for the Second World Congress Against the Commercial Sexual Exploitation of Children; and to the Economic and Social Research Council of Great Britain for funding a study of tourist-related prostitution in Jamaica and the Dominican Republic, undertaken with Jacqueline Sánchez Taylor (Award no.: R000237625), an ongoing research project, with Bridget Anderson, Esther Bott and Inka Stock, on the markets for migrant sex and domestic workers in Spain and the UK (Award no.: R000239794), and a research seminar series, 'Beyond Contract: Borders, Bodies and Bonds' (Award no.: R451265075) (co-organized with Jacqueline Sánchez Taylor, Bridget Anderson, Laura Brace, Jo Phoenix and Nirmal Puwar); and to the International Institute for the Sociology of Law (IISL), which hosted a workshop on 'Child Abuse and Exploitation: Social, Legal and Political Dilemmas', May 29–30, 2003 (co-organized with Kate Wilson), all of which have contributed enormously to the empirical materials and theoretical arguments presented in this book. I am also intellectually indebted to all those who participated in the 'Beyond Contract' seminar series and who attended the IISL workshop.

Especially warm thanks go to the following people, who – though they may not agree with the arguments put forward in this book – have over the years variously inspired me, supported me and/or supplied me with useful information, contacts and references: Laura Agustín, Alan Aldridge, Rutvica Andrijasevic, Anne Badger, Tricia Barnett, Della Cavner, Roger Cox, Jo Doezema, Ann Gray, Hanne Helth, John Hoffman, Jude Jones, Vernon Jones, June Kane, Liz Kelly, Kamala Kempadoo, Hilary Kinnell, Travis Kong, Anders Lisborg, Sue Parker, Tatania Pishkina, David Prosser, Vanessa Pupavac, Nirmal Puwar, Maia Rusakova, Hélène Sackstein,

Jeremy Seabrook, Karen Stenson, Nick Stevenson, Sun Wen Bin, Patrizia Testaí, Helen Vietch, Tracey Warren, Jackie West, Mel Wraight, and, above all, Esther Bott. I owe a particular debt to Dick Geary, Iman Hashim, Jim Kincaid and Jacqueline Sánchez Taylor, who read draft chapters of this book and gave me encouraging and very helpful feedback. Many thanks also to the anonymous referees who provided detailed comments on a draft manuscript of this book, and to my editor, Emma Longstaff, for her assistance and advice.

Though the weaknesses of this book are entirely my own responsibility, any strengths that may be found in it are certainly a reflection of the theoretical and political insight and intellectual generosity of three people – Ola Florin, Bridget Anderson and Laura Brace. What they have given me in the course of writing this book goes beyond gratitude.

Though it seems a poor reward for all the kindness they have shown me (they deserve something much cheerier), I dedicate this book to those whose affection, care and humour kept me going whilst writing it: Inez Grummitt (light of my life), Laura Brace, Matt Clark, Bridget Anderson, Ola Florin, Esther Bott, Django O'Connell Davidson, June Gregory, Frances Brace, Kayleigh Irwin, and, last but never least, Jacqueline Sánchez Taylor.

# Introduction

The author of a book on children in the global sex trade might reasonably be expected to have some particular and specialist interest in children and childhood. I therefore feel the need to start by confessing that I do not. My interest in children's presence in the sex trade originates in a concern with political, theoretical and empirical questions about sex commerce, and not about children as such. Another confession is that despite – or perhaps because of – my involvement with international policy debates on the commercial sexual exploitation of children (CSEC) over the past nine years,[1] this book is not born of a sense of particular moral or political outrage about children's presence in the global sex trade. I do not mean that I am indifferent to the fate of children who work in prostitution, or who are abused and exploited for purposes of producing pornography, or who have no option but to trade sexual access to their bodies in order to survive on the streets or in refugee camps or in prisons. I am as morally and emotionally moved as the next person by accounts of the horrors that such children endure.

However, I am uncomfortable with what I view as a more general impulse to separate children out as a special case when speaking of economic, social and political problems, as though the only way we can invite people to care about armed conflict or famine or poverty, for example, is by demonstrating the terrible impact these phenomena have on *children*; or as though it is possible to rank human misery, and be somehow less troubled by the fact that adults are sleeping rough, or working in dangerous and exploitative conditions, or being subjected to violence and abuse, than by the fact that children are subject to the same thing. This process of ranking also goes on within our concern for children as a separate and special group, and I am especially troubled by the fact that the idea of child sexual abuse and commercial sexual exploitation carries such enormous charge – the fact that politicians, journalists and ordinary folk not only seem to be unanimous that the sexual use of children is intolerable, but also to wish to loudly and publicly advertise that unanimity, and yet seem so much less eager to publicly deplore the fact that there are children in the world who are malnourished, without access to clean water, dying from preventable diseases, exploited in sweatshops and on plantations, and so on.

The elevation of phenomena such as child prostitution and pornography to a matter of international concern, deserving of two United Nations world congresses and a plethora of new laws and policies, reinforces this sense that the sexual exploitation of children is uniquely terrible. It suggests that while we may be just about able to stomach the idea that children go hungry, or without education, or without medical attention, or labour long hours in appalling conditions, as decent, civilized human beings we cannot possibly accept that a child is at this moment working as a prostitute or being sexually abused for the production of pornography.

I have no wish to contribute to the discourse that constructs CSEC as 'the rape of innocence' or 'innocence destroyed', thereby implying that it is 'innocence', rather than human beings, that needs safeguarding (see Kitzinger, 1997). Indeed, this book is as much concerned to critique that discourse as it is to explore evidence on children's presence in the global sex trade. It therefore begins by asking why it should be that adult–child sexual contact elicits such intense emotions, and why it is that over the past two decades in the West especially we have been urged so insistently to emote about sexual child abuse and exploitation.

Chapter 1 argues that contemporary concerns about sexual child abuse have to be understood against the backcloth of much deeper anxieties about the ordering of social and political relations in late-modern Western societies. In particular, they need to be set against disquiet about contract as the guiding and universal principle of human sociality. For even though contract and contractual relations have been 'held up as moral experiences, the route to self-development and agency' (Brace, 2003, p. 1), the more that contract is universalized, such that every aspect of both men's and women's experience (our 'private' sexual and emotional lives as well as our 'public' political and economic lives) is understood as determined by nothing more than a series of implicit and explicit contracts to which each party freely consents and from which each party may freely withdraw, the more our 'freedom' comes to appear as a burden, a threat to sociality rather than its guarantor. Children, who are socially constructed as beyond or outside contract, promise a refuge from this existential horror, at least so long as we can be certain of their fundamental difference from ourselves. Thus we cherish the innocence, dependency, helplessness and asexuality of 'the child', and rage against 'the paedophile' who defiles it.

The following chapters then explore evidence and debates on child prostitution, 'trafficked' and migrant children's presence in prostitution, paedophilia and child pornography, and 'child sex tourism'. The boundary troubles presented by the categories used to 'make sense' of these phenomena are a recurring theme. So, for example, whilst those who campaign against CSEC follow the United Nations' Convention on the Rights of the Child in defining children as persons under the age of 18, and insist on a firm line of demarcation between adult and child prostitution, this conceptual boundary does not reflect the realities of sex commerce in the contemporary world. Those aged above and below 18 often work alongside each other, in the same conditions, serving the same clients. Moreover, the same structural factors can underpin both adults' and children's entry into the sex trade and make them vulnerable within it (poverty, uneven economic development, social exclusion, drug addiction, racism, domestic violence, homophobia, and so on). Why limit our concern to persons under the age of 18?

The answer, according to liberal feminists as well as to people involved in campaigns against CSEC, is that adults are in a position to make choices, whereas children are incapable of making an informed decision about whether or not to trade sex. Yet this is to assume that the social categories 'adult' and 'child' refer to monolithic, homogeneous groups, and so to overlook the realities of many people's lived experience. A crack-addicted 38-year-old is not necessarily better positioned than a non-drug-using 17-year-old to make choices about prostitution, and equally we should recognize that some children (even quite young children), like some adults, are faced with such a forlorn set of alternatives that they can and do decide that selling sex is their least-worst option. Furthermore, people below as well as above the age of 18 can and do make strategic use of the exchange value that attaches to sex in pursuit of certain goals (such as day-to-day survival, migration to a safer or more affluent country, increased status and respect in one's own community, social mobility, independence from unsatisfactory parents or husbands, escape from institutional care).

The idea of a sharp and meaningful line between adult and child prostitution is strongly challenged by feminists who campaign for the abolition of prostitution. They argue that *all* sex commerce is an expression of patriarchal power relations, a form of male violence, and a violation of fundamental human rights to dignity and bodily integrity; *all* women and children who prostitute are victims of sexual slavery (for instance, Barry, 1995; Jeffreys, 1997; Hughes, 2000). However, this position is based on an equally problematic disregard for the diverse and complex realities of the lives of those who trade sex in the contemporary world, as well as on the ethically dubious assumption that those who are *treated* as objects by others actually *are* evacuated of all capacity for autonomy and agency.

This book is concerned to deconstruct the presumed boundary between adults and children in the sex trade, but not in order to insist that all those who trade sex should be treated as one homogeneous group. Rather, my hope is that by exploring the nature, causes and meaning of diversity in children's experiences of sexual oppression, abuse and exploitation, and looking at parallels between the experiences of some adults and some children, I can convince readers that we need to tell more complicated stories about the global sex trade than those that are currently popularized in much media coverage, campaigning literature and academic treatments of the topic. In particular, I hope to persuade readers of the need for stories that recognize the very real differences between human beings in terms of their capacity for self-protection and autonomy, and the extent and severity of the abuse and exploitation to which people (adult as well as child) can be subject within the global sex trade, but that do not insist on a cast-list consisting only of paedophile monsters and innocent children, or of slaves, sinners and saviours.

# 1  Beyond Contract?

## Dualist Legacies, Late-Modern Anxieties and the Sanctity of the Child

The sexual abuse of children has been the focus of much attention and great anxiety in Western societies over the past twenty-odd years, and two features of the discourse that surrounds the phenomenon are particularly noteworthy. First of all, there is an extremely high level of consensus about the wrongness of sexual contact between adults and children and an acceptance, even an expectation, that such contact will inspire intense and violent emotions. Where popular opinion is divided on adults who smack and otherwise physically chastise children in their care, there is virtually unanimous condemnation of adults who use children for their own sexual gratification. People speak of feeling physically sickened by media coverage of cases of child sexual abuse, and 'the paedophile' is one of the most loathed and feared figures in the contemporary Western world. On a number of recent occasions in Britain and the United States, otherwise ordinary, decent, law-abiding folk have come together as angry mobs, either gathering outside courts to shriek abuse and threaten to lynch men on trial for sexual murders of children, or attacking the homes of men who are so much as suspected of having a record of sexual offending against children. Many feel that no punishment can ever be enough for these monstrous perverts. As a leader article in a popular British tabloid recently put it, 'The law must have an iron fist to smash those who prey on children' (*The Sun*, 12 August 2003, p. 8).

The belief that children are harmed by sexual abuse is not enough, in itself, to explain the ferocity and turbulence of the emotions it arouses. There are many other ways in which children's lives can be blighted, even ended, none of which carry quite the same emotional charge. If a child is killed or maimed in a drink- or careless-driving traffic accident, people are often angry as well as saddened, but 'drink drivers' and 'dangerous drivers' are not socially constructed as icons of evil, even though they are certainly responsible for many, many more child deaths in any given year than are paedophiles.[1] And even if we turn to cases involving the deliberate harming of children's bodies by adults, responses differ according to whether the child's body has been violated for sexual purposes or for other reasons. Consider, for example, the differential response to child-killing by parents and the sexual murder of children by strangers. In Britain, the latter attracts intense media and public interest, and can dominate the news for periods of days or even weeks, yet when a child is murdered by his own parents or guardians, it rarely makes national news headlines. This is reflected in the processing of such cases within the criminal justice system. In the three years up to December 2000, police in England and Wales dealt with 492 cases – more than three per week – in which children under the age of 10 had been killed by parents or carers. In 61 per cent of cases, no charge was brought, and only 27 per cent ended in conviction, compared with 90 per cent in which a child was killed by a stranger (Dyer, 2002). Again, most people are dismayed by the idea of children dying as a result of parental brutality or neglect, but the horror inspired by such cases is rarely of the same proportions or intensity as the horror inspired by sexual attacks on children.

Or consider the fact that over five million of the world's children per year 'die from illnesses and other conditions caused by the environments in which they live, learn and play' (WHO, 2003). Diarrhoea, caused by lack of access to a clean water supply, is thought to account for 12 per cent of deaths of children aged under 5 in developing countries; malaria kills approximately one million children per year, mostly in sub-Saharan Africa (WHO, 2003). Children in at least sixty-eight countries are at risk from land-mines contaminating the land they live on – Angola, for instance, 'has an estimated 10 million land-mines and an amputee population of 70,000, of whom 8,000 are children' (UNICEF, 2003). Some 300,000 children are believed to be serving as soldiers in current armed conflicts (CSC, 2001), and amongst the estimated 250 million working children between the ages of 5 and 14, there are thought to be over 50 million children aged between 5 and 11 working in hazardous circumstances (ILO, 1996). Such statistics are widely reported in the West, and further publicized by charitable organizations. Most Westerners thus know, even if only in the most general of terms, that vast numbers of the world's children live and die in wretched and miserable circumstances. When forced to think about this reality, many people – probably the majority – are emotionally moved. They are saddened, and often express feelings of helplessness (they would like to help in some way, but the problem is overwhelming) and/or wish to donate money or time to charities that seek to alleviate children's suffering. But few people would describe themselves as *revolted* by the knowledge that at this moment a child is dying from hunger or preventable disease, or undertaking hazardous and back-breaking labour.

Similarly, when cases are brought to light in which adults have forced children to beg, steal, act as drugs mules or as unpaid servants, the adults involved certainly become objects of moral opprobrium. And yet it would be surprising to hear someone say that he retches when he reads about these forms of abuse and exploitation, or that she would gladly throw the switch to electrocute any adult who had exploited a child domestic worker, for example. But such sentiments are often voiced in relation to cases of sexual child abuse. (By contrast, when Tony Martin, a British man who shot and killed a 16-year-old boy who was burgling his home in 1999, was given a life sentence for murder, many people described the verdict as 'monstrous'. Martin received thousands of supportive letters in prison, and his recent parole after less than three years' imprisonment has been heralded by his supporters as a victory for commonsense, and a reassertion of the right to defend private property. Interestingly, Martin's appeal against the verdict rested in part on the claim that he suffered from a personality disorder which diminished his responsibility, and which was linked to his experience of sexual abuse as a child: BBC News online, 2003.)

The idea of adult–child sexual contact appears to evoke something more than sorrow, consternation and indignation, then. It also arouses disgust. Indeed, the disgust it stirs is potentially so all-consuming that the victim as well as the perpetrator can be enveloped in it. Thus, children who have been sexually abused sometimes find themselves ostracized or rejected instead of comforted by parents, family or community. Meanwhile, those who have experienced sexual abuse in childhood often report strong and violent emotions not simply or necessarily about their abuser, but more particularly about themselves – all too frequently, they are dogged by feelings of self-disgust, self-loathing, self-contempt. The fact that adult–child sexual contact inspires such disgust should alert us to its political import, for, as William Miller has observed:

> Some emotions, among which disgust and its close cousin contempt are the most prominent, have intensely political significance. They work to hierarchize our political order: in some settings they do the work of maintaining hierarchy; in other settings they constitute righteously presented claims for superiority; in yet other settings they are themselves elicited as an indication of one's proper placement in the social order. Disgust evaluates (negatively) what it touches, proclaims the meanness and inferiority of its object. (1997, p. 9)

In other words, the social emotions that attach to the sexual abuse of children in contemporary Western societies tell us as much, if not more, about the hierarchies we hold dear as they tell us about the value we place on protecting the vulnerable and defenceless in our midst.

A second important point to note about late twentieth- and early twenty-first-century Western discourse on the sexual abuse of children is that it constructs sexual child abuse as a problem that is rapidly growing, all-pervasive and also insoluble. Chris Jenks observes that 'child abuse is not an original event, there has never been a historical period nor a particular society in which children were not exploited, sexually molested and subjected to physical and psychological violence' (1996, p. 92), and although the reporting of sexual child abuse has increased dramatically in recent years, there is no real way to support the claim that the incidence of such abuse has grown. However, academic, policy and professional interest in child abuse in general and sexual child abuse in particular has expanded rapidly in the West over the past twenty or so years. Indeed, the latter has now become big business for 'academics, for publishing, for mental health (treatment and recovery) services' (Itzin, 2000, p. 2). It has also become big media business, for it seems that despite finding the idea of adult–child sexual contact horrible and disgusting (or more likely *because* it disgusts), the general public has an almost insatiable appetite for tales about the sexual abuse of children.

The stories that are told and retold in newspapers, magazines and books, as well as on talk shows and in soap operas, to satisfy this appetite in the USA have been very elegantly deconstructed by James Kincaid (1998), and his analysis can equally be applied to popular narratives of child molesting in Canada, Australia and Western European countries. Scandal after scandal and revelation after revelation construct a tale in which child molesters are almost everywhere – on street corners and in playgrounds, in schools and nurseries, amusement arcades, scout camps, churches, even in Disneyland – and have molested almost everyone from the most famous of film stars through to the woman next door. Such stories also dwell on the consequences of sexual child abuse for the victim, cataloguing the many and various ways in which the damage done may manifest itself, so that virtually any social or emotional ill or dysfunction becomes explicable through reference to abuse. These are stories about an epidemic of child molesting, a terror lurking in every nook and cranny, a horror that touches all of us, and there is 'no solution and no ending' to this narrative (Kincaid, 1998, p. 10). We become more vigilant, and invest more in policing the 'paedophiles' and 'perverts' who threaten our children, only to discover that the problem is even more extensive than we had previously realized (Kincaid, 1998).

Campaigns against the commercial sexual exploitation of children, which gathered steam during the 1990s, were shaped by and also helped to reinforce these narratives of child molesting. Just as child abuse is not an original event, so we can say that there is nothing new about the 'commercial sexual exploitation of children' (CSEC) except the term itself. Where prostitution has existed, so too has what would now be deemed 'child prostitution', and for as long as people have been taking erotic photographs of adults, they have also been producing 'child pornography'. As with child abuse more generally, it would be virtually impossible to produce empirical evidence either to support or to refute the claim that more children are commercially sexually exploited today than ever before, or indeed to measure the extent of the phenomenon in the contemporary world. And yet it is widely believed that CSEC is a huge and growing problem. Its supposed exponential growth represents, according to campaigners, the dark side of globalization and recent technological advances, and adds another layer of horror to the sexual abuse of children: the idea that there are people who profit from promoting and organizing 'the most abhorrent of crimes – sexual molestation of children' (ECPAT, 1996, p. 10).

CSEC, we are told, 'is a form of violence against the child which amounts to forced labour and a contemporary form of slavery' (ECPAT, 1999, p. 7), and in tales of CSEC, the cast-list of evil-doers is longer still than in stories of non-commercial child molesting. The paedophiles and perverts who abuse children are joined by mafia thugs and other hardened criminals, by callous parents who sell their children into sexual slavery in order to finance the purchase of satellite television, by 'intermediaries, pimps and sometimes even corrupt local authorities earning big money from this life-long psychological and physical injury of children' (Lindgren, 1996, p. 3). And the fate of the victims is even more emphatically sealed. Campaigners tell us that commercially sexually exploited children are often 'so severely injured that it is not possible to rehabilitate them to a normal life. Most children who end up in the sex industry are also soon infected with HIV/Aids or other illnesses and die before they are adults' (Radda Barnen, 1996, p. 16). Indeed, the centrality of this particular story-line to campaigns against CSEC is well illustrated by the fact that all delegates to the First World Congress Against the Commercial Sexual Exploitation of Children in Stockholm, 1996, were given a copy of a book titled *Rosario is Dead* (Axelsson, 1996), which recounts the story a Filipino child who died as a result of sexual abuse at the hands of a tourist client. The same themes are picked up and reworked by journalists. Heather Montgomery cites two newspaper articles detailing the experience of children sold into prostitution in Thai brothels by their parents, then 'rescued by good outsiders for a brief period of happiness before dying' (2001, p. 23). She continues:

> In countless other articles, the pattern is repeated: betrayal, abuse, rescue, death. There is a neatness and coherence to this story which is compelling; no loose ends and a predictable outcome. The reader is invited to be outraged at the story, and to pity the victims, but ultimately, there is no escape from the plot and nothing that can be done to help these children. Once the story begins, it can only end, unhappily ever after, with the child's death. (2001, p. 23)

And again, the struggle against those who would prey on children is one of epic proportions, not least because they are at the same time everywhere and nowhere. One moment 'the sex exploiter' appears as an unimaginable fiend, the next as the most ordinary of men, or the most prominent of citizens. As with narratives about non-commercial sexual child abuse, we are presented with a paradox: sexual interest in children is monstrous and unthinkable and yet at the same time rampant; only the most depraved of perverts could wish to use child prostitutes or child pornography, and yet there is a huge and growing market for children's bodies. As Kincaid remarks:

> The story is, in short, cagily baited, mysterious, self-perpetuating, inescapable. It is a story of monsters and purity, sunshine and darkness, of being chased by the beast and finding your feet in glue, of tunnels opening onto other tunnels, of exits leading to dead walls. Our story of child molesting is a story of nightmare, the literary territory of the Gothic. On the face of it, the Gothic is not a promising form for casting social problems. Instead of offering solutions, such tales tend to paralyse; they do not move forward but circle back to one more hopeless encounter with the demon. Why would we want that? (1998, p. 10)

Jenks' (1996) discussion of the mythology of child abuse addresses a similar question. In using the term 'mythology' and talking about the stories that are told about child molesting, neither author seeks to deny or minimize the fact of abuse. What they draw attention to, however, is that child abuse is simultaneously real and 'a device for constituting a reality' (Jenks, 1996, p. 98), and that the stories that we tell about child molesting are not merely factual accounts of specific instances of abuse. These narratives also serve a wider purpose, telling us what it means to be an Adult, what it means to be a Child, and what it is that endangers these social categories. They thus help us to 'make sense' of ourselves, the social world we inhabit, and perceived threats to our social connections. A key sociological question thus becomes, 'Why has child abuse recently become "a way of making sense" of such vivid dimensions?' (Jenks, 1996, p. 98). How can we explain the strong current appetite for tales of child abuse? What is going on that we are so eager to be reminded what it means to be Adult or Child, and how do stories about an epidemic of child molesting and about CSEC as 'modern slavery' speak to contemporary anxieties about social identities and connections?

  I want to address these questions first by thinking in more general terms about the way in which the relationship between individual and society has been imagined in dominant post-Enlightenment Western thought, and exploring threats to this framework for interpreting the social in late-modern Western societies. Following Jenks (1996), I will then argue that in the uncertain ethical landscape we currently occupy, 'children' and 'childhood' have assumed enormous significance. Collectively and individually, we look to 'the Child' to give meaning and coherence to our lives, to tell us who we are and what we hold dear, to provide a bulwark against the encroaching tides of change, and to reassure us that at least *some* of our social connections are fixed, indissoluble and beyond contract. But children only provide us such reassurance so long as we can be certain of their fundamental difference from ourselves. Thus we insist upon the innocence, dependency, helplessness and asexuality of 'the child', and dread the 'paedophiles' (and other assorted monsters) who would defile it.

## Modernity, Contract and the Public/Private Binary

In contemporary Western societies, the dominant conceptual framework used to make sense of relations of power and dependency is still powerfully shaped by a tradition of liberal political thought that dates back some three hundred years, and that accords a fundamental role to contract and contractual relations in the management of our political and economic lives. This is a theoretical tradition within which modernity implies a radical disjuncture with a past where the mass of ordinary people were subject to the paternal rule of kings, chieftains, patricians, lords, masters, and so on; a past in which one's position in the social order, and with it one's rights, duties and responsibilities, was fixed at birth; a past in which individual economic action was fettered by a plethora of customary rules and regulations designed to preserve the existing status quo. Modern society, by contrast, is held to have its roots in a social contract that guarantees people both political and economic freedom. Though this notion of a 'social contract' is complex and contested even within liberal theory, the basic idea is that in modern capitalist democracies, each person is born free and equal and equipped with certain natural rights. However, our reason tells us it is in our best interest to make a pact, or contract, with other members of society to surrender political authority to a state that will act on every person's behalf. The state is thus the amalgamation of individual wills, and creates a framework that protects the natural rights of all individuals. The individual citizen has duties of citizenship, but these are based on consent (rather than superstition, or blind deference to, or fear of, an absolute authority), and each citizen enjoys equal, civil freedom.

Classical social contract theory of the seventeenth and eighteenth centuries paved the way for contract to be more generally celebrated as the principal basis for human association in modern, free societies. It provided a way in which

> to think about society as a series of explicit and implicit contracts which its members make with each other, and to define the essence of a just society as one whose members were free to make whatever contracts they wished with each other, as opposed to earlier forms of society in which people inherited or were ascribed a fixed *status* defined by their kinship. This led to the idea that people had an implicit contract with themselves; they owned their selves as property over which they therefore exercised control, and aspects of which they could lend or hire out to others. (MacInnes, 1998, pp. 5–6)

It is not difficult to see how liberal commentators move from here to the assertion that capitalism and political freedom go hand in hand (see, for example, Friedman, 1962). In modern capitalist societies, no one is born to serve or to rule; no king, lord or despot has a customary right to direct or consume the labour of his God-given inferiors. Instead, individuals are all constructed as civil equals, and are free to sell their labour or the products of their labour to the highest bidder. The story of freedom through contract, which 'makes sense of' economic and political arrangements in liberal capitalist democracies, is one of Western societies' most important and popular myths (Pateman, 1988).

It is also a story that both reflects and reinforces a more general tendency within Western post-Enlightenment thought to conceive of social and political reality in terms of binaries or dualisms, a tendency that has recently been powerfully critiqued by feminist theorists. A central element of modern Western 'dichotomous thinking' (Prokhovnic, 1999) concerns the idea of a fundamental split between what are imagined as the 'public' realm of political, civil and economic life and the 'private' realm of the household and family. Indeed, the whole notion of modernity 'as the outcome of a break, as a radical contrast with what preceded it' (Cavarero, 1992, p. 32) rests crucially upon this dichotomy, for the newness of 'modernity' is invariably discovered, defined and explained within what is constructed as the 'public' sphere. Since women have historically been excluded from this realm, typologies and theories developed on the basis of past/present and private/public dualisms tend to produce highly gendered accounts of social and political developments (Sayer, 1991).

Certainly, if attention is focused on the civil and legal position of women (especially that of married women) in eighteenth- and nineteenth-century Western societies, the newness of modernity is not immediately apparent. Throughout most of the nineteenth century in Britain, for example, 'the legal and civil position of a wife resembled that of a slave', for the wife had no independent legal existence (Pateman, 1988, p. 119). She lived under the 'cover' of her husband, who had a right to his wife's obedience and her labour, a claim that was legally enforceable by violence. Wives could even be sold by husbands at public auction. Thus, in her groundbreaking book *The Sexual Contract*, Carole Pateman argues that social contract theorists told only half the story that explains 'the binding authority of the state and civil law', and 'the legitimacy of modern civil government' (1988, p. 1). Behind the story of the social contract is that of the sexual contract, and while

> The social contract is a story of freedom, the sexual contract is a story of subjection . . . the character of civil freedom cannot be understood without the missing half of the story that reveals how men's patriarchal right over women is established through contract. Civil freedom is not universal. Civil freedom is a masculine attribute and depends upon patriarchal right. (Pateman, 1988, p. 2)

The story of freedom through contract does not, then, describe a straightforward shift from tyranny to universal political freedom. Rather it is a tale about hegemonic power relations being transformed from a patriarchy within which the father (or king as a father figure) exercised paternal rule over both women and other men, 'to a fraternity, in which men get the right to rule over their women in the private, domestic sphere, but agree on a contract of social order of equality among themselves within the public, political sphere' (Yuval-Davis, 1997, p. 79). Civil and legal freedom and formal citizenship were initially granted not to individuals, but to *men* 'in their capacity as members and representatives of a family (i.e, a group of non-citizens)' (Vogel, 1989, p. 2, cited in Yuval-Davis, 1997, p. 79). The 'abstract individual' with entitlement to universal rights and freedoms and the capacity to contract was adult and male, with attributes deemed 'masculine' – women and children were lumped together and excluded from full citizenship. Thus, the concept of citizenship mapped onto a series of dualisms that are both gendered and aged (see below).

The tension between liberalism's ideal of universal civil freedom and the blunt and highly visible facts of women's political subordination to men in modern societies is not a recent discovery or preoccupation.[2] The classic, but always somewhat precarious, solution has been to explain it as a reflection of natural differences between men and women, in particular, as an expression of their 'sexual difference'. Indeed, women's sexual difference has long been taken as a central, defining feature of their Otherness. All the myriad ways in which men and women are the same as physical, embodied, 'object-beings' (the fact that we all need to eat, drink, sleep, expel bodily wastes, that we all age, are all at risk of disease, and so on) count for nothing against the difference between men and women in terms of their roles in biological reproduction. It is women's reproductive capacities that are held to root them in, and make them incapable of transcending, nature; it is through reference to their sexual difference (and all that is imagined to follow from it, such as a capacity to nurture and care for others) that women are defined as objects, rather than fully autonomous, sovereign subjects. In this sense, the subject–object binary is

| Public, adult male, citizen | Private, female/child, non-citizen |
|---|---|
| Abstract, disembodied, mind | Particular, embodied, rooted in nature |
| Rational, able to apply dispassionate reason and standards of justice | Emotional, irrational, subject to desire and passion; unable to apply standards of justice |
| Impartial, concerned with public interest | Partial, preoccupied with private, domestic concerns |
| Independent, active, heroic and strong | Dependent, passive, weak |
| Able to contract | Unable to contract |
| **Subject** | **Object** |

*Source:* Adapted from Lister, 1997, p. 69.

foundational to the list of dualisms shown here (Beauvoir, 1972, [1949], p. 29; Dickenson, 1997).

And yet despite their Otherness, women have never been *completely* excluded from 'civil society'. Though constructed as men's subordinates in the private sphere, and denied equality in the public sphere of economic and political life, women have none the less always been understood to have a political contribution to make and a political duty to perform. And paradoxically, 'Their political duty (like their exclusion from citizenship) derives from their difference from men, notably their capacity for mother-hood' (Pateman, 1992, p. 19). The contradiction of women's simultaneous inclusion within and exclusion from the political community on grounds of their sexual difference has long posed difficulties for feminist political strategy. What Pateman terms 'Wollstonecraft's dilemma' (because Mary Wollstonecraft argued both for equality for women *and* the recognition of women's difference) remains a very real problem for feminists:

> to demand 'equality' is to strive for equality with men (to call for the 'rights of men and citizens' to be extended to women), which means that women must become (like) men ... [But] to insist, like some con-temporary feminists, that women's distinctive attributes, capacities and activities be revalued and treated as a contribution to citizenship is to demand the impossible; such 'difference' is precisely what patriarchal citizenship excludes. (Pateman, 1992, p. 20)

## The Pursuit of Equality and Late-Modern Anxieties

Feminist struggles for formal 'equality' made great headway in the West-ern world throughout the twentieth century, and for the purposes of this chapter, the important point to note is that as women have gradually won the rights of men and citizens, so the problem of equality versus difference has increasingly become an issue for mainstream social and political the-orists, as well as for politicians, policy-makers, journalists and 'ordinary' people. In popular discourse, the dilemma does not normally appear as a problem of feminist political strategy, of course, but more as a set of anxieties about the ordering of the 'private' sphere. So, for example, there is much ado about how to balance women's rights to equal standing in the public sphere against their supposed right to express, enjoy and be recog-nized for their 'essential' womanhood (again generally understood as their capacity for motherhood).[3] And there is unease about whether, if women are successful in their pursuit of equality with men, they will continue to fulfil their historic roles as child-bearers and -carers. What will happen if, as independent, solitary individuals, as full subjects, they choose not to have children, or not to perform the domestic and caring labour that is so essential to the reproduction of citizens, workers and society? The falling birth rate in most Western societies since the end of the twentieth century, aligned with questions about who is going to care for their ageing populations, provides grist for these fears.

The increasing recognition of women as subjects generates another set of anxieties about the reproduction of community, for women's sexual difference has also traditionally been the key to maintaining the boundaries of community in the sense that, as objects of exchange between men, women have served to reproduce social links between the male members of the community. Following Lévi-Strauss (1971), Gayle Rubin observes that 'marriages are a most basic form of gift exchange, in which it is women who are the most precious of gifts' (1997, p. 36), and that 'If it is women who are being transacted, then it is the men who give and take them who are linked, the woman being a conduit of a relationship rather than a partner to it' (1997, p. 37). Such traditions were not immediately abandoned with the advent of 'modernity'; indeed, marriage has continued to represent an important means through which men forge social linkages with other men in modern Western liberal societies. And even today, vestiges of the traditional gift exchange persist (for instance, in the custom that dictates that the father 'gives away' the bride, and that upon marriage, the woman surrenders her father's name and takes on that of her new 'master').

The more that liberal principles of equality and self-ownership are applied to men and women alike, and gender equality is realized in the 'public' realm of economic and political life, the more that women are in a position to refuse their traditional position as 'gifts' and to do as they please with their sexuality. And freed from their economic dependence on and political subordination to men, what guarantee is there that women will choose to reproduce the existing boundaries and relations of community (see Chow, 1999)? What if women stop subordinating their sexuality to socially generative ends? As shown by the huge amount of air-time and print devoted to the social problem supposedly represented by rising divorce rates and the impermanence of marriage-like relationships in contemporary Western societies, these kinds of questions do actually worry many people.

This connects to another set of late-modern anxieties about the ordering of relations between men and women in the 'private' realm. So long as men and women are imagined as entirely different in terms of their essential natures and physical, emotional and intellectual capacities, then it is possible to interpret traditional sex roles within the home as symbiotic, as an expression of mutual dependence, rather than as hierarchical. Thus, difference has not always appeared as inequality, even when it involves palpable asymmetries of power. Indeed, in the nineteenth century, there was a sustained attempt to frame the wife's subordination to her husband in terms of 'ethical love and equal dignity' (Vogel, 2000, p. 182). Despite the more general shift from sacrament to contract (such that relations of power and dependency in society as a whole were no longer viewed as God-given), marriage 'remained embedded in the religious framework that tied the rights and duties of married men and women to procreation' (Brace, 2003, p. 3). And in this sense, 'The civil sacredness of marriage created a terrain where modern society was protected against the disruptive forces of modernity' (Vogel, 2000, p. 195).

Marriage may have appeared increasingly less sacred through the twentieth century, but the husband's authority and the wife's subjection continued to be popularly understood as a form of mutuality rather than a relation of domination. In the conventional nuclear family of the 1950s, 1960s and 1970s (and perhaps beyond?), the rights and freedoms enjoyed by men were not generally socially and cognitively interpreted as oppressive to women. Men's power in the household was humanized and justified through appeal to the story of sexual difference (authority falls to the man because he is by nature more able, rational and worldly-wise), rather than denied and concealed by the fiction of contract. Interpreted as such, it posed no threat to the permanency of marriage or the social connections established through it – women did not, on the whole, leave their husbands because they failed to take on an equal share of household or child-care tasks, or because their husbands made financial and other decisions without fully consulting them.

But as women are increasingly incorporated into civil society as men's equals, so this strategy for establishing enduring social connections appears increasingly fragile. What will happen if the logic of gender egalitarianism in the public sphere is extended to the private realm? How are men going to know that they are men, and women that they are women, if there is no division of labour by gender, and if men no longer exercise authority over weaker, less rational wives or partners (if men no longer 'wear the trousers' in their households)? And if the sameness of men and women, rather than their difference, becomes more visible and more significant for the day-to-day management and ordering of the private sphere, such that men and women are equally responsible for all the tasks necessary to the daily reproduction of households, and carry equal authority, how can a state of reciprocal dependency be ensured? What is there left to protect us from modernity's disruptive forces?

Such anxieties became so central and compelling in the 1990s that even the most mainstream of sociologists began to concern themselves with them. So, for example, Anthony Giddens' (1992) book *The Transformation of Intimacy* addresses questions about the 'democratization' of sexual relationships, arguing that the values that inform the public realm in liberal democracies can be, are being, and should be extended to relationships in the private sphere. And in prescribing and celebrating intimacy as democracy, involving 'pure' relationships based on equality, autonomy, respect, trust, openness, accountability, and so on, Giddens is effectively arguing that contract should become the principle of human association in the private as well as the public realm:

> A pure relationship... refers to a situation where a social relation is entered into for its own sake, for what can be derived by each person from a sustained association with another; and which is continued only in so far as it is thought by both parties to deliver enough satisfactions for each individual to stay within it. (1992, p. 58)

All relationships which approximate to the pure form maintain an implicit 'rolling contract' to which appeal may be made by either partner when situations arise felt to be unfair or oppressive. The rolling contract is a constitutional device which underlies, but is also open to negotiation through, open discussion by partners about the nature of the relationship. (p. 192)

But the 'pure' relationship, it seems, necessarily offers only an insecure connection between people, for its 'purity' lies in the fact that each party is in a position to freely retract from it. And without faith in a reciprocal dependency between men and women decreed by God or fixed by nature, what is there to bind them together and ensure that they contribute to the stability and future of society? If contract comes to replace status in the private domain of our sexual and family lives, what is to prevent the private from mirroring the public realm, which is to say, what is to stop it from fragmenting into a multitude of atomized, self-seeking, solitary individuals, thinking only of their own individual rights and pleasures, pursuing only their own personal advantage?

The apprehensions discussed here are, it seems to me, the inevitable outcome of the tension between the two halves of the myth that is fundamental to making sense of relations of power and dependency in Western liberal democracies, namely the stories of the social and the sexual contracts. Followed to its conclusion, the logic of the story of civil equality and freedom through contract undermines the sexual contract, and without the sexual contract, the social contract becomes a frail and precarious basis for sociality. For the more that society is imagined as founded in nothing other than a series of explicit and implicit contracts which its members freely make and from which they can freely withdraw, the more 'the individual witnesses a diminution of their points of attachment to a collective life, or at best a recognition of the utterly transitory nature of such points of attachment' (Jenks, 1996, p. 110). And the more that individuals are severed from the security of faith in permanent, collective attachments, experiencing themselves as, precisely, *individuals*, the greater their existential angst. Thus, in contemporary Western societies, people's consciousness of themselves as authors of their own destiny weighs heavily upon them – we have to choose how we live and take responsibility for it, 'knowing that as mortal beings, our choices are always limited and disappointing, that our awareness of and control over ourselves can never be complete, and that one day our bodies will die' (MacInnes, 1998, p. 13).

## The Sanctity of the Child

Where can we turn for release from the predicament outlined above? One solution is, as Laura Brace points out, to fetishize children:

since the nineteenth century, as we have accepted an increasingly contractual and civil, and so less sacred, version of marriage, we have displaced something of this sacredness onto children, and it is they who
are expected to protect us against the disruptive forces of modernity.
They are, for example, expected to act as points of connection between
otherwise atomized, separate and isolated individuals. Children are vital
to many people's sense of community and connection, and they often
act as conduits for collective concerns. (2003, p. 3)

Children are the 'gift' that couples can give to each other in order to secure
their own relationship as well as to establish social links with each other's
kin. Children are also vehicles for other social relations, for parenthood
both demands and permits forms of ethical integration into civil society
that are not generally open to non-parents. Indeed, parenthood offers a
veritable host of points of attachment to collective life and experience, especially to those who are relatively affluent.[4] In the context of the growing
anxiety about our connections to each other and to society as a whole, children have assumed immense significance. 'The child is the source of the
last remaining, irrevocable, unexchangeable primary relationship. Partners come and go. The child stays' (Beck, 1992, p. 118), and 'The trust
that was previously anticipated from marriage, partnership, friendship,
class solidarity and so on, is now invested more generally in the child'
(Jenks, 1996, p. 107). Children and childhood are 're-enchanted', and
become the 'sustainable, reliable, trustworthy' repositories of 'the now
outmoded treasury of social sentiments that they have come to represent'
(Jenks, 1996, p. 108).

However, and it is a very important proviso, children can only serve
this function and protect us from the spectre of atomization, separation
and loneliness because their social relations with us and ours with them
are imagined as founded on something other than explicit or implicit contracts. Indeed, though Giddens asserts that the emergence of the 'pure
relationship' holds the promise of democracy not only in the area of sexuality but also in those of parent–child relations, he does not, one assumes,
intend to suggest that a new-born baby could enter into a social relation
with its parents 'for its own sake, for what can be derived by each person
from a sustained association with another' (1992, p. 188), or to recom-
mend that a parent should continue her or his relationship with a young
child only in so far as the relationship is thought to deliver enough satisfaction to the parent to stay within it (i.e. enter into what he has defined
as a 'pure relationship', p. 58). Aligned to this (and central to the perception of children's *commercial* sexual exploitation as uniquely horrifying),
children can act as repositories for sentiments such as altruism and care
because they are excluded from, and deemed incapable of, participation
in the market. For if children are unable to enter into market relations of
exchange, if they depend on us to mediate those relations for them, then
we cannot approach our relationships with them in the same way that we
approach our relationships with other adults.

It is children's dependency on adults, and adults' corresponding duty of care towards them, that turns parenthood into a moral domain, and makes it possible for children to serve as points of connection between otherwise solitary individuals. There is no 'rolling contract' to which parents can appeal when they feel oppressed by their baby's nocturnal wakefulness, their toddler's temper tantrums, their youngster's incessant questions – after all, the child did not ask to be born. And no matter how unruly, petulant or otherwise disappointing a child proves to be, a parent cannot simply cease to feed, clothe and house her. If a parent cannot just withdraw from her or his relationship with a child, neither can the social links established through that relationship be simply terminated at whim. Children's 'quasi-mystical power of social linkage'[5] thus rests crucially upon their dependency, and this is of enormous significance for contemporary Western discourse on child sexual abuse and exploitation.

## Connections Imperilled

If our relationships with children are imagined to anchor us in a natural, fixed and certain moral and social realm because, unlike any of our other relationships, they are not governed by implicit or explicit contracts, then we *need* children to be unlike us. This helps to explain why, in contemporary Western societies, the social categories of 'Child' and 'Adult' are discursively constructed 'by reference to one another, so that we know what it is to be a Child because it is to be Other than Adult, and vice versa' (Ribbens McCarthy et al., 2000, p. 787). In particular, being a child means 'not being rational, mature and independent; not possessing rational autonomy' (Brace, 2003, p. 1), and so being incapable of contracting. Imputing these qualities to children confers on adults not a 'right' in the modern liberal sense, but a duty, to exercise particular kinds of authority over them. In modern Western societies, asymmetries of power that exist between other social groups (employers and workers, men and women, white and black, for example) are increasingly denied or concealed behind the fiction of contract and civil equality (see Patterson, 1982). But no attempt is made to hide the ties of personal dependence between children and their carers, or to camouflage the vastly asymmetrical power relations that exist between children and adults. And where in contemporary Western democracies, husbands can no longer demand obedience from wives, and white people can no longer demand that black people show them deference and respect, adults still generally expect that children will obey them, defer to them and respect them simply on the basis of their status as adults.

Yet the powers adults (neighbours, bus drivers, librarians, shop-keepers, and so on, as well as parents, other adult relatives and teachers) exercise over children are rarely considered oppressive. Instead they are viewed as desirable, necessary and humane, and this is not least because although children are constructed as 'not-adults', it is recognized that they will eventually develop into adults. Adults only claim temporary authority over children, and they exercise this authority in the children's interests – to protect them from themselves and others, and to ensure that they develop the qualities necessary to their future existence as adults. This model of adults' power over children as legitimate because grounded in their role as 'caretakers' has a long history within liberal thought (see Archard, 1993), and draws attention to another sense in which we *need* children to be different from us. So long as we see children as dependent, helpless, incompetent, innocent and Other, the exercise of 'personalistic power'[6] over them makes sense cognitively and socially, even though we frown on the exercise of this type of power over any other social group.

But children's physical, psychological and emotional dependency on adults decreases over time. As it does so, adults' absolute rule over them becomes increasingly difficult to legitimate in terms that are acceptable within liberal democracies. The parent who directs and controls all aspects of a 3-year-old child's life (what she eats, drinks, wears and watches on TV, where she goes and when and with whom, etc.) is popularly viewed as responsible; a parent who attempted to do the same with a 17-year-old child would be widely regarded as domineering. Similarly, children's mystical powers of social linkage diminish (though they do not entirely disappear) as they get older. Aunts and uncles start to forget their birthdays, parents are no longer expected to attend the social events to which their children are invited, no longer feel obliged to huddle together in groups whilst their children take exercise or play in the park (indeed, teenagers generally go to great lengths to conceal their lives from their parents and to conceal their parents from their friends). Couples cannot easily tell themselves that they must stay together 'for the sake of' their adult children.

Since childhood is a socially constructed category, its boundaries vary historically and within and between societies (Ariès, 1962; Pilcher, 1995). Greater awareness of its socially constructed nature means that in late-modern Western societies, childhood has become a focus of public as well as academic debate. Among other things, people worry about the point at which parental rule should be replaced by some more democratic arrangement, about the degree of autonomy that should be granted to children of different ages, about the age at which children are capable of some degree of participation in markets as consumers and as workers, about whether the parent–child relation should be viewed as indissoluble, and about the moral obligations this relation confers on parents of young children and on adult children of elderly parents. So, for example, people fret about whether children today are remaining dependent on their parents for too long (as suggested by recent UK market research that found parents bribing their twenty-something-year-old children with £5,000 'golden goodbyes' in an attempt to make them 'forgo the creature comforts of the family home for "real" life and a mortgage', Frith, 2003, p. 3). But, on the other hand, people worry that children are being 'almost coerced into growing up too fast and far too soon by ... pressures to succeed, to conform, to be in fashion, to be "cool", and to have anything and everything immediately – especially if it's the designer label of the day', as asserted by Jim O'Neill, chairman of the Professional Association of Teachers in his opening speech at the association's 2003 conference (cited in Woodward, 2003).

Concepts of authority and dependency are central to questions about child abuse, for, as Jenks notes, 'Dependency rests on a need and an authority in the provision of that need – abuse requires the misuse or corruption of that authority'(1996, p. 111). Child abuse thus becomes a foil against which broader anxieties about childhood and adults' political authority over children can be debated. Are children endangered by the freedoms they are granted? Jim O'Neill, quoted above, for example, went on to despair at the 'erosion of childhood and childhood innocence' in the UK today, evidenced by, among other things, plans to introduce sex education for 5-year-olds (cited in Woodward, 2003). Meanwhile, new concerns about children's access to the internet, and how this may leave them open to abuse by strangers met in chat-rooms, now add to long-standing anxieties about children's vulnerability to attack by 'predatory paedophiles' if they are given the freedom to play outside the home. But people are also worried about the negative side-effects of measures to protect children from sexual abuse. Are we perhaps endangering children by giving them too *little* freedom and independence? If they stay indoors watching TV instead of going out to play, will they become unhealthy and obese? What impact will the regime of close surveillance under which most Western children now live have on their emotional and psychological development? Don't we risk destroying children's supposedly innocent and trusting nature if we teach them to suspect that every adult they meet may be a paedophile just waiting for a chance to interfere with them? Have things swung too far the other way, so that where once parents and other carers were blithely unaware even of the possibility that a child could be sexually abused, now they are afraid to bathe children, cuddle them or show them any physical affection in case they find themselves accused of sexual abuse?

Chris Jenks asserts that 'dependency is no longer a taken-for-granted feature of the relationship between adults and children, what with de-mands for charters of children's rights, [and] with children "divorcing" parents' (1996, p. 110). This may need to be qualified so far as relation-ships between adults and young children are concerned, but I think his central argument holds good:

> Children have become both the testing ground for the necessity of in-dependence in the constitution of human subjectivity and also the sym-bolic refuge of the desirability of trust, dependency and care in human

relations. In this latter role 'childhood' sustains the 'meta-narrative' of society itself and abuse, both real and supposed, expresses our current ambivalence towards and impotence in the face of constantly emergent structural conditions. As we see less coherence and sustained meaning in the experience of our own subjectivity and our relationships with others, we witness more symbolic abuse of children. (1996, p. 111)

In contemporary Western societies, we *need* children to be passive, helpless and dependent, to be objects not subjects, for only then can they serve as conduits for our relationships with others; we *need* them to be empty, evacuated of individuality and agency, innocent and trusting, for only then can we inscribe on them the meaning that is lacking in the rest of our lives. And yet this fetishized view of 'childhood' as a state of dependency, innocence and vulnerability is difficult to sustain, especially when children themselves often refuse to co-operate with it (what with their demands for designer labels, their often superior competence with new technologies such as mobile phones, computer games and the internet, and so on). Witnessing and, perhaps more crucially, endlessly talking about abuse of children and of childhood by paedophiles provides a means through which to reassert a vision of 'children' as vacant, vulnerable and dependent, as the opposite of sex, the opposite of us, and so also a vision of ourselves as 'adults' (see Kincaid, 1998). The discourse of 'innocence raped', 'innocence betrayed', 'innocence murdered', reassures us not simply that children are helpless innocents, but also that *we* adults all agree that children need care and protection; that children are not 'fair game' in love; that there is a limit to our acceptance of processes of marketization – we may be willing to submit all other aspects of human experience to the ruthless logic of the market, but we will not tolerate children being treated as commercial objects.

In these convictions we find perhaps the only sure evidence of our own humanity, the only certainty about our essential nature, for it points to a form of human association that is governed by principles that not only pre-date contract, but are seemingly beyond contract. Our humanity is preserved so long as the social contract that allows us to arrange all our political, social and economic relationships on the basis of self-interest, and to sustain them only to the extent that both parties deliver enough satisfactions for each individual to stay within them, has a flip-side; so long as we can believe we are all party to an implicit covenant to care about children, and not to use them for our own private ends, especially not to use them for ends that conflict with the dominant vision of childhood as a state of innocence, dependency and Otherness. The 'paedophile' visibly and dramatically breaks this covenant by using children for purposes of sexual gratification. By condemning paedophiles as unnatural, monstrous, inhuman, Others, we reassure ourselves that the rest of us are restrained by the covenant.

## The Impossibility of Children in the Sex Trade

Where notions of 'innocence' and 'purity' have figured prominently in Western post-Enlightenment discourse on childhood, discourses on prostitution have centred upon ideas of corruption, pollution and impurity (Ennew, 1986). This means there is a sense in which children's involvement in sex commerce is, for most of those socialized in Euro-American societies, almost literally inconceivable. It cannot be readily accommodated within the conceptual schema that is generally used to make sense of either childhood or prostitution. If a child is a *prostitute* (and therefore supposedly dirty, rapacious, sexually knowing, instrumental and predatory upon the frailty of men), then she cannot truly be a *child* (and therefore supposedly innocent, asexual, naïve and dependent upon adults' wisdom, economic support and protection), and vice versa. The idea of children's presence in the global sex trade is widely experienced as profoundly disturbing not least because it carries the potential to rupture the imagined boundaries that serve to ring-fence both 'childhood' and 'commercial sex'. In so doing, it threatens to undermine other key pillars of the conceptual framework that is employed to structure, explain and give meaning to social relations in late-modern Western societies, in rather the same way that any attempt to rearrange individual components of a house of cards imperils the entire edifice, for, as has been seen, we *need* children to be dependent, protected, objects rather than subjects of social exchange.

One way out of this impasse is to treat children's involvement in the sex trade as a form of 'modern slavery', and/or as a straightforward subset of the more general phenomenon of child sexual abuse, since these phenomena have been discursively constructed in such a way as to reinforce rather than destabilize the house of cards. Subsumed within what James Kincaid (1998) refers to as 'cultural narratives of child molesting', or represented as 'slavery', the ideas of child prostitution and child pornography remain shocking and dreadful to countenance, but they no longer endanger dominant assumptions about generational, sexual, economic, social or political relations in Western liberal democracies. Indeed, the reverse is true. By bringing the 'commercial sexual exploitation of children' under the umbrella of the dominant moral and political discourse that insists upon and celebrates the innocence, asexuality and dependency of the child, children's presence in the global sex trade is transformed into a phenomenon that underscores the rightness of liberal concepts and values.

This book argues that, ultimately, it is impossible to address the commercial sexual exploitation of children (CSEC) without also knocking down liberalism's house of cards. Its foundations in the story of freedom through contract, and the binaries that serve as its key pillars (Adult/Child, subject/object, public/private, modern/traditional, consent/force, freedom/slavery, and, as will be seen in the following chapter, civilized/barbaric, white/non-white), make CSEC appear intolerable, and yet also encourage us to tolerate the material inequalities and asymmetries of power that underpin children's presence in the sex trade, as well as other forms of abuse and exploitation affecting both adults and children. My argument is that we cannot rescue children by insisting that *they* alone are beyond contract. We have to find other ways of imagining and structuring *our* interdependence as human beings.

# 2 Prostitutes, Children and Slaves

We will gather in Stockholm for the first World Congress Against the Commercial Sexual Exploitation of Children. We will express our outrage at the sexual exploitation of children. And as governments – together with concerned individuals everywhere – we will make our commitment to a global partnership which will bring an end to this contemporary form of slavery.

ECPAT, *Newsletter* (1996)

The social categories 'Adult' and 'Child' are imagined in opposition to one another, and are also fundamental to people's moral identity in contemporary Western societies (Ribbens McCarthy et al., 2000, p. 787). 'Prostitute' and 'Slave' are also constructed in relation to an imagined opposite, and they too are categories that tell us what we are by showing us what we are not – the virtuous and respectable woman knows herself as such because she is not a 'Prostitute'; we know ourselves to be free because we are not 'Slaves'. They are also all categories that map onto a more fundamental dualism in Western thought, namely, the subject–object binary. The Child, the Prostitute and the Slave are socially imagined as the objects, not the subjects or authors, of social exchange. As cultural figures, they symbolize and embody our fear of engulfment, infantilization, exclusion and dishonour. To refer to anyone as a 'slave', to describe another adult as 'childish', or to call a woman a 'whore' are thus all extremely powerful insults, and when people say that they have been treated like slaves, prostitutes or children, it communicates their sense that they have been humiliated, stripped of dignity, denied recognition as full human subjects and agents.

At the same time, those deemed to actually *be* children or slaves have very often been the focus of intense sentiment – as objects, they can be pitied much more freely and much more intensely than can those who are viewed as authoring and controlling their own destiny. The suffering of the prostitute can evoke a similarly sentimental response, providing there is no suspicion that she actively chose her wretched condition (see Gilfoyle, 1992). Brought together in the idea of a 'child sex slave', these social categories add up to a particularly potent symbol of undeserved suffering, one that can be used to great effect for fund-raising and lobbying purposes. Unsurprisingly, then, the metaphor of slavery has figured prominently in campaigns against the commercial sexual exploitation of children (CSEC), and is taken by many to capture in a very straightforward way the essence of the harm that it represents. However, as this chapter sets out to show, a number of moral, political and theoretical problems attend on the treatment of child prostitution as a 'contemporary form of slavery'.

## The Anomaly of Prostitution

Imagined as a woman or girl who trades sex for cash or other benefits, 'the Prostitute' disrupts what are imagined as natural binaries and so troubles categories and classifications that are central to the way in which sense is made of social and political relations. As a female, she is (or should be) sexually continent, pure, modest and passive, and yet as a prostitute, she is seemingly sexually indiscriminate, voracious, immodest and active; as a female, she is (or should be) naturally passive and dependent on a husband, father or brother, and yet as a prostitute, she is seemingly active and in-dependent. And because, in most societies, gender inequalities mean that most women are economically dependent on men, so that most heterosex-ual sexual relationships have an economic element to them, the existence of the prostitute threatens the certainty of other key cultural categories; in particular, those of 'wife' or 'virtuous woman/girl': 'The only difference between women who sell themselves in prostitution and those who sell themselves in marriage is in the price and the length of time the contract runs' (Marro, cited in Beauvoir, 1972 [1949], p. 569).

The ambiguities and boundary loss implied by prostitution may help to explain the hugely negative stigma that is commonly attached to female prostitutes, and their cultural association with filth, disease, decay and death (Pheterson, 1989; O'Neill 1997). As Mary Douglas famously put it, dirt is 'matter out of place', and 'our pollution behaviour is the reac-tion which condemns any object or idea likely to confuse or contradict cherished classifications' (2002, p. 45). She goes on to note that cultural categories, as public matters, are not easily subject to revision, and yet

> they cannot neglect the challenge of aberrant forms. Any given system of classification must give rise to anomalies, and any given culture must confront events which seem to defy its assumptions. It cannot ignore the anomalies which its scheme produces, except at risk of forfeiting confidence. This is why ... we find in any culture worthy of the name various provisions for dealing with ambiguous or anomalous events. (2002, p. 48)

The social and legal provisions that different societies have devised to deal with the ambiguities of prostitution could form the subject of another entire book. Here the important point to note is simply that there is cross-cultural and historical variation in terms of how people diffuse the threat to cherished categories posed by the anomalous figure of the prostitute woman. In some societies – past and present – the anomaly is dealt with by attempts to physically exterminate the female prostitute, for example by stoning, such that she does not live to contradict the definition of 'woman' as sexually pure and passive. In others, however, attempts are made to rescue the cultural categories that are imperilled by prostitution by re-casting female prostitutes as a separate and different class of persons. They are not *really* women – a prostitute is 'a woman with half the woman gone, and that half containing all that elevates her nature, leaving her a mere instrument of impurity', as William Acton put it in 1870 (cited in Bell, 1994, p. 55); or as Pietro Aretino wrote in *The Life of Courtesans*, 1534 (and this is quoted approvingly by Richard Goodall in his 1995 defence of prostitution), 'a whore is not a woman. She is a whore' (Goodall, 1995, p. 93).

Re-labelled as natural born 'whore' rather than 'woman', the female prostitute is no longer anomalous, and there need be no anxiety or confusion over her place in the social order. She can be accepted (though inferiorized) as a necessary feature of the social fabric. Thus, prostitution has often been likened to a sewer and understood to serve a vital function, for in containing men's excess sexual urges, it protects the purity of 'good' women and girls ('Prostitution . . . is the security valve for the honour of families and it is as necessary in societies as garbage dumps, drainage and sewerage system, etc.', Barrios et al., 1892, cited in Nencel, 2001, p. 15). And, providing prostitutes are geographically and socially isolated from 'honest' women, they pose no threat of pollution, just as human detritus does not endanger or disgust so long as it flows in a sewer. This traditional view of prostitution as an unpleasant but inevitable and necessary feature of human society persists even to this day (and at policy level generally leads to an emphasis on preventing prostitutes from contaminating 'respectable' society, i.e. subjecting them to forms of surveillance and control that would rarely be imposed on other citizens), as does the equally traditional view of prostitution as sin and the castigation of both prostitutes and their clients (which at policy level translates into calls for prohibition).

Although such models of prostitution sit comfortably with traditional beliefs about gender, they are incompatible with key tenets of modern liberal thought discussed in the previous chapter. If people are authors of their own destinies, then no woman is born to prostitute, and no man is incapable of controlling his sexual impulses. And the fact that prostitution is generally organized along the same lines as other forms of commodity exchange invites uncomfortable comparisons with economic transactions that are socially sanctioned, such as wage-labour. Could it be that prostitution is a contract like any other?

This is a difficult question for liberals, for there is a longstanding tension in liberal political thought regarding the relationship between the body, property and labour. John Locke stated that 'Every man has a property in his own person. This nobody has any right to but himself. The labour of his body, and the work of his hands, we may say, are properly his' (Locke, 1993, p. 274). This dictum allows for the commodification of a person's bodily capacity to labour, and for the construction of the wage-labour contract as a moral experience. Yet as Bridget Anderson notes, because he viewed the body as God-given and sacred, Locke also considered that 'A man does not stand in the same relation to his body as he does to any other type of property. . . . So a man does not have the right to kill himself, or put himself into slavery, because he is the work of God' (2000, p. 3). The liberal concept of property in the person thus leaves room for debate about what can, and cannot, properly be commodified and contractually exchanged across a market without moral harm. Among other things, it leaves unanswered questions about whether or not a woman has a right to put herself into prostitution. Do the body's sexual capacities constitute property in the person, or is it impossible to detach sex from person-hood without moral harm? Do laws prohibiting prostitution violate the prostitute's natural right to engage in voluntary transfers of her rightful property, or does the prostitution contract itself violate her natural right to dignity (O'Connell Davidson, 2002)? Such questions complicate inter-national policy debate on prostitution, which is already politically fraught for a number of other reasons.

### International Debates on Prostitution: Division and Consensus

Though prostitution is known to be a significant feature of economic life in many nations, regardless of their overall level of economic development,[1] there is much cross-national variation in terms of the scale and visibility of the commercial sex market, and in terms of social norms and attitudes regarding prostitution. And while laws pertaining to prostitution are gen-erally informed by one of three basic models (prohibition/suppression; legalization/regulation; or decriminalization/toleration, see Davis, 1993), there is also much variation between countries in terms of the details of prostitution law and law enforcement practice. These legal and so-cial disparities simultaneously reflect and generate significant differences between nations in terms of public and political discourse on commer-cial sex. The extent and nature of such national differences represent a major impediment to achieving any international consensus regarding adult prostitution, and disputes over how best to approach prostitution cannot be resolved through appeal to dominant liberal discourse on hu-man rights, for, as noted above, liberal understandings of property in the person and individual rights to voluntarily contractually exchange such property do not inform a single or consistent position on commercial sex.

Thus we find that although prostitution has been explicitly addressed within a number of United Nations conventions since 1949, the pronouncements and recommendations emanating from the UN do not add up to a consistent or coherent position on prostitution involving adults (see Kempadoo, 1999a). This reflects member states' inability to agree upon whether the international community should be attempting to eradicate all forms of prostitution, or whether a distinction should be made between forced and child prostitution (which should be outlawed) and prostitution that is voluntarily chosen by adults (which should be tolerated or regulated). Over the past two decades, international debates on prostitution and associated issues such as 'trafficking' have progressively polarized around these two positions, and the exchange between groups campaigning for the total abolition of prostitution and those lobbying for the recognition of 'free choice' prostitution as a legitimate form of work has become increasingly acrimonious.

International differences and divisions are less pronounced in relation to child prostitution. The UN Convention on the Rights of the Child (1989), ratified by over 190 countries (Social Care Group, 1999), defines the child as a person below the age of 18 and explicitly calls on states to protect children from all forms of sexual exploitation. There are also a number of other instruments that offer the child international legal protection against exploitation in prostitution (NGO Group for the Convention on the Rights of the Child, 1996). Moreover, in most countries where prostitution is legally regulated rather than prohibited, it is already a requirement that persons must be over the age of 18 (sometimes over 21) in order to register as a prostitute or to take up employment in a brothel. And where a legal policy of suppression is in place, there are already often provisions to impose particular penalties on those who encourage or profit from the prostitution of minors. This does not, of course, mean that those under the age of 18 actually *are* universally legally protected against prostitution. There are plenty of gaps and loopholes in many countries' legislation on the commercial sexual exploitation of children, and law enforcement practice is often lax. However, there are few, if any, politicians or lobby groups who would actively argue against the principle of completely abolishing child prostitution, and many are comfortable with the position expressed by Vitit Muntarbhorn at the first World Congress against the Commercial Sexual Exploitation of Children: 'I do not pass judgement on the pros and cons of adult prostitution. However, child prostitution is inadmissible – it is tantamount to exploitation and victimization of the child because it undermines the child's development. It is detrimental to the child both physically and emotionally, and it is in breach of the child's rights' (1996, p. 10). Thus, adult prostitution is understood to pose complex moral and political questions about individual liberty, sexual morality, property in the person, free choice and contractual consent, and it is a brave (or Swedish) liberal who passes judgement on it. But child prostitution is another matter. Why?

## The Child as Object

Liberal thinkers have long argued that since children have not developed the capacity for reason, they are not qualified for the exercise of freedom; indeed, as John Locke put it, to grant freedom to one who is without reason is 'to thrust him out amongst Brutes, and abandon him to a state as wretched, and as much beneath that of a Man, as theirs' (cited in Archard, 1993, p. 7). Similarly, John Stuart Mill held that the adult's independence over any form of conduct that 'merely concerns himself' is absolute – 'Over himself, over his own body and mind, the individual is sovereign' (Mill, 1910 [1859], p. 13), but argued that children – at least those who have not yet reached 'the maturity of their faculties' – cannot be granted this kind of self-sovereignty: 'Those who are still in a state to require being taken care of by others must be protected against their own actions as well as against external injury' (p. 13). There can be no 'voluntary' child prostitution, then, because children are incapable of making a free and informed choice to enter prostitution. Child prostitution thus 'amounts to forced labour and a contemporary form of slavery' (ECPAT, 1999).

On first inspection, Mill's proviso that the liberty principle apply only to those who have developed the capacity for rational thought may seem politically uncontroversial (to allow 5-year-olds the liberty to trade sex in exchange for trips to Disneyland if they chose to do so, for instance, would be neglectful rather than respectful of their autonomy). And yet I think the fact that Mill employed the same arguments in defence of colonialism should give pause for thought. Mill held that where human beings in 'civilized' societies (namely most European societies) were in the maturity of their faculties and 'had attained the capacity of being guided to their own improvement by conviction or persuasion', all non-European societies were 'backward' – their peoples were in a state of 'nonage' or 'infancy' (cited in Parekh, 1995, p. 93). Africa was a continent without a history; China and India, in fact the whole of the East, had been 'stationary' for thousands of years. Such 'backward' societies could not be improved by free and equal discussion, and if they were to be further improved, 'it must be by foreigners' (cited in Parekh, 1995, p. 93).

As these were moral and political infants, below the age of consent, Mill held that a 'parental despotism' by a 'superior people' was perfectly legitimate, in the interests of the colonized even, for it would help to raise them to a higher stage of development (Parekh, 1995, p. 93). 'Civilized' and 'primitive' (or 'barbarous', 'savage' or 'wild') can thus be added to the list of dualisms constructed and reproduced in classical liberal thought that were discussed in the previous chapter (modern/pre-modern, free/unfree, public/private, reason/emotion, independent/dependent, masculine/feminine, adult/child) (see Mills, 1998; Puwar, 2004). The interconnections between these dualisms are significant for contemporary debates on the commercial sexual exploitation of children, especially the construction of child prostitution as a form of 'slavery'. It strikes me that the discourse on child prostitutes as 'sex slaves' is one that sets out not simply to rescue individual children who are exploited within the sex trade, but also to redeem certain cherished cultural categories.

Take, for example, the way in which child prostitution is understood by Ron O'Grady, the founder member of End Child Prostitution in Asian Tourism (ECPAT), a Bangkok-based NGO which had its roots in a tourism pressure group (the Ecumenical Coalition on Third World Tourism). His account is important, for ECPAT is widely regarded as having played a central role in transforming child prostitution into an issue of international concern, debate and policy attention, and so has exerted a powerful influence on public and political discourse on CSEC (Black, 1995; Montgomery, 2001). The key elements of ECPAT's concerns about child prostitution are to be found in *The ECPAT Story* (O'Grady, 1996). The book opens by stating:

> Child prostitution has a long history in Asia. For centuries India maintained a system of temple prostitution or devadasis and it still lingers on in rural areas today. In China and Central Asia the wealthy have long considered sex with a young pre-pubescent girl, preferably a virgin, to be the best way to ensure wealth and vigour. Such customs were written into the religious and social traditions of the entire society but ... the enlightenment of the first half of the twentieth century saw education become more widespread in Asia and the ideals of democracy, equality and the rights of women and children began to be accepted more readily in some quarters. (p. 9)

However, O'Grady continues, the 'growth towards a more enlightened society has suffered a setback with the revival of widespread child prostitution' in recent decades (p. 9). The demand, he tells us, comes partly from low-income local men who have discovered that it is cheaper to use child prostitutes, partly from locals who wrongly assume that a child is less likely to be infected with AIDS and other STDs. However, 'the largest determinant in the recent growth of child prostitution appears to have come from foreign abusers' – foreign military personnel, seamen, expatriate workers and paedophiles from Western countries (p. 10).

By focusing on Asia and failing to note the fact that child prostitution also exists in 'enlightened' Western societies that are formally committed to 'ideals of democracy and equality', this account implicitly reproduces the imagined opposition between pre-modern and modern, barbarous and civilized, 'oriental' and 'occidental' societies. Indeed, it is these dichotomies that make the behaviour of Western paedophiles, tourists and expatriates so very shocking. After all, unenlightened and uncivilized folk might be expected to sexually abuse children (indeed, their maltreatment of women and children is part of what makes them primitive and barbarous), but for members of a 'civilized' society to behave in this way is intolerable. It can be and must be stopped. (For the sake of the children, or because it endangers the presumed boundary between civilization and barbarity?)

O'Grady also notes that ECPAT's decision to 'campaign to end child prostitution and nothing else' often had to be defended against those who argued that the problem could not be treated in isolation (p. 19). First, there were those who held that child prostitution was caused by poverty, and that ECPAT should therefore look at the root causes of poverty and focus on strategies to provide economic alternatives for children vulnerable to CSEC. But, O'Grady comments, there were already development agencies working on poverty alleviation, and besides, 'it is too simplistic to reduce the issue of child prostitution to a question of poverty alone' (p. 20) (more will be said about this in the following chapter). Next, there were those who opposed all forms of prostitution, whether involving adults or children, and who tried to persuade ECPAT to campaign more generally for the abolition of prostitution. O'Grady remarks that he feels some sympathy for this view, especially when confronted with evidence of adult women who were also subject to slavery-like conditions in prostitution, but

> it is also a fact that prostitution (both male and female) is legal in many countries and that, when there is an element of choice in the decision to become a prostitute, the moral issue is far from clear. The prostitution of young children is a much clearer issue. With children the consent of the child is never present, or, if it appears to be, it will be because of blackmail or manipulation on the part of the adult. (p. 20)

Finally, ECPAT came under pressure from those who believed the organization should be campaigning against child sexual abuse in general, rather than commercial sexual exploitation in particular. O'Grady defends the idea of a boundary between commercial and non-commercial forms of child sexual abuse as follows: 'There is a qualitative (and usually quantitative) difference between the commercial sexual abuse of a child kept in slavery, required nightly to serve the demands of several different adults, and the more usual form of child sexual abuse which may happen less frequently and often within the circle of family and friends' (pp. 20–1). This is pretty flimsy stuff. If the moral issue centres on consent, and O'Grady accepts that some adults are forced into prostitution, why focus only on 'child slaves'? And if the concern is with the non-consensual sexual use of children, can it really make a difference how frequently a child was raped or whether the child was raped within what is imagined as the 'private' realm of family and friends or the 'public' realm of the market? The fact that ECPAT sought to erect and defend these boundaries reflects, I believe, its narrow concern with what its founder members viewed as the operation of an immoral market, a market that was unacceptable because within it, children become 'commercial sexual objects available for short-term hire' (O'Grady, 1996, p. 11). This narrow concern can be understood, at least at one level, as expressing anxieties about the maintenance of key cultural classifications. Child prostitution seemingly collapses conceptual matrixes that in liberal thought are quite distinct. It turns 'the child' into 'a prostitute' (a sexual and a market actor), so potentially disrupting both a model of children as innocent, asexual, passive, dependent, unable to contract, the opposite of adults, and a model of the market as a benign site in which sovereign subjects and civil equals meet to engage in voluntary, mutual, contractual exchanges.

The metaphor of slavery offers a means by which to make the otherwise incompatible categories of 'child' and 'prostitute' congruent. If children are incapable of making choices, then child prostitutes are objects and 'sex slaves'; and if child prostitutes are objects and 'sex slaves', then we can be certain that there has been no element of choice in their decision to prostitute. But is it really so easy to hive child prostitution off from adult prostitution, and does the concept of 'slavery' help us to grasp the realities of children's experience of prostitution in the contemporary world?

### The Variability of Prostitution

In any given country, prostitution can take many organizational forms and involve very different employment relations, working conditions and earnings. There is variation in terms of the settings in which prostitute–client transactions are arranged and executed (brothels, massage parlours, hair salons, lap-dance clubs, restaurants, bars, private apartments, hotels, streets, beaches, truck stops, roadside lay-bys, to name but a few), and the extent and nature of third-party involvement in prostitution (some prostitutes work independently, others are directly or indirectly employed by a third party, some enter into contracts of indenture, some are confined in brothels and forced to prostitute, and so on). Third-party involvement does not map tidily onto the settings from which prostitutes work, and whether involved in 'indoor' or 'outdoor' prostitution, prostitutes may be controlled by an extremely abusive third party, or working completely independently, or somewhere between these two extremes. The degree of direct economic exploitation to which prostitutes are exposed thus spans a continuum from absolute (as when a third party appropriates all of the money garnered through an individual's prostitution) to entirely absent (as when a person who prostitutes independently keeps all of her or his earnings). Prostitutes' experience of violence, at the hands of both third parties and clients, also varies, and though some of those who work in the sex trade are at very high risk of assault, others are not (West, 1992; Scambler and Scambler, 1997; O'Connell Davidson, 1998; Weitzer, 2000).

Next we should note that though generally understood to refer to cash-for-sex transactions, prostitution is not always or necessarily arranged as a simple and instantaneous commodity exchange ($x$ sum of money for $y$ service). It can also entail less explicitly contractual and more diffuse exchanges (what is sometimes termed 'open-ended prostitution'). The latter can shade off into longer-term relationships within which one party provides domestic labour and/or companionship, as well as sexual services, in exchange for a range of benefits (a place to live, financial support, help with setting up a business, assistance in migrating from a developing to a rich country, and so on) (Hobson and Heung, 1998; O'Connell Davidson, 1998; Sánchez Taylor, 2001a). The boundary between commercial and non-commercial sexual relationships is neither sharp nor impermeable, so that, as noted earlier, the cultural categories of 'wife' and 'whore', 'good' and 'bad' girls and women, are always somewhat precarious. And even when prostitution is arranged as a commodity exchange like any other, it does not preclude the possibility of more diffuse relationships developing between prostitutes and regular clients.

Taken together, all this means that 'prostitution' does not refer to a uniform experience. There is a hierarchy or continuum in terms of earnings, working conditions and the degree of control that individuals exercise over the details of their own prostitution, and the experience of those at the top of the hierarchy is vastly different from, some would say incomparable to, that of individuals on the lowest rungs of the sex trade. And the subjective experience of prostitution differs not simply because the power relations it implies vary, but also because people come to prostitution with very different personal histories, different attitudes towards sex commerce, and different qualities as individuals that leave them either better or worse equipped to manage their experience (O'Connell Davidson, 1998).

Where do children fit into this complex and differentiated phenomenon? I think it would certainly be true to say that nowhere in the world are persons under the age of 18 to be found amongst those sex workers who enjoy the highest earnings, best conditions and greatest control over their working lives, and that they are often found in the lowliest, most exploited and most vulnerable positions in the sex trade. But as the following chapter will show, children are not always forced, manipulated or 'blackmailed' into prostitution by adults. Instead, many children trade sex as part of a survival strategy in just the same way that many adults 'choose' prostitution because it is the only or best means of subsisting open to them. And crucially for the purposes of this chapter, when children are discovered on the bottom rungs of the prostitution hierarchy, forced by third parties to submit to harsh work routines, unprotected sex, beatings, and so on, they are rarely alone but instead work alongside adults in the same conditions. So, for example, in research on Burmese prostitutes in Thai brothels, almost all of Hnin Hnin Pyne's (1995) interviewees reported having been tricked or sold into brothel prostitution by husbands or boyfriends, friends or, in most cases, strangers who had brought them from Burma to Thailand on the promise of jobs as waitresses, maids or food vendors. The fee paid to the recruiter by the brothel owner was constructed as a 'debt' that the individual who had been sold then had to work off through prostitution.

The experience of 17-year-old Aye Aye was typical of those who had been forced into prostitution in this way:

> Aye Aye had been kept in Thailand for three years at two different brothels. When rescued, she was living on the fifth floor of the brothel, which had a pool hall and a bar on the first two floors. The building housed approximately one hundred women. From noon until two in the morning, Aye Aye, wearing a numbered button, would sit behind a glass partition, while men ogled her and others from across the room. She would watch television while waiting for her number to be called. She served about twelve to twenty men a day. (Pyne, 1995, pp. 215–16)

But Aye Aye was not forced into prostitution or subject to these working practices *because* she was below the age of 18, nor would she have been immediately released upon reaching her eighteenth birthday. Pyne's study included a sample of 43 Burmese brothel prostitutes in Ranong, a Thai town close to the Burmese border, 41 of whom had been forced into prostitution in the manner described above. The ages of these women 'ranged from eighteen to thirty-seven, although the majority (72.1 percent) were in their late teens and early twenties' (Pyne, 1995, p. 218). Likewise, research in Thailand, India, Bangladesh, Pakistan, Brazil and the Czech Republic shows that those prostitutes who are debt-bonded and/or confined in brothel prostitution are by no means all below the age of 18 (Truong, 1990; Sutton, 1994; Lim, 1998; Brown, 2000; Uddin et al., 2001; Saeed, 2002; Siden, 2002).

It is also important to note that where women and girls are subject to abuse and confinement by employers, very often the police and other state actors (immigration officials, local officials who license businesses, etc.) systematically collude in and profit from their oppression, and/or further violate their human rights. So, for instance, in one police raid on brothels in Ranong in 1993, 148 Burmese women and girls were 'rescued' by the Thai police. Following the raid, the women and girls 'were arrested by the Thai police as illegal immigrants and kept in appalling conditions for months' (Montgomery, 2001, p. 31). Investigations by human rights groups suggest there had been widespread collusion by Thai officials in the initial trafficking and subsequent confinement of these women and girls in the brothels (Montgomery, 2001). In Bangladesh, the system through which prostitution is legally regulated bestows upon local officials and police the power to license or register sex workers, thereby giving the police enormous control over the supply of labour for brothels. Bribes from brothel owners provide the police with a regular income, and they are often complicit with the financial exploitation of forced and underage prostitutes, as well as using their powers to extort sexual services from sex workers in brothel districts (Uddin et al., 2001).

What possible grounds could there be for distinguishing between adult and child victims of the practices and structures described above? It is sometimes asserted that children, 'because of their young age and lack of control, are more vulnerable to being sold by parents or guardians and to being tricked, coerced, abducted or kidnapped by unscrupulous adults' (Lim, 1998, p. 176), and are therefore more likely to be subject to forced labour or enslavement in the sex trade. Yet even if this is the case, we know that some people over the age of 18 are subject to this type of abuse and exploitation. So why would any campaign that sought to combat this 'modern form of slavery' focus its concern on *children*? Could it be that the discourse on CSEC as modern slavery is as much concerned to protect cherished components of a liberal system of classification, in particular, to preserve Adult and Child, and 'slavery' and 'freedom', as oppositional categories, as it is to rescue any human being who is actually subject to abusive employment practices in the sex trade?

## Slavery and Freedom

Much scholarly attention has been paid to the problem of how to define slavery, not least because, as Laura Brace observes, 'it is often argued that in order to understand liberty and autonomy, we need to know how to recognise their opposites' (2004, p. 160). For liberals in particular, she continues, 'this has meant striving to draw bright lines between slavery as a wrong or a logical impossibility and individual autonomy as a good and a right' (pp. 160–1). Yet evidence about the social relations of the real world has long hampered and still impedes philosophical efforts to clearly demarcate autonomy and slavery, or free and unfree labour, as oppositional categories. Put crudely, the problem is that even when understood as defined in the Slavery Convention of the League of Nations (1926), which states that slavery is 'the status or conditions of a person over whom any or all of the powers attaching to the right of ownership are exercised', slavery implies a *package* of unfreedoms, not all of which are unique to the condition. Thus, slavery has certain features in common with other forms of unfree labour, such as debt bondage, serfdom, servitude and forced labour.

    More problematic still, the form of free wage labour that liberals fondly imagine as a defining characteristic of 'modernity' (based on a voluntary, mutual contract between worker and employer from which each party may freely retract) did not miraculously appear with industrialization in Western countries. Employment relations in the eighteenth and nineteenth centuries, in 'modern' manufacturing as well as other sectors, were shaped by traditional forms of servitude and thus implied some of the unfreedoms that are classically associated with slavery. For example, in Britain, the Master and Servants Act (which was not repealed until 1875) allowed employers to arbitrarily impose fines for poor performance or attitude, and prevented workers from freely withdrawing their labour, which was owned by the master for the duration of the contract (often a period of twelve months) (Palmer, 1983). Meanwhile, European labour power for the colonies was often recruited and retained using a system of indentured servitude under which

> an individual entered a legal contract which bound him or her to a master for a fixed number of years.... The individual was obliged to make labour power available to the master who appropriated the total product of the labourer's labour power and who, in return, was responsible for the costs of transport, subsistence and reproduction. (Miles, 1987, p. 76)

Following the abolition of the slave trade and then slavery, a new form of indenture was introduced to bring labourers from India, China and Africa to the Caribbean (Potts, 1990; Ramdin, 1994). Again, these workers were bound to employers by restrictions placed upon their 'economic and political freedom to dispose of labour power' (Miles, 1987, pp. 89–90). And even in the twentieth century, the employment contracts imposed on supposedly 'free' workers in the colonies were often but 'a fig leaf concealing actual slavery', or 'enslavement ... masked by a legal transaction: the agreement between the slave owner, designated in the contract as the hirer, and the slave, designated in the contract as the seller of labour' (Nzula et al., 1979, p. 82). Nor can we comfort ourselves with the idea that in the contemporary world, those who are formally constructed as 'free' wage workers are universally protected from all of the unfreedoms associated with slavery. The Asian Migrant Centre's yearbook is full of reports of 'free' wage workers in a variety of sectors and a range of countries who have been denied basic human rights and freedoms, for example (AMC, 2000), and children are amongst those who are not legally or socially constructed as 'slaves', but yet live and work in conditions similar to those experienced by enslaved persons (see, for example, Seabrook, 2001).

And so far as a bright line between slavery and freedom is concerned, the problem is not just that a multitude of sins can be and have been incorporated under the heading 'free wage labour', but also that the experience of people legally constructed as slaves has never been homogeneous. Whilst acknowledging that the institution of slavery was 'brutally – and all too often murderously – inhuman', historians increasingly urge us to recognize the fact that 'relations between owners and slaves were infinitely more complex than [the] polar model of dominance and submission would suggest' (Geary, 2004, see also Archer, 1988; Lott, 1998). In Brazil in the eighteenth and nineteenth centuries, for instance, there was a good deal of diversity in terms of slave employment. 'On many plantations ... slaves worked together with freed men', some slaves worked in specialized occupations, and there were even cases in which 'slaves were actually entrusted with the management of entire estates and found themselves in a position to accumulate capital and buy their freedom' (Geary, 2004). There have also been times and places in which the labour performed by individual slaves (even though very much in the minority amongst enslaved persons) has been less arduous than that performed by individual free wage workers, for example the labour of African and Indian children kept as pets by wealthy English families in the eighteenth century (Fryer, 1984; Visram, 2002) as compared to that of 'free' child workers in factories in England during the same period. Thus, if we are concerned with slavery as a form of labour exploitation, there is no clear, clean line between it and 'free' wage labour. Slavery stands at one pole of a continuum of exploitation, shading off into servitude and other forms of exploitation, rather than existing as a wholly separate, isolated phenomenon.

Perhaps not surprisingly then, in seeking to draw 'bright lines' between slavery and freedom, liberals have tended to emphasize the excluded political and legal status of slaves rather than dwell too closely upon their economic exploitation. Hence the unique horror of slavery is widely held to be the fact that it treats human beings as property, chattels to be bought, sold or given as gifts, treated as nothing but 'an extension of the will of another, without any rights needing to be recognized, lacking almost all formal acknowledgement of human worth and therefore all honour' (Turley, 2000, p. 6). But so far as questions about treating human beings as property are concerned, matters are again not entirely clear-cut. The League of Nations' definition of slavery as 'the status or conditions of a person over whom any or all of the powers attaching to the right of ownership are exercised' does not completely distinguish the master–slave relation from every other social relationship, for some of the powers attaching to the right of ownership can be and often are also exercised over spouses, employees, professional athletes and, of course, children (see Patterson, 1982; Brace, 2004).

Thus, individual components of the package of unfreedoms (legal, moral and economic) associated with slavery have been and are also experienced by groups that, although sometimes *compared* to slaves, are not socially imagined as 'slaves' (wives, children, wage workers). One feature of slavery that does appear to be singular concerns the dishonour of the slave. According to Orlando Patterson (1982), slavery is a form of social death. A slave is not only a person without power, but also a person without natality. Slaves' connections to their own blood relations, their ancestors, parents and children, are severed, and their natal alienation means that they cease to belong, in their own right, 'to any legitimate social order' (Patterson, 1982, p. 5). They must therefore depend absolutely upon their master for their identity as well as their physical existence. They live in the 'shadow cast by the owner', and the slave is thus 'a symbol of extreme dependency, objectifying other people's fears of being effaced, losing their continuing links and their home in the social world' (Brace, 2004, p. 169).

This social death (the absence of an independent identity and exclusion from civil society, and thus the inability to make claims, either on other people or on property) is intimately connected with the slave's dishonour, something that many commentators hold is grounded in slavery's origins 'in defeat and capture, and to its continuing basis in violence' (Brace, 2004, p. 170; see also Blackburn, 1988). As Patterson notes, 'Archetypically, slavery was a substitute for death in war', but 'The condition of slavery did not absolve or erase the prospect of death. Slavery was not a pardon; it was, peculiarly, a conditional commutation. The execution was suspended only as long as the slave acquiesced in his powerlessness' (1982, p. 5). In accepting social death in place of actual, physical death, every moment of the slave's life thus testifies to and compounds the original dishonour of 'choosing' the humiliation of slavery in place of death (see also Yavetz, 1988, p. 158).

If, traditionally, the ultimate humiliation for a man has been defeat in warfare, for a woman or girl it has been the loss of her sexual 'honour'. The rape victim or the 'adulteress' may be required to pay with her life (as, for example, in the recent case of Safiyatu Huseini, a northern Nigerian woman condemned to be stoned to death under *sharia* law for the 'crime' of having been raped and impregnated by a man to whom she was not married: Dowden, 2002), but she is also often propelled into what is traditionally imagined as another form of social death – prostitution (see, for instance, Kannabiran, 1996). 'Whore' and 'slave' have historically been gendered terms to refer to persons without honour (thus Othello refers to Desdemona as a 'whore' and a 'strumpet' when he believes she has betrayed him, and to Cassio and Iago as 'slave' when he thinks they have done likewise). Indeed, the strong cultural associations between slavery and dishonour strike me as a very good reason for urging caution with regard to the indiscriminate use of the term 'slavery' in relation to prostitution.

More generally, it is important to recognize the problems associated 'with setting up slavery as either about social exclusion or about labour, and with insisting that it has to be understood either as the opposite of belonging or as the opposite of freedom' (Brace, 2004, p. 171). Such dichotomous thinking 'misses the connections and continuities between labour, morality and honour and between self-ownership and community' (Brace, 2004, p. 171). If the term 'slavery' is to be used in relation to prostitution, then it is necessary to look closely at the specifics of the culture and economics of unfree prostitution in any given setting. This is not only important in terms of understanding the complex interplay between political exclusion and labour exploitation in shaping the experience of prostitution, but also in terms of identifying and prioritizing policy responses. Let me illustrate with an example.

## Unfree Prostitution in Context

In a number of South Asian countries, there are socially and geographically isolated brothel districts in which whole communities (men, women and children) are directly or indirectly economically dependent on prostitution (INSAF, 1995; Brown, 2000; Uddin et al., 2001; Saeed, 2002). These communities may live in a particular 'quarter' of a city, or 'in the case of those outside the big towns, the brothel communities have a separate existence as a special kind of village, which at first glance looks like a typical squatter or slum settlement' (Uddin et al., 2001. p. 18). As Uddin et al. note on the basis of research in two such communities in Bangladesh, 'There is a hierarchy of sex workers at the core of each brothel community.' The most powerful are the *bariwalis* and *shordarnis*, women who have worked their way up through the sex work hierarchy and now own housing and/or land, and 'have amassed sufficient income and influence to act as community leaders' (2001, p. 25). *Shordarnis* are also the women who 'recruit and manage bonded prostitutes, known as *chukris*'. As the least powerful of sex workers, *chukris* are positioned at the base of the community hierarchy:

> *chukri* . . . denotes a girl sold to a *shordarni* or *bariwali*. The older woman pays the basic living expenses of the *chukri*, who in return hands over all the earnings from her sex work. After a period ranging from a few months to several years, a *chukri* will buy her way out of the contract, in a settlement mediated by the *shalish* [local form of arbitration]. The sum she pays to her *shordarni* or *bariwali* may be quite considerable. Customarily a *chukri* borrows this money from another *shordarni/bariwali*. This procedure elevates her status from *chukri* to *bharatia*, or tenant sex worker, at which point she is said to have become 'clever'. Some *chukris* escape from the brothel, usually going on to another one where at least they are not bonded. (p. 25)

There are features of this form of prostitution that resemble aspects of slavery, as traditionally understood. Indeed, Uddin et al. observe that *chukris* 'began their lives outside the world of the brothel, and were abducted or procured and sold on to a *shordarni* or *bariwali* in a deal which reduces them to sexual slaves' (p. 44). Yet it is important to note that unfreedom is not necessarily a permanent condition. An elaborate cultural system, featuring both economic and social elements, exists through which both the prostitute's status within the community and her earnings and working conditions can be shifted. It would certainly be possible to compare the system through which *chukris* buy themselves out of bondage to the phenomenon of manumission, but this should not obscure the significance of the *chukri*'s impermanent status for subjective understandings of power relations within the community. In the brothel culture, *shordarnis* are respected rather than depicted as villains and criminals, and bonded girls often aspire to become *shordarnis* or *bariwalis* one day, for this is 'the pinnacle of a sex worker's career' (Uddin et al., 2001, p. 25).

Three further points. First, not all child prostitutes in such brothel districts are bonded workers. Girls who are born to sex workers and raised in the brothel community also enter prostitution. Unlike *chukris*, they enjoy 'some freedom of action within the brothel compound'; however, they do not necessarily exercise much control over the details of their prostitution or the earnings gleaned through it (Uddin et al., 2001, pp. 42–4). Indeed, there is an expectation that such children will hand over all their earnings to their mothers or guardians, who are often entirely economically dependent upon them. None the less, bonded and non-bonded prostitutes, both adult and child, work alongside each other in these communities. Second, the degree of economic exploitation involved in child prostitution in the brothel districts (for both bonded and non-bonded prostitutes) is not fundamentally different from that involved in other forms of child labour in Bangladesh, such as domestic work or work in *bidi* (cigarette) factories (Uddin et al., 2001, p. 45). However, and this third point is crucial, both adult and child prostitutes are socially constructed as profoundly inferior Others by the wider political community in which they live. Indeed, so great is the stigma attaching to prostitution in Bangladeshi society that some brothel communities even have to have their own graveyards because sex workers' bodies will not normally be accepted by regular graveyards for burial (Uddin et al., 2001, p. 22). And though the Bangladeshi state does not officially sanction the forms of prostitution described above (the legal status of prostitutes and prostitution is ambiguous, and the sale of children and the use of bonded labour are illegal), neither does it offer women and girls effective protection from abuse and exploitation. Indeed, as noted earlier, the police derive a regular income from prostitution, and are often complicit with the exploitation of unfree and underage prostitutes.

Compare the situation of a *chukri* in a Bangladeshi brothel district with the following case, involving Nikita, a 16-year-old orphaned girl from the Czech Republic. Having been fired from her job as a seamstress, Nikita turned to street prostitution to subsist. On the second day working the streets she was kidnapped by men who smuggled her to the Netherlands, where she was sold on to a group that forced her to work in a sex club. Here, a man (presumably a client) 'saw her suffering and many traces of abuse and helped her to get out of prostitution. He provided a hiding address and called the police' (Wolthius, 2002, p. 1). As Nikita was abducted, sold, confined, unpaid and forced into a given work-rate through the use of violence, she too could be described as treated like a slave, and her situation is certainly what many commentators have in mind when they speak of child prostitution and sex trafficking as forms of modern slavery. But again, I would urge caution, for unless the term 'slavery' is used carefully, paying close attention to contextual variations regarding the configuration of slavery's constituent elements within different socioeconomic systems (see Patterson, 1982, p. 26), to the different 'cultures' of slavery, and to the role that the state plays in creating the legal and social framework within which people are enslaved, then it serves only to further Otherize and objectify the prostitute. Certainly, it does not assist in the development of realistic, context-appropriate policy goals and priorities.

So, for instance, in Bangladesh, female prostitutes are socially constructed as pariahs and stripped of ties and claims to community belonging in a way that resembles social death, and this is not unconnected to the forms of labour exploitation to which they are subjected within prostitution. In the Netherlands, female prostitutes are not imagined or treated in the same way (indeed, adult prostitutes, at least those who are EU citizens, are afforded certain rights and protections as workers). Such differences are of enormous significance in relation to policy, for interventions that may help to protect women and children from abuse and violence in one context may actually make them more vulnerable in another. It is one thing to call for closer police surveillance of sex clubs and the closure of establishments in which girls like Nikita are found in the Netherlands, but quite another to do so in Bangladesh, for, as Uddin et al. note:

> From time to time . . . there are calls for the closing down of certain broth-els and the 'rehabilitation' of sex workers. Such proposals are nominally inspired by religious and moral concern, but often disguise an intention to take over property and land occupied by brothel communities estab-lished over many years. They entail the eviction of sex workers from their homes and communities, and therefore the loss of the small measure of security they possess. The sex workers also know that 'rehabilitation' in the mainstream of Bangladeshi society is impracticable: they will not be accepted. (2001, p. 18)

Sex workers therefore resist such campaigns, though not always success-fully.

If the concept of slavery is to contribute anything to analysis or policy-making in relation to child prostitution, then it must be used in the context of more detailed and systematic assessments of the specific unfreedoms associated with specific forms of prostitution in specific locations. For where the notion of 'the Slave' is used merely as a rhetorical device to bridge the social categories of 'Child' and 'Prostitute', there is a danger of implying that only the innocent child can truly be a slave, and is a 'slave' regardless of the actual circumstances surrounding her prostitution. This may allow for the protection of the conceptual binaries that are held dear in liberal democracies (Adult/Child, freedom/slavery, civilized/barbaric, virtuous woman/whore), but it does not necessarily promise to safeguard the interests of those who are currently subject to slavery-like employment practices in the sex trade. Indeed, the discourse on CSEC as modern slavery makes it possible for governments and international policy-makers to sideline questions about human, civil and labour rights abuses affecting prostitutes of all ages, including violations perpetrated by state actors. And last but not least, it deflects attention from questions about the structural conditions that encourage many children independently to use prostitution as a strategy for survival, questions that form the focus of the following chapter.

# 3 On Child Prostitutes as Objects, Victims and Subjects

The United Nations Convention on the Rights of the Child (CRC) is the most ratified instrument of international law and affords children rights to protection, provision and participation, including, in Article 34, protection against all forms of sexual exploitation and abuse. However, since it defines 'children' as persons below the age of 18, the term 'child' spans what is inevitably a condition of complete and absolute dependence on older carers through to what may be a state of partial or complete independence from such carers, or, indeed, a state in which the person has acquired responsibility towards older or younger dependants. Within any given country, children are further divided by their gender, class, race, ethnicity and/or 'caste', as well as by their nationality and/or immigration status, and there are also global divisions and cross-national differences to take into account. Differences between 'childhoods' nationally and cross-nationally, and divisions between children in terms of age, gender, class, race, 'caste', nationality, disability, and so on, are clearly relevant to any analysis of children's presence in the sex trade. A 17-year-old British boy trading sex on the streets of London and a 10-year-old Cambodian girl in brothel prostitution in Phnom Penh are unlikely to have entered prostitution in the same way or for the same reasons, for example.

Those involved in campaigns against the commercial sexual exploitation of children do generally recognize that children enter prostitution by different routes and for different reasons (sometimes even that they occupy different positions in the prostitution hierarchy). Yet they do not invite us to dwell too long upon the meaning of that diversity. Instead, one of the central themes of campaigns against CSEC is that no matter why children started to trade sex, no matter what form their prostitution takes or why they remain in it, no matter what their age or their subjective view of their involvement in prostitution, trading sex violates children's rights as set out under Article 34 of the CRC. It endangers children's mental and physical health, undermines their development, and, since children by virtue of their immaturity, lack of experience, susceptibility to peer pressure as well as manipulation and exploitation by adults, can never give free and informed consent to a sexual-economic exchange, child prostitution is always an intolerable form of forced labour, a form of modern slavery (UNICEF, ECPAT, NGO Group for the Convention on the Rights of the Child, 1996, p. 1; ECPAT, 1999, p. 8).

The classification of child prostitution as 'forced labour' or 'slavery' and the discursive separation of adult and child prostitution through an emphasis on children's inability to *choose* prostitution have encouraged the popularizing of some extremely simplistic ideas about the nature of the problem and appropriate policy responses to it. For example, it is widely assumed that, since children are passive, dependent, vulnerable and incapable of choosing to prostitute, children who sell sex must have been forced to do so by an adult or adults. The individual morality of those who compel children to prostitute then becomes the focus of attention and concern, and the stage is set for a parade of the world's best-beloved folk devils – paedophiles, perverts, homosexuals, pimps, mafia thugs, human traffickers, heartless and greedy parents. Constructed in this way, CSEC is heaven not just for tabloid journalists, but also for populist politicians who have nothing to lose and much to gain by making crude and sweeping statements about eradicating child prostitution by punishing the monstrous perverts, evil brothel keepers and vile traffickers who are responsible.

Presented as a problem of individual morality, child prostitution appears as a fairly straightforward criminal justice and law enforcement issue. Certainly, it does not raise any complicated or threatening questions about the global political and economic order, or about inequalities of class, gender, race or ethnicity within nations. All we need to do is smoke out and hunt down the baddies. And even if we turn to more sophisticated commentaries in the literature provided by those campaigning against CSEC, child prostitution is often linked to 'a decline in values' as well as to structural inequalities (Muntarbhorn, 2001, p. 12). In particular, campaigners are keen to stress that whilst poverty may play a role in the phenomenon, there is no direct causal relationship between poverty and child prostitution (not all poor children sell sex), and 'poverty should not be seen as a pretext for justifying the sexual exploitation of children' (Muntarbhorn, 2001, p. 7). We should instead be thinking of the 'poverty-plus' factor, and the 'plus' is often taken to refer to the moral feebleness, or plain wickedness, of adults who should be providing the child with care and protection (see, for example, O'Grady, 1993; Kane, 1998, p. 57).

There are good reasons for challenging any analysis that treats poverty as a necessary and sufficient condition for prostitution, whether involving adults or children, and it is certainly true that some children – poor or not – end up in prostitution as a direct result of actions taken by adults, actions that I think can properly be described as immoral. Yet the prominence given in campaigns against CSEC to cases in which children have been sold or directly forced into prostitution by adults serves to reinforce a totalizing model of childhood that assumes all children always stand in a very particular relation to adults and the wider community – one of helplessness and dependency. This bolsters the impression that the solution to the problem lies primarily in better laws and stronger law enforcement. And as this chapter sets out to show, it also rests upon and reproduces subject/object and agent/victim dualisms that obscure both the realities of the lives of many children who sell sex, and the continuities between their experience and that of prostitutes aged over 18.

### Poverty-Plus?

There is much evidence to suggest that it is those children who are already disadvantaged by a range of economic, social and political factors who are most likely to end up in the sex trade. So, for example, children who are affected by cataclysmic events (armed conflict, civil war, ethnic and racial violence, famine and environmental degradation and disasters) are at high risk of involvement in sex commerce (UNHCR, 2001; HRW, 2002; Higate, 2003). Some 10 million out of the world's 21.5 million refugees and other persons of concern are under the age of 18 (UNHCR, 2000), and adolescent refugees in particular often have to fend for themselves, and may also have to assume adult responsibilities such as caring for siblings. Studies in Bosnia, Liberia and Colombia suggest that refugee and displaced children aged between 12 and 18 sometimes trade sex for official papers, privileges for themselves or their relatives, clothes and food, and/or protection, as well as for cash (Kadjar-Hamouda, 1996).

There are also links between poverty, HIV/AIDS and child prostitution. At the end of 1999, USAID estimated that 13.2 million of the world's children aged under 15 had lost their mother or both parents as a result of AIDS, and that 90 per cent of these children live in sub-Saharan Africa. It is further estimated that '44 million children in the 34 countries hardest hit by HIV/AIDS will have lost one or both parents from all causes, but primarily from AIDS, by 2010' (USAID, 2000, p. 1). The vast majority of children orphaned by AIDS struggle to subsist, often also to support siblings. Again, this can precipitate involvement in commercial sex. Other tragedies that are less immediate and dramatic, but equally calamitous, also impact on children's lives and can be associated with entry into prostitution. Writing in the late 1990s, Castells noted that over the past three decades, 'the poorest 20 percent of the world's people have seen their share of global income decline from 2.3 percent to 1.4 percent. . . . Meanwhile, the share of the richest 20 percent has risen from 70 percent to 85 percent' (1998, pp. 80–1). This polarization is occurring both between and within nations, and has been exacerbated by the pursuit of neo-liberal policies for fiscal discipline and economic restructuring. In undermining welfare benefits and minimum wage levels, and cutting the subsidies that made housing, transport, child care, education and health care more affordable, neo-liberal economic reforms in both affluent and developing nations have intensified many of the pressures that lead children to work and live on the streets (Mickelson, 2000, p. 272). And whether in Canada, Zambia, Brazil, Romania or Cambodia, children who live and work on the streets very often end up trading sex for cash, food, drugs, shelter and/or protection.

At the same time as intensifying poverty and unemployment amongst already vulnerable women and youth, global economic restructuring has also encouraged an expansion of the commercial sex industry. For example, since the 1970s, world financial institutions have encouraged indebted nations in Latin America and South-East Asia to respond to economic crisis by developing tourism and/or 'non-traditional' export industries such as gold, diamonds and timber (Kempadoo, 1999a). One side-effect of such development policies is the creation of a highly concentrated, effective demand for prostitution: affluent tourists seeking 'entertainment', and predominantly male migrant workers in isolated mining and logging regions with cash to spend on 'recreation'. Such demand is met by adolescents as well as adult women (Silvestre et al., 1994; Feingold, 1998, 2000; Kempadoo, 1999a; Xie Guangmao, 2000; O'Connell Davidson, 2001b; O'Connell Davidson and Sánchez Taylor, 2001).

But though we can identify global political and economic factors that leave children, as well as adults, in conditions where they must struggle for the basic necessities of life, human beings are clearly not *propelled* into any given course of action by such forces. Structural constraints and pressures do not cause particular forms of social action in the same way that, for instance, the force of gravity causes a person who leaps from a tenth-floor window to fall. This is something campaigners are often quick to remind us with regard to impoverished adults who sell or debt-bond their children into prostitution, but it is also relevant to people below the age of 18. What is it, outside or beyond poverty, that leads children to enter prostitution?

Existing research evidence on different types of child prostitution in different parts of the world does not point to a simple, single answer to this question. Instead, it draws attention to a range of 'push' and 'pull' factors, including: the use of force, deception or manipulation; poverty, hunger or economic need; social and political marginalization; familial neglect and abuse; experience of sexual victimization; peer influence; drug addiction; children's consumerism; children's desire for independence, excitement and/or experience; children's sense of duty towards and/or responsibility for their kin. In the campaigning as well as the academic literature, it is generally recognized that none of these factors, on their own, are enough to precipitate a child's entry into prostitution (a hungry child does not immediately turn to prostitution to obtain food; teenagers do not necessarily start to prostitute because they cannot afford to buy the latest designer clothes; a child who has been raped or sexually abused does not automatically decide to start selling sex). Rather, children's presence in prostitution is usually understood to result from some combination of the factors listed above.

So, for example, Laura Mayorga and Pilar Velasquez (1999) discuss the interplay between economic and social factors, and experiences of neglect, abuse and abandonment as factors precipitating children's entry into prostitution in Colombia. Their research focused on girls and young women working independently in street prostitution in Cartagena, serving demand from local men and tourists. Cartagena is in one of the poorest regions of Colombia, a region in which 70 per cent of the inhabitants 'are unable to satisfy their basic human needs', and where the 'rate of malnourishment for children is 10.4 percent, the highest in Colombia' (Mayorga and Velasquez, 1999, p. 163). The girls and young women they interviewed all reported having grown up in poverty, and five out of thirteen stated that hunger was 'an immediate factor that motivated them to have sex for money the first time' (p. 164). But the children who identified lack of food as a factor precipitating entry into prostitution were not motivated to exchange sex for money by hunger alone. It was also 'the caregiver's attitude about providing food for the child ... that appears to have made the child feel rejected and willing to leave home for the life of the streets' (p. 164). In some cases, sexual abuse as well as hunger and neglect played a role in the child's eventual participation in prostitution, for the decision to trade sex sometimes followed a sexual relationship with an adult male.

Children's presence in prostitution in affluent countries can come about as a result of a similar mix of pressures. Adolescents – male and female – who sell sex are often 'runaways', escaping abusive family situations or institutional care (Ennew, 1986; Kinnell, 1991; O'Neill, 1997; Bagley, 1999; McIntyre, 1999; Melrose et al., 1999; Morse et al., 1999; Kelly and Regan, 2000a; O'Neill and Barberet, 2000; Connell and Hart, 2003). Having made a bid for independence by leaving home or care, many find themselves homeless, without means of support, and unable to find employment. Trading sex is one means of subsisting. Drugs can also play a key role in keeping children and young women and men in prostitution. A striking finding of Melrose et al.'s research in Britain concerned 'the relative youthfulness of those who are already heavily involved in using highly addictive substances such as heroin and crack' (1999, p. 59), and using street prostitution as a means of supporting their own and their boyfriends' substance use (see also McKeganey and Barnard, 1996; Dodd, 2002; Connell and Hart, 2003; Cusick et al., 2003). To this we should add that studies in North American cities in particular have found that a very large percentage of adolescents in prostitution have a prior history of sexual victimization and/or physical abuse in their younger childhood (Silbert and Pines, 1981; Bagley, 1999; McIntyre, 1999). However, whilst in many cases neglectful and/or abusive parents or guardians could be said to have set in motion a chain of events that ultimately led to the child's involvement in the sex trade, the link between sexual abuse and prostitution, like that between poverty and prostitution, is not direct or unmediated.

The studies discussed thus far show that not all children in prostitution have been 'sold for sex' – the 'poverty-plus' factor is not always an adult who sells, lures or brutalizes a child into prostitution. Shivanandan Khan's (1999) collection of life-stories from men and boys who trade sex in India complicates the picture further by reminding us that many children do not even have parents or guardians to betray them, and also by pointing to the role children themselves can play in other children's prostitution. The following excerpt is taken from an interview with 'Rafiq', a 10-year-old orphan who lives at the railway station in Calcutta:

> For the last two years I have been here on my own. Well not really on my own as I am with the other boys here. We are a gang. Our gang is about 20 boys and girls, mainly boys. The oldest is 14 and we have one boy who is seven. None of us have families. We live here sleeping near the station. I am always hungry. We all are. We beg here . . . sometimes we thieve. . . . Other times we help passengers with their luggage and they give us a little money. . . . But all this is never enough . . . for food. I first had sex when I was seven, just after I joined the gang. Ramesh was the leader then. . . . He was then 14. We usually all sleep together, and it was cold that night. I was the youngest and Ramesh chose me to keep him warm. . . . It was about one year later that I got paid to do this sex thing with an older boy who was in a different gang. He was about 16, and he gave me five rupees. . . . I felt a lot of pain, but the money bought me food. Then Ramesh showed me this toilet, where lots of men come for sex with each other. . . . I began to earn money through selling my arse. . . . Maybe I can make 100 rupees a week, and I used to give some of it to Ramesh. Now I give it to Debanuj. He is the leader now that Ramesh is gone. (p. 205)

Inadequate or non-existent welfare provision for persons under the age of 18, combined with peer suggestion or pressure, can lead children to start prostituting in affluent as well as poor countries. For example, one of the Glasgow sex workers interviewed by McKeganey and Barnard (1996, pp. 24–5) describes her entry into prostitution as follows:

> I was homeless at 16 and I was staying with a girl in Ruchazie, I wasn't getting any money from the social security because I was under 18, all I had was my lodging allowance and she was threatening to throw me out if I didnae get any money. She'd been on the street before and basically it was a case of either I did it or I was out on the street.

In a study of child prostitution in Addis Ababa, girls describe being procured for clients by friends of their own age already working in prostitution (Zelalem, 1998), and Heather Montgomery's (1998, 2001) research on children involved in the sex trade in a tourist resort in Thailand provides an extraordinarily rich and thought-provoking insight into the phenomenon of child 'pimps'. Indeed, Montgomery observes that whilst popular myths about child prostitution make it 'inconceivable that children should pimp for each other and take a cut of the earnings of another child who has become a prostitute...this is exactly what does happen as part of the children's survival strategies' (2001, p. 92).

Economically desperate children who have friends or acquaintances working in prostitution may also be more likely to start trading sex not because they are coerced by older children, but simply because they can see that prostitution offers a means of subsistence, and/or a way to escape the indignities of poverty and the crushing, hopeless tedium of life in an impoverished rural area. So, for example, Jacqueline Sánchez Taylor and I interviewed teenage girls in Cuba who had migrated from rural villages to tourist areas to prostitute not because they would have starved had they remained at home, nor always because their home life was abusive, but because their lives in the villages were an unremitting struggle simply to exist, empty of all interest, excitement or hope. For them, the economic blockade of Cuba imposed by the USA meant sharing a single ill-fitting pair of shoes with a sibling, trying to keep their home clean without detergents, to wash themselves without soap, to cook without cooking oil, having to put up with headaches, period pains and scabies because treatments for minor ailments were unavailable, staying in after dark because there were no street lights and no places of entertainment, and so on. So when friends told them that in tourist areas it would be possible to make enough money to buy shoes and clothes, to earn hard currency that would enable them to access items like shampoo, pain killers and cooking oil in the unofficial economy, and that in tourist areas there were bars, music, bright lights, opportunities for adventure and pleasure, many of them went (O'Connell Davidson and Sánchez Taylor, 1996a).

Or consider recent research in Namibia that involved individual and focus group interviews with 148 sex workers, some above and some below the age of 18, most of whom were involved in outdoor forms of prostitution, and worked independently of any pimp or third party (Hubbard, 2002). More than half had experienced some form of abuse in childhood, and only 10 per cent described themselves as having experienced a 'good life' as a child, but almost all interviewees reported that they started to prostitute because of poverty, joblessness and the need to support their dependants. Asked why she had started to prostitute, a 17-year-old replied:

> I have a 2 year old daughter. The father of my daughter is in jail. I am living with my mother, two brothers and my daughter. I started doing sex work at the age of 15 years only because there was no one who could look after my daughter.... I support my child, my mother and my two brothers. (cited in Hubbard, 2002, p. 88)

Both adults and children in this study made the decision to enter prostitution following attempts to survive by taking on domestic work or other casual jobs, and finding such work to be poorly paid and insecure. They were thus urgently seeking other and better earning opportunities, and decided to try prostitution either at the suggestion of a friend or an acquaintance already in sex work, or after having observed sex work on the streets or in clubs or bars: 'word of mouth played a big role as friends tell friends about this way of making money . . . sex work was the last and often desperate choice for most of the respondents to earn money' (Hubbard, 2002, p. 89).

### Factoring in Other Forms of Oppression

Since 'the Child' as a social category is defined by its asexuality, as well as its dependence and passivity, children's experience of homophobia has received little attention in the anti-CSEC campaign literature. And yet there is evidence to suggest that this can be an important contributory factor in children's prostitution. Boushaba et al.'s (1999) research with 172 male sex workers in Morocco found that those who identified as homosexual had entered prostitution at a younger age than heterosexual males, with most having started to sell sex by the age of 15. For many, 'sex work was not simply a means of economic survival, but also a source of refuge from the hostility of those around them, and particularly their family. It also provided the opportunity to live their own sexuality' (p. 270). These boys and young men were at high risk of violence from clients, thugs and muggers on the street, but many also reported having experienced violence at the hands of their fathers or older brothers. Homophobia in the wider society further locked them into prostitution, for employers were unlikely to take them on. As one male sex worker put it, 'When you are a *pede* in Morocco you don't have much future' (p. 271).

For these Moroccan boys, the experience of violence, rejection by family members and social exclusion (often exacerbated by imprisonment for their involvement in prostitution) 'encourages a greater dependence on sex work as a means of survival' (p. 271). It can also promote a sense of solidarity and group belonging amongst sex workers, and lead to a positive evaluation of clients, especially those from supposedly more tolerant countries. One of Boushaba et al.'s interviewees said that he was waiting for his 'Swedish friend': He's going to come over this summer. I hope he will take me back with him. Over there, you can be very successful particularly if you are young, good looking and dark skinned' (p. 271). And even in countries that are imagined to be tolerant of diversity, child prostitution can be linked in complex ways to sexual abuse, homophobia and economic need. For instance, Barbara Gibson's collection of life-stories from boys who sell sex in Britain includes an account provided by Jason, a boy brought up in Wales in what he describes as a very loving and caring family, but who was bullied by other children from a young age because he was considered feminine in appearance and demeanour. 'Growing up at school was a nightmare. People say it was the best years of their life, they'd love to go back and do it all again ... I'd rather be hanged' (Gibson, 1995, p. 29). He continues:

> I was six years old when I started to fantasize about men. I used to think about sex and men. . . . When I was ten, I remember being in the public toilets and I saw all these holes in the wall. . . . I started looking through them and I saw these men getting off together. . . . I was trembling. . . . I had these sexual feelings and so I left my cubicle door open and someone came in. He fondled me down there while he masturbated himself. . . . It was all over when he came two minutes later. He slipped a £5 note into my hand. As soon as I came out of the toilet I burst into tears. . . . A year later, when I was eleven, I went back to the toilets to make money. (pp. 29–30)

By the time he was 13, Jason was earning around £100 per week from prostitution and 'It was having all this money that got me through big school. Instead of people calling me names, I was the most popular kid in school because I had all this money' (p. 31). At the age of 16, he moved to London. Without entitlement to housing or other welfare benefits, without qualifications, and too young to obtain anything but the most low-paid, menial work, he relied on street prostitution to subsist.

Racism is also significant for the analysis of prostitution, both adult and child. Discrimination against racial and ethnic minority groups often leaves women and girls with few options for economic survival other than domestic work or prostitution (see, for example, Mayorga and Velasquez, 1999), and, in a world where 'sex is raced and race is sexed' (Nagel, 2003, p. 10), there are other senses in which racism can link to participation in the sex trade. Jacqueline Sánchez Taylor's (2001a, 2001b) work on tourist-related sex commerce in the Caribbean, for instance, draws attention to the relationship between the social devaluation and sexualization of black bodies, on the one hand, and men and boys' willingness to enter into sexual-economic exchanges with tourist women, on the other. For teenagers as well as adult men, performing the stereotype of the sexually powerful black male with tourist women can be subjectively experienced as empowering, as well as yielding much needed material and financial benefits. Thus, while the pigmentocracy that operates in most Caribbean societies increases darker-skinned adults and children's chances of living in poverty, sexualized racisms, which have often been internalized by local black men and boys, appear to offer opportunities for social honour and affirmation.

And last but not least, oppression that comes in the form of rigid social attitudes towards female sexuality and the stigmatization of sexually 'impure' girls and women is a contributory factor in many children's involvement in the sex trade. In Colombia, for example, a girl who left home and started to prostitute at the age of 10 told how she had asked her adoptive mother if she could return home. The answer was 'No', because she had 'already been damaged'. Her adoptive mother would not accept her because she 'was going to set a bad example for her daughter' (Mayorga and Velasquez, 1999, p. 167). She therefore had little choice but to continue to trade sex to survive.

The International Labour Organization's Convention (No. 29) Concerning Forced Labour (1932) states that 'the term "forced or compulsory labour" shall mean all work or service which is exacted from any person under the menace of any penalty and for which the said person has not offered himself voluntarily'. Clearly, the latter clause would not apply in relation to children's prostitution, for, as noted earlier, children are deemed incapable of voluntarily entering a prostitution contract with a client, or consenting to work for a third-party organizer of prostitution. But as the studies reviewed thus far have shown, the assumption that child prostitutes' sexual labour is always *exacted* from them under the menace of some penalty is simply not borne out by evidence on children's involvement in the sex trade. Indeed, the research discussed above makes grim reading not because it describes a world in which children have been turned into 'commercial sexual *objects* available for short-term hire' (O'Grady, 1996, p. 11, emphasis added), but rather because it provides a glimpse of a world in which children, as human *subjects*, have been faced with such bleak choices. This highlights something that is seldom discussed in the campaigning literature on child prostitution, namely the significance of children's agency – their existence as conscious and purposive (albeit massively constrained) actors – for their presence in and experience of prostitution.

## Children as Agents

When children are imagined as a homogeneous group, defined by their passivity, helplessness, dependence and irrationality, it is impossible to imagine them as either faced by or capable of making choices. In the dominant discourse on CSEC, the alternatives for children are set up as a simple opposition between good and evil – between the physical and emotional development of the child, on the one hand, and commercial sexual exploitation, on the other (and, of course, it is not the child who chooses either of these options, but an adult who makes a decision, for good or ill, on the child's behalf). The contrast is made between a pleasant and sheltered childhood in the bosom of the family which leads to healthy and 'correct' development, and a 'lost', 'stolen' or 'raped' childhood leading to life-long physical and psychological damage (or worse) for those children who are forced to leave the protected environment of home (Montgomery, 2001, p. 57). This is not a contrast that makes sense so far as any of the under-18s in the studies mentioned thus far are concerned, and if we are genuinely concerned to understand what leads children to sell sex, it is incumbent on us to think seriously about the alternatives that actually face many persons under 18.

Montgomery observes that the children she studied in prostitution in Thailand had generally tried other forms of work, but the jobs open to 'poor, unskilled, women and children in the town are badly paid and often backbreaking' (2001, p. 98). She continues:

> The rubbish dump is close to where they live, but there is little money to be made there and it involves plenty of risks. The rats, the filth and the smell are all deeply unappealing, and the risk of injury and infections from broken glass or jagged metal is high. Selling food is another option, but there are start-up costs which would involve savings that most people do not have and the financial returns are not as high as in prostitution. In comparison with the jobs available, prostitution is well paid. . . . Without the school-leaving certificates which are necessary for any sort of office or shop work, and lacking any vocational training, the children's only other option, besides sorting rubbish, is begging, which is seen as a poor choice as earnings fluctuate greatly. (p. 98)

In many countries, domestic work in private households often represents the main or only earning opportunity for girls apart from prostitution. This is largely because such work is socially and politically constructed as not 'real' employment but an extension of women and girls' 'natural' role in the household (Anderson, 2000). However, domestic work is not only associated with low-paid jobs often involving arduous labour undertaken in extremely poor conditions, but is also a sector in which both adult and child workers lack protection and are often highly vulnerable to a range of abuses (Blanchet, 1996; Anderson, 2000; Anderson and O'Connell Davidson, 2003). The only work that the children interviewed by Mayorga and Velasquez had experienced apart from prostitution was domestic work, and their accounts of their experience as domestic workers in private households revealed 'lives trapped by broken promises and economic blackmail. They described having worked, largely, in exchange for food and lodging' (1999, p. 171). One interviewee, Cristina, described how, at the age of 14, she had run away from home and worked in prostitution but hated it so much that she decided to try employment as a live-in domestic worker. However, her working and living conditions were so poor that she left and returned to prostitution (p. 171). Physical and sexual violence against adult and child domestic workers is not uncommon (Blanchet, 1996; Mayorga, 1998; SACCS, 1999). Indeed, the experience of sexual violence at the hands of an employer can be a factor that precipitates women and children's movement from domestic work into prostitution (see, for example, Brown, 2000, p. 38).

Children are, of course, unlikely to be fully informed about the potential consequences of the decision to sell sex. Rafiq, for instance, may not factor the possibility of HIV infection into his choice between the pain and discomfort of sex and that of hunger; Cristina may not have been fully informed as to whether the statistical probability of being raped and beaten in sex work is higher or lower than in domestic work when she decided to return to prostitution. But many children – especially those who live in difficult circumstances – do none the less evaluate the choices they face on the basis of knowledge and experience, albeit limited and partial. Children, as much as adults, can and do act upon the basis of their subjective evaluation of the different options open to them. And because children are social beings, ideas about honour, duty and/or social status can also inform their subjective evaluation of different possible courses of action. Again, Montgomery's research in Thailand is particularly instructive, for it draws attention to the fact that children who trade sex have their own discourses about what they are doing and why, discourses that give meaning to and guide their social action:

> However incomplete and contradictory children's justifications for their lives are, and however little they perceive the wider social relations that they labour under, the child prostitutes in Baan Nua do use what little control they have to make life more bearable. The children have tangible markers of status and hierarchy, and by moving up, or aspiring to move up, within this hierarchy, they claim some sense of control over the world. While child prostitutes are often viewed by outsiders as a homogeneous group, forced into involuntary prostitution, they do not see themselves that way. In Baan Nua, there is a great internal differentiation in the group, and in their classificatory system there is a distinction between those who have no power to refuse or negotiate and those who do. (2001, p. 91)

Even young children experience social emotions such as shame (if any reader doubts this, ask yourself how old you were the first time you experienced a sense of public humiliation). In the community of Baan Nua, as elsewhere in the world, the poorest families command the least respect, and individuals who are powerless and can be treated as objects by others are socially devalued. Children's action within prostitution is guided not simply or even always by the desire to eat rather than starve, but also by the desire for social esteem and a sense of honour:

> Lek was first procured at the age of three by her neighbour. At that age she had no power to refuse or negotiate, and for many years she had a very low status in Baan Nua because she was a child who could be forced to do whatever she was told. As she has grown up, however, her status in the community has improved, so that now she too procures younger children.... In Lek's case the status she receives in so doing is particularly gratifying. She and her family are especially poor... and often viewed as being at the bottom of the community, and it hurts her that she is looked down upon by so many. (Montgomery, 2001, p. 93)

It is more generally the case that earning opportunities in the informal economy are ranked on status hierarchies of gender, age, race and relative economic position. In Latin America and the Caribbean, for example, it is boys not girls who work as shoe-shiners, but shoe-shine is also viewed as child's work. For a teenage boy to rely on shoe-shine for his income would be subjectively experienced as humiliating, in some countries, probably much more humiliating than engaging in certain forms of sex work. Indeed, there are contexts in which boys' participation in sexual-economic exchanges represents not just a strategy for economic survival or advancement (even though they are that), but also a means through which to demonstrate oneself 'manly' and 'not gay', and to earn respect from peers and older men (Moya and García, 1999; Sánchez Taylor, 2001a).[1] And even though the stigma of female prostitution is such that it can rarely be entirely erased either by visible financial success or by association with 'high class' clients, there are none the less girls who use prostitution as a means to escape a situation that they subjectively perceive as more painful, debasing and soul-destroying than trading sex.

Children are 'active in the construction and determination of their own social lives' (Jenks, 1996, p. 51), and this is true of child prostitutes, as well as children in general. It does not, of course, mean that they can control the conditions in which they live or that they should be viewed as authors of their own destinies. To the extent that they make their own social lives, they, like adults, do so in circumstances that are given to them by history. But to understand why many children end up selling sex, it is none the less important to think about children as agents, as *existent* rather than nascent social and emotional beings. It is only when children are recognized as such that we can begin to grasp the complexity of the links between prostitution and factors such as poverty, neglect, abuse, homophobia and racism. Very often it is precisely because children – like adults – experience these factors as blotting out their subjectivity and individuality that they view prostitution as the lesser of two evils. There is no dignity in poverty. Children who must go hungry, ragged and barefoot, or who only manage to eke the barest subsistence from performing tasks they find demeaning, can feel just as humiliated as an adult in the same position. Children who are neglected, or physically and verbally abused, by their carers, or who are forced to conform to the grimly regimented, emotionally empty routine of life in a large state-run orphanage, or who are constantly made the objects of homophobic bullying and denied opportunities to express their sexuality, can experience this as an extinguishing of themselves as full persons. To run away, even if that means using prostitution as a means of survival, can thus be experienced as an assertion of the self as subject, not as being transformed into an object.

Scheper-Hughes has noted, 'In writing against cultures and institutions of fear and domination', it is important to find a middle ground between reducing those who suffer oppression to object-like victims and romanticizing the tactics they employ to survive as a form of heroic resistance. The 'destructive signature of poverty' must be acknowledged, but so too must the 'creative, if often contradictory, means' that people use to stay alive and to exist in the world in which they find themselves (Scheper-Hughes, 1992, p. 533, cited in Nencel, 2001, p. 221). This holds good in relation to persons below, as well as above, the age of 18, as well as in relation to other forms of oppression, such as racism and homophobia. Children like Rafiq, Lek or Jason are not resisting their oppression or realizing themselves as free and autonomous beings when they sell sex, but they are none the less social agents making choices between the bleak alternatives on offer to them. And recognizing that children, as well as adults, can and do use sex as a resource should also alert us to another set of boundary troubles.

### Boundary Troubles Revisited

In popular Western thought, two key sets of assumptions serve to delineate prostitution from non-commercial heterosexual sexual relationships. First, it is assumed that unlike marriage and/or sexual relationships based on mutual desire or romantic love, prostitution involves a form of sexual interaction that is brief, instrumental and businesslike in character, hence 'prostitution' is taken to refer to the narrow and explicit exchange of sexual services for payment in cash or kind. Second, the term 'prostitute' is held to describe a person (or more usually a woman) who makes a living by selling such services, and it is assumed that such a woman is easily separated from wives, girlfriends and other non-prostitute women by her willingness to enter indiscriminately into narrowly focused, cash-for-sex exchanges with a series of anonymous others. But it is only possible to ring-fence prostitution in this way by keeping our eyes firmly shut to the fact that in most societies, gender inequalities mean that heterosexual sexual relationships are very often also economic relationships. Indeed, Simone de Beauvoir once remarked that from the standpoint of economics, the prostitute's position corresponds to that of the married woman: 'For both the sexual act is a service; the one is hired for life by one man; the other has several clients who pay her by the piece. The one is protected by one male against all the others; the other is defended by all against the exclusive tyranny of each' (1972, p. 569). In a world of material and political inequalities, there can be no firm boundary between sex for economic gain or personal advantage, and sex for its own sake (or for love or duty). Instead, there is a continuum. At one pole are those sexual encounters within which one party participates *only* because s/he is paid or forced to do so, at the other pole are those in which people genuinely exchange only love for love, or lust for lust, or obligation for obligation. But in between are a range of encounters and relationships within which a relatively less powerful party pursues social or economic advantage, as well as sexual pleasure and/or emotional sustenance (see Sánchez Taylor, 2001a). This is because, as Zalduondo and Bernard point out,

> sex is a resource with both symbolic and material value. As a source of sensual and emotional pleasure, and/or as a means of acquiring so-cial capital (including prestige, debt, etc.), sex plays multiple roles in

personal relationships and broader social alliances (e.g., through marriage). In addition, for persons with characteristics sexually desirable by
others, sex has exchange value, and so can function importantly in individual strategies for personal advancement and/or economic survival.
(1995, pp. 157–8)

It follows that people – both above and below the age of 18 – can and often
do enter into sexual-economic exchanges in what is imagined as the 'private' sphere, as well as in the 'public' realm of the market (Zalduondo and
Bernard, 1995; Kempadoo, 2001). In settings where poverty is widespread,
the close connections between sexual and economic life can encourage
children's involvement in what some commentators term 'transactional
sex', that is, 'sex with one person, consistently, in exchange for economic
or "in kind" support' (Williams, 1999, p. 20). So, for instance, studies
in Jamaica as well as in a number of African countries show that girls
(and sometimes boys) as well as adult women sometimes rely on the
exchange value attaching to sex, entering into relatively long-lasting relationships with older men ('Boops' or 'Sugar Daddies') within which sex
is exchanged for gifts and/or basic necessities (Chikwenya et al., 1997;
Williams, 1999; Wood and Jewkes, 2001; Simpson, 2001).

Providing that children are imagined as a homogeneous group, defined
by their passivity, asexuality and innocence, sexual-economic exchanges
between adults and children that occur in non-commercial contexts present
no moral, political or legal challenges. When a paedophile assumes the
role of 'benefactor' to a young child who is impoverished and/or homeless, providing her or him with clothing, school books, food, perhaps even
a place to live, in exchange for a relatively long-term and stable sexual relationship, he or she clearly transgresses socially agreed codes and
conventions, as well as laws, regarding relationships between adults and
children. Similarly, when men provide long-term economic support to impoverished families in exchange for regular sexual contact with a small
child on the assumption that young children pose no threat of sexually
transmitted disease, there is no question but that it represents a form of
sexual child abuse. But 'transactional sex' involving teenagers takes us
onto more difficult terrain. Here, we are talking about adults providing
adolescent sexual partners with long-term financial support, gifts, accommodation and/or access to entertainment and a life-style that would
otherwise be beyond the younger person's reach. This happens in affluent
countries as well as in the developing world, but wherever it takes place,
the young people's motivations are often similar to those identified by the
authors of a study on sex and violence among Xhosa Township (South
Africa) youth:

> poverty, mind-numbing boredom and the lack of opportunities or
> prospects for advancement contribute to young people investing substan-
> tial personal effort in the few arenas where entertainment and success
> are achievable, most notably their sexual relationships. These become

an important vehicle for gaining (or losing) respect and 'position' among peers, as well as for material benefit. (Wood and Jewkes, 2001, p. 318)

The 'Sugar Daddy' does not usually need to force the young person into a sexual relationship, and providing that the child concerned is above the legal age of sexual consent, there is rarely anything in national law to prevent such arrangements.[2] Is there any reason to differentiate between an impoverished 16-year-old who trades sex with many different adults in exchange for cash, clothes and other benefits (i.e. a 'victim of an intolerable form of forced labour' in CSEC-speak), and an impoverished 16-year-old who does the same thing with one adult? In this regard, we should also note that in many countries – both affluent and developing – it is legally possible for a child aged 15, 16 or 17 to marry (Lederer, 1996), and so potentially for an adult to enter into a perfectly legal exchange of economic support for sex with a child. Again, why differentiate between a teenager who trades sex with many men in order to subsist, and a teenager who is expected to provide sex to a husband upon whom she depends for her subsistence? Certainly, the consequences for a child's health are not always very different. Recent research on age differences in sexual partners and risk of HIV-1 infection in rural Uganda suggests that many HIV-positive adolescent girls were infected by an older husband, for example (Kelly et al., 2003), and girls who use non-commercial sexual relationships as part of a strategy for economic survival or personal advancement can experience violence at the hands of husbands, boyfriends or Sugar Daddies.

Yet failure to differentiate between the two would lead us into a very tangled web, for the fact is that, far from transgressing dominant social conventions in relation to sexual life, the relationship between Sugar Daddy and adolescent or between husband and teenage bride often mirrors (albeit perhaps in an exaggerated form) inequalities that are quite normal in heterosexual relationships in most societies. It is not uncommon to find an (often huge) imbalance of economic, social and political power between heterosexual lovers and spouses, yet few people would accept the proposition that this makes most men 'sex exploiters' in relation to their wives or girlfriends. Indeed, when women or girls seek out more powerful husbands or boyfriends, they are often accused of being mercenary 'gold-diggers' rather than viewed as victims of exploitation. This tension is evident in commentaries on transactional sex, and public reactions are particularly ambivalent when people suspect that teenagers may be participating in sexual-economic relationships with older men not for basic survival, but for luxury goods.

In Japan, school girls' involvement in 'compensated dating' (*enjo kosai*) is often viewed as signalling the child's moral laxity as well as being read as a sign of a more general social malaise (*Japan Times*, 1998). Meanwhile, a researcher who recently studied the 'Sugar Daddy' phenomenon in Kenya commented, 'Young women actively seek partners who are willing to spend money ... and often initiate relationships with older men' (IRIN, 2003). At the same time, she said, the girls were often driven to such relationships by dire circumstances: 'we can't paint them as villains, but we can't see them as innocents either' (IRIN, 2003; see also Williams, 1999, p. 26). It seems that the further we move from the story about small children kidnapped and held in sexual slavery, the less certain we are about who are the goodies and who are the baddies, who are the victims and who the victimizers, who is object and who is subject. Moral certainty evaporates once attention is focused on what is imagined as the 'private' realm of sexual and family life, rather than upon the market. We lose the plot, or, at least, we find ourselves immersed in quite a different narrative.

### Victims of Childhood?

John Hoffman (2001) has commented on the difference between the notion of a 'victim', which refers to a person or group subject to violence, and 'victimhood', which refers to a pathology and ideology within which persons/groups see themselves, or are seen by others, as mere objects, without the capacity to defend their own interests or those of others (i.e. without power). This distinction can inform responses to human pain and suffering. Violence against those who are cloaked by the mantle of victimhood tends to elicit a stronger emotional reaction than does violence against those who are socially imagined as full subjects. There are, of course, complicated and often compelling reasons for feeling a particularly intense horror and distress about violence against extremely vulnerable human beings. However, it is also necessary to recognize the possibility that people or groups can be victims of victimhood (i.e. harmed by the fact that they are socially imagined as objects, without subjectivity or agency), and that ideologies of victimhood can encourage the minimization or denial of injuries to persons and groups who are constructed as subjects, rather than objects (see also Lamb, 1999).

The social construction of children as powerless objects all too easily translates into a stereotypical image of the victimized child, such that a child who does not conform to the stereotype (a child who is not pathetic, helpless, doe-eyed and innocent) cannot be imagined as a victim. Thus, children who develop strategies for fighting back or coping with conditions of deprivation are often viewed with great unease (Montgomery, 2001, p. 27). Victimhood is also gendered, and emotional and legal responses to children who trade sex for money, a place to live, and so on, differ according to the sex of the child and the adult involved. In France, for example, a 35-year-old female teacher was recently given a one-month suspended prison sentence for having a sexual relationship with a boy aged 14. She met the boy, who suffered abuse as a child, at a special school, and gave him a room in her flat: 'The public prosecutor ... refused prosecution demands for a three-month sentence, and said [she] had helped the young man in some ways. Her lawyer . . . said the verdict was a gesture to appease strict moralists' (Webster, 1999, p. 15). If the gender identities of the adult and child involved in this case were reversed, would the relationship have been described in the same terms?

Male adolescents who exchange sex with adult women for cash or other benefits are rarely understood as harmed by the experience in the same way as their female counterparts, for the cultural vocabulary of victimization is a 'far more pervasive theme in female than in male development' (Haaken, 1999, p. 25). As a result, teenage boys who trade sex do not necessarily narrate their experience in the same way that teenage girls do. In published accounts of adolescent boys' entry into prostitution, they appear to be more likely than girls to stress their own agency, including their sexual agency (Gibson, 1995; Davies and Feldman, 1999; Laurindino da Silva, 1999). This observation could be interpreted in different ways – do the blinkers of gender ideology prevent boys from seeing their own victimization, or prevent girls from seeing their own agency? For the purposes of this chapter, however, the real point is that children do not all stand in a single, uniform relation either to adults or to their communities. And, as boys and girls of different ages, different racial/ethnic identities and sexual orientations, not to mention individual personalities and qualities, children who trade sex do not all alike conform to dominant models of the 'innocent victim'.

Those involved in fund raising for children's charities are all too well aware that 'childlike' children elicit a more generous response from the general public, and those seeking to build popular support for campaigns against CSEC know that the less ambiguous the child's status as both child and victim is in stories about child prostitution, the more likely it is that people will agree to the proposition that child prostitution is an intolerable form of forced labour. Asked to choose between the following two accounts of a child's entry into prostitution, it is fairly obvious which would be more effective for fund raising and lobbying purposes:

> When I first met one of these children, 12-year-old Dah Vit, it was clear she had been tortured. Cigarette burns scarred her wrists and hands. We were sitting in the back room of a brothel . . . Dah Vit was close to tears. She had ended up in the village of Svay Pak a long way from home in Vietnam, after being sold by her mother for US$200. (ECPAT, 1998, p. 5)

> When I was 16 I went to a pub with a pal and he kept going to the toilet and coming back with money. He told me he was wanking old queens for £5 a go. He said it was easy money so I had a go. (Davies and Feldman, 1999, p. 6)

Perhaps understandably, then, public-awareness-raising materials produced by those campaigning against CSEC have, through the use of particular images (broken rose-buds, discarded toys, small children being led away by large, shadowy male figures), and examples of cases involving children aged between 3 and 12 and/or children who are subject to slavery-like practices by an employer or pimp, kept the focus of attention firmly on the sexual exploitation of those who readily fit with dominant cultural tropes of 'childhood'. Within this, any recognition is lost of children as agents, as human beings who, though massively constrained by structures and forces beyond their control or even understanding, none the less may attempt to pursue their own interests and desires.

In this sense, campaigns against CSEC could be said to be out of kilter with the principles that inform the Convention on the Rights of the Child, which extends to children rights of participation (as well as rights to provision and protection), thereby representing 'children as subjects or agents, capable of exercising for themselves certain fundamental powers' (Archard, 2003, p. 4). And yet the fact that campaigners clearly struggle to find any way of representing commercially sexually exploited children as agents or of incorporating the principle of participation into strategies to combat CSEC[3] should alert us to more fundamental tensions within the CRC. For though this convention does establish 'a discursive space . . . within which children are . . . seen as individuals, whose autonomy should be safeguarded and fostered', it also reiterates children's separateness and difference from adults (James, et al., 1998, pp. 6–7). And because it gives rights to children 'only and in so far as they are children', it necessarily enshrines and universalizes a particular understanding of children and childhood (Archard, 2003, p. 3). Critics argue that the CRC actually encodes the modern Western liberal conception of childhood, within which children are understood to be immature, irrational, incompetent, dependent and asocial beings, who must pass through a standard series of steps in order gradually to acquire competencies and develop into 'full' human beings (i.e. fully autonomous, rational adults) (Boyden, 1990; James, et al., 1998; Seabrook, 2001).

Even the age boundary of childhood accepted by the CRC (18) seemingly reflects the interests and experience of the affluent in the affluent world. In Western societies, a combination of government policies on housing, health care, education, employment and taxation serves to force children into dependence on adults until the age of 18 (and even beyond, as is the case for many young adults in Britain, where the Labour government is aiming to ensure that 50 per cent of young people go to university, but will not fund their access to higher education). This gradual and politically constructed increase in the upper age limit of childhood as a period in which human beings require special protection is related primarily, though not exclusively, to the growing demand for a professional and qualified workforce, for 'as the length of time needed for education and training extends', so young people tend 'to assume later and later in life the responsibilities of earning a living, marriage and childbearing' (Black, 1995, p. 87). By contrast, in economically developing nations (and even in poorer families in affluent countries), it is not the norm for young people to remain in education or training and in a state of complete economic dependency until their eighteenth birthday.

The discursive construction of CSEC as 'forced labour' and the violation of childhood 'innocence' likewise assumes that a particular model of childhood (as a state of passivity and dependence) can be universalized and extended to cover both young children and adolescents up to the age of 18. It follows that, for anti-CSEC campaigners, the notion of autonomy has limited application in relation to commercially sexually exploited children. They should have the right to speak and be heard, to have their wishes taken into account by adults (judges, social workers, teachers, parents, etc.) after they have been rescued from prostitution, and, more generally, efforts should be made to encourage children's participation in plans and programmes designed to combat CSEC. But it is not necessary to consider whether, as subjects and agents, children might prefer the company of their fellow gay sex workers to that of their homophobic family, might prefer to sell sex than to pick rubbish or work in domestic service, might prefer to live on the streets, even if it means trading sex, than in institutional care, because children ought never to have to face such choices. They ought to be enjoying the secure and dignified 'childhood' and decent standards of living promised to them by the CRC.

In reality, however, there are millions of people in the world who, long before the age of 18, have had to assume responsibilities, face discrimination, suffer losses, endure hardships and make choices that a middle-class adult from an affluent society will never have to assume, face, endure or choose. Some of them trade sex as part of a strategy for coping with the circumstances in which they find themselves. And they do not find themselves in these circumstances simply because they are 'children', but also because they are members of impoverished communities, and/or groups that are socially, economically and politically disadvantaged on grounds of race, ethnicity or caste, or groups that are forgotten, feared or despised by the wider community (homeless, gay, slum-dwellers, drug users) (see Ennew, 1986, p. 1). The CRC does actually recognize the interdependence and indivisibility of children's rights, and those who campaign against CSEC also sometimes acknowledge the fact that children's rights to protection from commercial sexual exploitation cannot be separated from their rights to decent economic and social standards of living. But the significance of this point is eclipsed by talk of child prostitution as 'forced labour' and 'slavery', as well as by the assumption that children's rights are divisible from adults' rights, and that children are defined by their passivity and dependence.

Patricia Williams' comments on the shortcomings of the liberal ideal of a 'colour-blind' society as a response to the problem of racism also ring true in relation to the campaign against CSEC:

> While I . . . embrace colour-blindness as a legitimate hope for the future,
> I worry that we tend to enshrine the notion with a kind of utopianism

whose naïvety will assure its elusiveness. In the material world ranging from playgrounds to politics, our ideals perhaps need more thoughtful, albeit more complicated, guardianship. By this I mean something more than the 'I think therefore it is' school of idealism. 'I don't think about colour, therefore your problems don't exist.' If only it were so easy. (1997, p. 2)

Is the utopianism embodied in dominant children's rights talk, with its emphasis on children's universal right to 'childhood' (even their 'right to happiness', Warburton and Camacho de la Cruz, 1996), likely to help any of the children discussed in this chapter? Or does its naïvety merely help us to keep our eyes wide shut to the structures and ideas that oppress them as members of particular groups (groups that include both adults and children)? As Judith Ennew observes in the conclusion to her seminal book *The Sexual Exploitation of Children*:

We need to broaden the sphere of morality to take into consideration all practices which involve a lack of respect for persons: systems of race, class, age and gender – in short, all inequalities and aggressions.... If moral debate is reduced to sexual matters, then all other inequalities are bound to be obscured by insistent screams of shock and horror – by exaggeration and distortion. As long as that process continues, children will be exploited sexually, racially, through their poverty, or simply because they are children. (1986, p. 147)

# 4 Child Migration and 'Trafficking'

This book is concerned, at one level, with the boundary troubles generated by attempts to classify social phenomena and social groups, and such problems are perhaps nowhere more acute or more politically significant than in relation to migration and migrants in the contemporary world. Who counts as 'a migrant', what counts as 'voluntary' or 'economic' migration, and what as 'forced' migration or 'asylum seeking'? Western social scientific research on 'migration' has very often been policy-driven – its definition of its subject matter as well as 'its research questions, methods and even findings are shaped by the political interests of governments and funding bodies' (Castles, 2003, p. 25). Very often, this means approaching migration as a problem, for governments are primarily concerned with forms of migration that are viewed as a threat to national sovereignty and security, and/or to national/racial/ethnic purity. Thus, a good deal of research attention has been paid to movements from poor or relatively economically disadvantaged countries to more affluent countries, from countries with predominantly black and brown populations to countries with predominantly white populations, from Muslim to Christian countries, while little interest has been shown in flows of affluent persons around the world. Tourists, gap-year students, international businesspeople and Western expatriates, for example, are not usually imagined as 'migrants', even though they may spend longer in a foreign country than, say, seasonal agricultural workers from poor countries who would be defined as 'migrant workers'.

As is the case with other social phenomena, academic and popular Western thought on migration is powerfully shaped by a series of binaries: internal versus international migration; voluntary versus forced; temporary versus permanent; legal versus illegal (King, 2002). And because these binaries map onto other dualisms central to Western understandings of the social world, they lead to accounts of migration that are gendered and aged, as well as raced. Thus, migration has traditionally been conceptualized and theorized through reference to adult men's movement, with women and child migrants typically imagined as merely tagging along behind the 'primary' male migrant (King, 2002, p. 97). Russell King (2002) argues very convincingly that the old dyads are increasingly inadequate to grasp the contemporary realities of migration, and this, it seems to me, is another reason why the issue of migration provokes such intense anxiety in late-modern Western societies. The forms of migration that we are currently witnessing and the migrants living in our midst do not fit neatly into the classifications, social categories and stereotypes that have so long served to 'make sense' of the phenomenon of 'immigration'. Gone (or so it seems to many) is the 'political refugee' of old – the elderly, bespectacled, brilliant, dissident male professor, forced into exile because he spoke out against a totalitarian regime, and in his place are 'gangs' of young male leather-jacketed Romanian Gypsies; gone (or integrated into mainstream British society) is the friendly, hard-working 'West Indian' migrant here to staff our health service or transport system, and in her place are veiled 'Muslims' whose economic contribution is unseen and uncertain, and Eastern European prostitutes, and Albanian children begging on the streets of London.

The intense contemporary policy and public interest in 'people smuggling' and 'trafficking in women and children' strikes me as, at least at one level, an attempt to reassert the old boundaries and binaries of migration (voluntary/forced, legal/illegal, male/female, adult/child), and so to reclaim the old certainties of a world order in which modern liberal states seemed to occupy the moral, as well as the economic, high-ground. The corpses that wash up on the beaches of southern Spain and Italy (and these amount to more than two thousand a year: Andrejavic, 2002; McGill, 2003), those in Britain found suffocated in a container lorry at Dover and drowned whilst cockle-picking at Morecambe Bay are not tragic testimony to the enormity of global political and economic inequalities and the inhumanity of the affluent world's immigration regimes – they speak only to the barbarity of the Other (the 'snakeheads', the 'mafia', the 'slave traders'). The human rights of the men, women and children held in detention centres for an indefinite period without trial are not being violated, for they may very well be 'bogus asylum seekers', rather than having a genuine claim to remain in the country. And should anyone doubt the civility of a state that refuses human beings both the right to work and entitlement to welfare benefits, the concept of 'trafficking' will come to the rescue. Because it serves to divide the deserving 'victims' from the undeserving 'illegal immigrants', we can all sleep easy, knowing that our governments have committed themselves to do all in their power to protect and assist those who truly merit help.

This chapter critically interrogates the notion of 'forced' and 'free' migration as oppositional categories, and the assumption that child migration can be treated as distinct from adult migration for analytical and political purposes. It argues that dominant discourse on 'child trafficking', like the discursive construction of child prostitution as 'forced labour' and 'modern slavery', serves to shore up a model of children as passive objects and eternal victims and to deflect attention from the structural factors that underpin children's presence in the global sex trade.

## What is 'Trafficking'?

In Europe and North America at the end of the nineteenth and start of the twentieth century, there was great public concern about 'White Slavery' – a term used to refer to 'the abduction and transport of white women for prostitution' (Doezema, 2002, p. 22). The phenomenon 'was covered widely in newspapers, a number of organisations were set up to combat it, and national and international legislation was adopted to stop the "trade"' (Doezema, 2002, p. 22); indeed, concerns about White Slavery eventually culminated in the UN Convention on the Suppression of Trafficking in Persons and the Exploitation of the Prostitution of Others (1949). A number of commentators have explored the 'cultural myth' of White Slavery, paying particular attention to the ways in which representations of the 'White Slave' (in newspaper reports, campaigning materials, popular fiction and later film) served as a foil for the expression of broader anxieties about social change, especially as regards sexuality, gender and familial relations, race, national identity, migration patterns and public health (Grittner, 1990; Gilfoyle, 1992; Chapkis, 1997; Doezema, 1999, 2001; Bartley, 2000). Stories of White Slavery typically featured wicked parents who sold their daughters to white slavers, or young and virginal country girls being lured to big cities where they were seduced, corrupted and ultimately destroyed. Disease and death were themes in both fictional and non-fictional accounts of prostitution at turn of the twentieth century: 'all assume that once a woman "falls" it is forever. The rigid boundaries of proper sexual behaviour make it impossible for any sexually experienced female . . . to regain respectability or virtue' (Gilfoyle, 1992, p. 155).

White Slave narratives were also formulated during a period of intense anxiety about race and immigration (Chapkis, 1997, p. 42), and stories of White Slavery clearly reflect these fears. Meanwhile, the very term 'White Slavery' marks the phenomenon off from the enslavement of black Africans, and valorizes whiteness. The moral content of White Slave stories focused on the despoliation of white girls' youth and innocence, inviting readers to understand this form of slavery as peculiarly disturbing and repugnant because it corrupts *white* females, the mothers of the nation and guardians of racial and national purity.

At the turn of the twenty-first century, 'trafficking' has once again emerged as an issue of intense public concern, although now the focus is not exclusively upon white women and girls, and in some quarters at least, it is accepted that people can be 'trafficked' into sectors and settings other than prostitution. However, it is cases involving women and girls forced into prostitution that have received the lion's share of media and research attention. I will provide but three examples of the kind of cases that have stimulated renewed concerns about the problem of 'trafficking'. The first involves a Nigerian girl, Charity Osatin, who was 'just 14 when her uncle's wife's brother – known to her as Uncle Sam – offered to take her on a holiday. But Charity soon found herself in a brothel in Lagos, where she was first raped then forced into prostitution' (Gillan, 2003, p. 2). Later she was to be brought to Europe to prostitute, and in preparation for this she, along with four other girls, was taken to a wood where various rites were performed. As she related:

> They cut us and told us it would be a secret.... I believed that I was going to die if I told anybody.... They kept some of my body stuff, my hair and nails, and it is still with them so I am still frightened of them. (Gillan, 2003, p. 2).

Charity and the other girls flew to London, with instructions to claim asylum and then, at a later date, to make contact with a man who would arrange their transport to Italy, where they would join many other Nigerian women and teenagers working in street prostitution to repay their 'debt' to third parties for airfares, accommodation, food, clothing, and so on. The second example is the case of a 15-year-old Cambodian girl:

> I lived with my mother in a little village . . . we never had enough food to eat and we were all hungry. There was a woman who sometimes came to our village. She . . . said she could find good jobs in the city for some of us girls. I wanted to go with her so when she came back I went for an interview with some others. There were two men with her and they asked us lots of questions. I was really happy because they chose me and two others to get jobs. We left the next day in a taxi and went to Phnom Penh. We thought we were going to work in a shop but instead they sold all of us to different brothels. (Brown, 2000, p. 90)

And finally, Petra, a Slovakian teenager, describes how she was forced into prostitution in Dubi, a town on the Czech–German border:

> I went to a disco with a girlfriend. They just grabbed me. They threw me in a car and drove me here. . . . They were Russian. They drove me here. I didn't want to do this. They beat me – badly. They gave me injections . . . they brought me to the bar. . . . I didn't want to work. I wouldn't do what I was told. They got very angry. They beat me up. They cut me with a knife. . . . I couldn't tell anyone. They threatened me. . . . They had my passport and papers. I was afraid if I went home they'd come after me. . . . Then they sold me. This guy bought me. (Siden, 2002, pp. 75–6)

There are many, many reports of cases such as these involving both adult women and girls under the age of 18 (Calder et al., 1997; Kelly and Regan, 2000b; Wolthuis, 2002; McGill, 2003; *Pravda*, 2003, for example), and they form the backbone of current alarm about 'trafficking in persons'. In the most general of terms, 'trafficking' is understood to involve the transportation of persons by means of coercion or deception into exploitative or slavery-like conditions, and it is viewed as a serious problem by a wide range of different agencies, organizations and lobby groups (including governments; law enforcement agents; feminists campaigning for the abolition of prostitution; migrant workers' and other labour organizations; child rights NGOs; sex workers' rights activists; and other human rights agencies and NGOs). And yet different groups identify trafficking as a problem for very different reasons and often have very different political agendas with regard to the issue, and this means that attempts to produce a precise definition of 'trafficking in persons' and to identify appropriate policy responses to it have provoked, and continue to provoke, much controversy (Anderson and O'Connell Davidson, 2002). There are two key strands to the 'trafficking' debates: one concerns tensions between governments' obligations to protect and promote human rights, and their desire to restrict irregular forms of migration; the other centres on conflicting views of the relationship between trafficking and prostitution.

## The Politics of 'Trafficking': Part 1

The voluntary/forced migration dichotomy is central to the way in which most governments understand their international and domestic obligations in respect of immigration. So, for example, states that are signatories to the 1951 UN Refugee Convention officially have a duty to recognize as refugees people who have been forced to leave their countries due to persecution on specific grounds, but simultaneously retain the right (some would say obligation) to control and restrict the entry of migrants who have voluntarily left their home country in pursuit of particular ends (such as economic advancement, educational opportunities, family reunion, and so on). In other words, governments generally approach migration as if it were *either* instrumentally motivated ('voluntary' labour migration, for instance) *or* politically driven (people have been forced to move by war, or 'ethnic cleansing', or because they face persecution on grounds of their religion, political beliefs or racial identity, for example).

But can all migrants who are not compelled to move under threat of death by another person or persons, and/or the illegitimate exercise of power by state actors, be described as migrating 'voluntarily'? Many migration scholars would answer no; indeed, Stephen Castles has recently called for a contemporary sociology of forced migration, one that allows us to 'analyse the new characteristics of forced migration in the epoch of globalization' (2003, p. 17). Such a sociology would recognize that displacement can come about as a result of many causes – development projects, environmental degradation, natural disaster, industrial accidents or pollution – and that in many cases, 'it is extremely hard to distinguish between environmental, economic and political factors' (Castles, 2003, p. 15). Processes of economic development and restructuring (especially those that accompany structural adjustment policies imposed by world financial institutions) can also have a devastating impact on the lives of the rural and urban poor. If the experience of human rights violations is what marks forced from voluntary migration, and if economic, social and cultural rights are recognized as being just as important as political and civil rights, then the term 'forced migration' should arguably extend to cover those who move in an attempt to escape poverty.

But to recognize, as I think we should, that people can be compelled to migrate by a complex mix of political, social, economic and environmental factors immediately blurs the line between voluntary and forced migration. How serious must the suffering caused by such factors be before we can say it *forced* a family or individual to migrate? Is it enough that their living standards have fallen and they are hopeless about their future, or must they face a stark and immediate choice between migration and starvation? Few governments would be happy to accept a definition of 'forced migration' that included all those migrants who are driven to leave their homes by circumstances beyond their control. Indeed, some politicians are currently pushing for an even more restricted definition of 'refugee' than that provided in the 1951 Convention, and the new and more restrictive asylum and immigration legislation adopted by a number of European governments is regarded by many as threatening to end 'the right of asylum in Europe, one of the most fundamental of all human rights' (Morrison, 2000, p. 29; see also Gallagher, 2001, 2002). Because immigration is constructed as a problem of national sovereignty and security, and because widespread racism and xenophobia mean that anti-immigration policies have great popular appeal, there is a political tension between governments' spoken commitment to protecting universal human rights and their desire to be seen to control and restrict immigration. Thus, governments will enthusiastically endorse Article 13 of the UN Universal Declaration on Human Rights (1948) which concerns the individual's right to *leave* any country, but refuse to countenance the idea of a human right to *enter* any country, even though to protect the right to exit a country without guaranteeing a corresponding right to enter another country is an entirely meaningless piece of sophistry.

In recent years, the term 'trafficking' has come to play an important role in sustaining the fiction that dominant liberal discourse on universal human rights is something more than simple sophistry. From a governmental and intergovernmental perspective, 'trafficking' has been framed as a crime control and prevention issue. The beauty of trafficking, constructed as a problem of organized transnational crime within which the 'mafia' of various countries purportedly make billions of dollars by kidnapping or luring passive and 'innocent' young women and children into sexual slavery, is that it apparently represents a form of forced migration that simultaneously involves the violation of the human rights of the 'trafficked' person *and* a threat to national sovereignty and security. With trafficking understood as such, governments can present more restrictive immigration controls as if they were measures designed to protect and promote human rights (Anderson and O'Connell Davidson, 2002).

## The Politics of 'Trafficking': Part 2

The deep divisions that bedevil feminist debate on prostitution in general (see McIntosh, 1996) also find expression in the more specific debate on 'trafficking'. On one side of the divide stand those who might be termed 'feminist abolitionists'. They argue that prostitution reduces women to bought objects, and is always and necessarily degrading and damaging to women. Thus, they recognize no distinction between 'forced' and 'free choice' prostitution – all prostitution is a form of sexual slavery, and trafficking is intrinsically connected to prostitution (Jeffreys, 1997; Raymond, 2001). In this account, migrant sex workers have all been sold, duped or abducted, or forced to prostitute because they are women, and because they are women they are 'homeless and poor' (Barry, 1995, p. 196). From this vantage point, measures to eradicate the market for commercial sex are anti-trafficking measures, and vice versa. On the other side of the divide stand feminists who adopt what might be termed a 'sex workers' rights' perspective. They reject the idea that prostitution is intrinsically or essentially degrading, and, treating prostitution as a form of service work, they make a strong distinction between 'free choice' prostitution by adults and all forms of forced and child prostitution. Whilst they believe the latter should be outlawed, they hold the former to be a job like any other (NSWP, 1999; P. Alexander, 1997). From this standpoint, it is the lack of protection for workers in the sex industry, rather than the existence of a market for commercial sex in itself, that leaves room for extremes of exploitation, including trafficking. The solution to the problem thus lies in bringing the sex sector above ground, and regulating it in the same way that other employment sectors are regulated.

The feminist abolitionist stance finds favour with religious and moral conservatives around the world, while the sex work lobby's position often finds favour with politicians of different political persuasions whose desire to demarcate 'voluntary' and 'forced' prostitution seemingly reflects a wish to limit their state's obligations to protect migrant sex workers. 'Trafficked' women may (at least in theory) be recognized as 'deserving' protection and support; those who are working 'voluntarily' can be summarily deported (or 'administratively removed' in British Immigration Office-speak). Indeed, some commentators argue that expressions of concern about the plight of victims of 'trafficking' are often used to justify the strengthening of legal frameworks that violate the civil and human rights of all those who work in prostitution, and/or that restrict all women's capacity to migrate (Doezema, 2002, p. 24).[1]

But the politics of trafficking discussed here are not seen as relevant to debates on CSEC, for, once again, children are another matter: 'Whilst there continues to be debate about the boundaries of forced adult prostitution, there is no dispute that prostitution of children is always, by definition, coercive and to be proscribed' (Esadze, 2003, p. 14). Those who recognize that the concept of 'trafficking' is difficult in relation to adults rarely discuss the same difficulties in relation to children. So, for instance, having noted many of the political and definitional problems associated with dominant approaches to trafficking in women, Derks states that 'The vulnerability of children, stemming from the bio-physiological, cognitive, behavioural and social changes taking place during the growth and maturation process, distinguishes children from adults...and thus also their trafficking situation' (2000, p. 14). But is it really so easy to separate questions about adult and child 'trafficking'? To answer this, it is necessary to examine the definitional problems posed by the concept of 'trafficking' in more detail.

### 'Trafficking' Defined?

Those campaigning against 'trafficking' are very certain about the scale and severity of the problem: 'No one now disputes that trafficking today has reached alarming proportions the magnitude of which affects many countries as countries of origin, transit and destination points' (Javate de Dios, 2002, p. 1). If no one disputes that trafficking has reached alarming proportions (and the international and national policy attention devoted to 'trafficking' in recent years suggests that large numbers of people are convinced that the problem is serious and growing), then we can surely be confident that everyone knows what trafficking is – after all, how can something vague and ill defined be globally monitored, measured, mapped and evaluated?

Until recently, there had been no international agreement as to the proper legal definition of trafficking. However, in November 2000, the UN Convention Against Transnational Organized Crime was adopted by the UN General Assembly, and with it two new protocols – one on smuggling of migrants and one on trafficking in persons (known as the Palermo protocols, because the Convention was opened to states' signature at a conference in Palermo, Italy). The inclusion of these protocols in this particular Convention reflects the extent to which 'illegal migration' is currently understood as part and parcel of a supposed 'security threat' posed by transnational crime (see Beare, 1999). Where smuggling is held to refer to situations in which the migrant gives full and informed consent to movement, trafficking is defined as:

    a) The recruitment, transportation, transfer, harbouring or receipt of persons, by means of the threat or use of force or other forms of coercion, of abduction, of fraud, of deception, of the abuse of power or of a position of vulnerability or of the giving or receiving of payments or benefits to achieve the consent of a person having control over another person, for the purpose of exploitation. Exploitation shall include, at a minimum, the exploitation of the prostitution of others or other forms of sexual exploitation, forced labour or services, slavery or practices similar to slavery, servitude or the removal of organs;

    b) The consent of a victim of trafficking in persons to the intended ex-
       ploitation set forth in subparagraph (a) of this article shall be irrelevant
       where any of the means set forth in subparagraph (a) have been used.
    c) The recruitment, transportation, transfer, harbouring or receipt of a
       child for the purpose of exploitation shall be considered 'trafficking
       in persons' even if this does not involve any of the means set forth in
       subparagraph (a) of this article;
    d) 'Child' shall mean any person under eighteen years of age.

Rather than describing a single, unitary act leading to one specific outcome, 'trafficking in persons' is thus being used as an umbrella term to
cover a *process* (recruitment, transportation and control) that can be organized in a variety of ways and involve a range of different actions and
outcomes. The flexibility of the protocol's definition of 'trafficking' makes
it difficult, perhaps impossible, to operationalize in a uniform way, since
different individuals may make different decisions as to which particular actions and outcomes, and in which particular combination, should be
included under its umbrella. For this reason alone, claims about the magnitude and growth of the phenomenon should be taken with a very large pinch
of salt. The problem is compounded by the fact that (a) the constituent
elements of trafficking may also be deemed to constitute other separate
or related phenomena (for instance, the condition of slavery is one of the
outcomes included in the protocol definition, but not all enslaved persons
are 'victims of trafficking'); and (b) some of the constituent elements
identified in the protocol definition of trafficking themselves present definitional problems within international law (there is no international consensus regarding the definition of 'servitude', or of 'sexual exploitation',
for example) (see Anderson and O'Connell Davidson, 2002). But these
are not the only weaknesses in the protocol's definition of 'trafficking'.

### Voluntary/Forced and Adult/Child Dualisms Revisited

To approach 'trafficking' as a subset of illegal migration is to rely on
an over-simplistic distinction between 'legal' and 'illegal' migration, a
dichotomy that 'fails to match many aspects of contemporary migrant
reality' (King, 2002, p. 93). Violence, confinement, coercion, deception
and exploitation can and do occur within both legally regulated and irregular systems of migration and employment, and within legal and illegal
systems of migration into private households. So far as definitions of trafficking are concerned, the problem is further complicated by the fact that
these abuses can vary in severity, which means they generate a continuum
of experience, rather than a simple either/or dichotomy. At one pole of the
continuum, we can find people who have been transported at gunpoint,
then forced to labour through the use of physical and sexual violence and
death threats against them or their loved ones back home – as, for instance,

in the exemplary cases of trafficking cited at the start of the chapter. At the other pole, we can find people who have not been charged exorbitant rates by recruiting agencies or deceived in any way about the employment for which they were recruited, and who are well paid and work in good conditions in an environment protective of their human and labour rights, and/or women and children who have migrated into private households as wives, au pairs or adopted kin with the assistance of agents, and who are well treated and living in conditions that allow them to realize their rights and aspirations. But between the two poles lies a range of experience (Anderson and O'Connell Davidson, 2002).

Just how exploitative does an employment relation have to be before we can say that a person has been recruited and transported 'for purposes of exploitation'? And exactly how deceived does a worker have to be about the nature and terms of the employment prior to migrating before s/he can properly be described as a 'victim of trafficking'? There are numerous different elements to the employment relation: hours of work, rates of pay, job content, work rate, working practices, living conditions, length of the contract, and so on. Is it enough for a worker to be deceived about just one of these elements by a recruiter, or must s/he be entirely duped about every aspect of her work in order to qualify as a trafficked person (Anderson and O'Connell Davidson, 2002)?

Since persons under the age of 18 are not debarred from all forms of employment, this problem arises in relation to child as well as adult 'trafficking'. Take the case of the 15-year-old Cambodian girl that was described at the start of this chapter. Had she been given shop work in Phnom Penh as promised instead of being sold into prostitution, she would not automatically be considered a 'victim of trafficking'. Instead, her status as 'trafficked' would depend on the degree of exploitation to which she was subject in shop work. If she had been locked into the building, forced to work without pay and raped and beaten by her employer, then most would agree that she had been 'trafficked'. But what if the exploitation was less dramatic? What if her recruiter had merely deceived her about how much she would be paid and the hours of work? What if nobody actually beat or raped her, if she was formally free to quit and return home, but unable to do so until she had saved her return fare out of her meagre earnings and therefore compelled to remain only by dull economic necessity?

Without a neutral measure of 'exploitation', it is also unclear how 'trafficking' is to be distinguished from the legal movement of women and children into households, for instance through marriage, adoption and fostering. Expectations regarding the amount of unpaid labour that women and children will provide within households vary cross-nationally and within nations, as do social norms regarding the powers that men can properly exercise over women and that adults can properly exercise over children. How bad does a woman's or child's experience need to be in order for the agents who facilitated her movement to be viewed as 'traffickers'? Must she be imprisoned in the household, starved, beaten, raped and forced to work all hours in order to qualify as a 'victim of trafficking'? Or should qualification extend to a 'mail order bride' or adopted child who does not enjoy all the freedoms and privileges that would normally be enjoyed by a middle-class, ethnic majority wife or child in the host country? Or is the threshold somewhere between the two?

The problem is well illustrated by recent reports highlighting the fact that some West African children are trafficked into domestic work the UK. The language used to describe this phenomenon in an article in the *Observer* is revealing. 'Children are being trafficked into domestic service in Britain to clean houses and do chores without pay', it begins (Hinsliff, 2003, p. 13). But in case readers are not immediately appalled by the idea of children cleaning house and doing chores without pay (perhaps some have been known to ask their own children to undertake cleaning chores without pay), it continues, 'The victims are mostly west African girls lured on the promise of a Western education, only to find themselves forced to do *heavy* chores for wealthy families' (emphasis added). Next, we are told that child servants are not uncommon in West Africa, and that it is professional *African* families who are believed to 'secretly hire' these trafficked children for 'childcare and chores'. The children 'are rarely paid, work long hours and are vulnerable to ill treatment', and

> It is thought that a significant percentage of up to 10,000 largely west African children thought to enter the UK for private fostering are in fact destined for an underground world of domestic service. 'They don't speak the language, and probably wouldn't go to school,' said a spokesman for Unicef. 'It is often assumed that the families are doing them a favour – "we brought them to Britain, they do the work for free in return". They may be told that if they approach the police they will be arrested'. (p. 13)

Leaving aside concerns about the nervous tone ('it is thought', 'thought to enter', 'probably wouldn't', 'often assumed', 'may be told'), and the way in which such reporting pathologizes a traditional practice (not just in West Africa) of sending children to live with more affluent kin in order that they may enjoy opportunities that their parents are unable to provide,[2] the key point to note is how inadequate the UN protocol's definition of trafficking is in relation to this problem. Unless we can say precisely what is meant by 'exploitation', then to define trafficking as the movement of persons for purposes of exploitation is to invite policy-makers and others to fall back on prejudices about what constitutes a 'proper' and 'tolerable' relationship between parent/guardian and child, or husband and wife, or employer and employee, or pimp and prostitute.

And the dangers of framing migration as an issue of transnational crime control and crime prevention, rather than a human rights issue, and assuming that migrants can be neatly divided into moral categories such as adult (strong, active, agent) and child (weak, passive, victim), and smuggled (complicit in a crime against the state) and trafficked (victim of a crime against the person), are well illustrated by the following three examples of child migration. A Moldovan diplomat was recently arrested, in Moldova, 'on suspicion of involvement in the illegal trafficking of a 9-year-old Moldovan girl to the United States in 1999' (BBC Monitoring Service, 2003a). The girl in question was suffering from several serious diseases, and has been adopted by an American family who have provided her with medical treatment; she now speaks English, is attending school, and feels well. Preliminary investigations suggest that the accusations are ill founded and that the adoption was made officially and legally, but none the less the Moldovan authorities have not ruled out the possibility of insisting on the child's return to Moldova.

Since the child was not moved for purposes of exploitation (or should we understand the American family who adopted her as exploiting her vulnerability in order to obtain the benefit of having a child to love and care for?), it is, on the face of things, hard to see why the diplomat was accused of 'trafficking' rather than 'smuggling'. But then, as children are constructed as passive objects, and as 'smuggled migrants' are deemed by the Palermo smuggling protocol 'to be acting voluntarily and, therefore, in less need of protection' (Gallagher, 2002, p. 12), what are we to make of this case? If it was true that the diplomat had broken the law to arrange her entry into the United States, and the Moldovan authorities reclaimed the child as a 'victim of trafficking', wresting her from her adoptive family and bringing her back to live in a state-run orphanage without medical care, should we celebrate this as a victory in the fight for fundamental human rights?

But when people who assist children who want to migrate are treated as 'smugglers', it merely draws attention to the conflict between states' desire to control and restrict immigration and their spoken commitment to promoting and protecting children's and human rights. This is illustrated by the case of a group of Ukrainian parents, working in the USA illegally and separated from their children for years, with no lawful means of being reunited with them, who had paid an emigrant from the USSR, now a US national, $US7,000–10,000 to arrange their children's illegal passage to the USA disguised as a church choir. All of those charged with immigration offences received suspended jail sentences, but 'This was not an easy decision, because on the one hand this is a crime, and on the other there are separated families' (BBC Monitoring Service, 2003b). By way of contrast, consider the fact that in a 1998 test case in California, the court ruled that it is legal for US parents to pay anything between US$25,000 and $40,000 to have their 'unruly' teenagers kidnapped, handcuffed and flown to a 'behaviour modification' centre in Jamaica where they are held, against their will, for a year or more. Here, 'parental choice was sacrosanct' (Steele-Perkins, 2003). So much for children's rights.

A third example of the inadequacies of the binaries that inform dominant discourse on child 'trafficking' comes from Iman Hashim's research in Tempane Natinaga, Ghana (2003). Her study not only shows that children who remain in their place of birth, working for their own families, can be subject to exploitation, but also that those who migrate to work may be positive about their experiences, for migrant work in many cases had afforded them 'the opportunity to develop important relationships or skills, and to earn an income which they had significant control over and which allowed them to buy the things necessary for their progression into adulthood' (Hashim, 2003, p. 12). Ironically, however, 'the moment they become migrants, particularly cash-migrants for a non-related individual', they become the subject of interest as child labourers and potentially 'victims of trafficking', rather than child workers (Hashim, 2003, p. 12).

### Continuums and Impermanence in Prostitution

As noted in chapter 2, there is immense diversity within prostitution in terms of its social organization. Although it would be quite wrong to assume that all those who enter into some kind of direct or indirect employment relation with a third party are abused, cheated and poorly paid, dependence on a third party does leave many sex workers open to another layer of abuse and exploitation, especially when they are employed in illegal or poorly monitored workplaces, and/or if their status as 'illegal immigrant', lack of language skills and local knowledge, and/or extreme youth leaves them reluctant or unable to seek assistance or redress against injustices and ill treatment. The greater the individual's dependence on middle agents and employers who are effectively unaccountable and unregulated, the more that these third parties enjoy the godlike power to choose between harming or helping her. Not every middle agent or employer who enjoys this power will choose to harm, for those who recruit labour for and/or employ workers in the sex trade are not a socially, morally or politically homogeneous category of persons, and do not all adopt the same approach to their economic activity. An important distinction needs to be made between those third parties whose involvement in prostitution (whether legal or illegal) is guided by 'normal', mainstream rules of business practice, and those whose involvement in prostitution takes the form of simple and often brutal extortion. Amongst the former group are people who, for either ethical or business reasons or both, have no interest whatsoever in exploiting the labour of trafficked/unfree persons. Indeed, there are cases in which club owners have sought ways in which to regularize the immigration status of the migrant sex workers they employ (Agustín, 2001), and in some countries third-party employers' associations are amongst those calling for the application of labour standards law to the sex industry. Such calls are often coupled with demands for clampdowns on street prostitution, and thus reflect employers' economic interests rather than any altruistic sentiment, but they none the less highlight the fact that not all third parties provide demand for 'trafficked'/unfree labour.

Even third parties who enter into highly exploitative contracts with prostitutes (for instance, those who use systems of indenture to tie workers to them for up to 18 months) cannot be treated as a morally homogeneous group. Some of them beat and cheat the women and children they exploit. Some do not use physical force and honour the terms of the contract (O'Connell Davidson, 2001b). The fact is that some third parties understand themselves as employers and are at some level concerned to win or manufacture the prostitute's consent to the arrangement that exists between them, no matter how exploitative that arrangement may actually be. Other third parties do not view the persons they exploit as 'employees', or seek to otherwise legitimize or normalize the powers that they exercise over prostitutes. Instead, they control and exploit prostitutes simply through the use of violence or its threat, and/or confinement, or else treat women and children as objects to be sold on to other third-party organizers of prostitution. The two 'types' of third party can co-exist even in the same physical place (see, for example, Siden, 2002). In the absence of any form of workplace monitoring or protection, and, worse still, in the presence of connivance by corrupt police officers and local officials, getting a 'good' or a 'bad' employer is simply a matter of luck for the women and children concerned.

Meanwhile, as Laura Agustín (2004) observes, debts are common among all kinds of migrants, and middle agents who arrange women and children's transportation to another country in exchange for a fee that must be paid off through prostitution are not all cut from the same cloth. Some rape and assault those in their power, and continue to extort money by threatening to harm their loved ones back home long after the initial debt has been repaid. Others merely wish to recoup their outlay on travel and documents and the fee for their services. And even if we turn to organized criminal involvement in 'trafficking', the experience of those they exploit is not uniform. Louise Shelley (2003), for example, identifies different models of 'business' practice followed by criminal groups in different regions, models that are associated with different levels of violence.

It follows that in prostitution as much as in other sectors, the abuse to which migrants – both above and below the age of 18 – may be subject in the migratory process and at the point of destination varies in severity, generating a continuum of experience, rather than a simple either/or dichotomy. At what point on the continuum do we say that the abuse and/or deception is so serious and the exploitation so extreme that the individual concerned has been 'trafficked' rather than 'smuggled' into prostitution? This may not appear as a problem in relation to children, since the Palermo trafficking protocol explicitly states that the recruitment, transportation, transfer, harbouring or receipt of a person under 18 for the purpose of exploitation shall be considered 'trafficking in persons' even if it has not involved the use of force, deception, coercion, and so on. But given that we are being asked to understand 'trafficking' as a *process* (not a specific event) that can affect persons aged above as well as below 18, the idea of a clear and morally significant boundary between adults and children is difficult to sustain.

Let me illustrate with a hypothetical case, but one that research in a number of South-East Asian countries suggests would not be unusual (Skrobanek et al., 1997; Feingold, 1998, 2000; Phongpaichit, 1999; O'Connell Davidson, 2001c). A 16-year-old Vietnamese girl accepts a broker's offer to take her to China or Thailand and arrange for her to enter into a contract of indenture that binds her to a brothel owner for a period of twelve months. She is a 'victim of trafficking' according to the protocol definition. Let us say she has been lucky, and her employer is a woman or man of honour who, after withholding her salary for one year and deducting the broker's fee and the costs of food, accommodation, clothing and any medical care she has received, pays her the sum she was initially promised. Now a 17-year-old, she is free to leave, or to stay on and prostitute in the brothel as a formally free worker. At this point, she will be able to earn relatively good money from prostitution, certainly a great deal more than she could earn in any alternative employment back home. She decides to stay. A year later, the brothel is raided by police and the girl, now 18, is picked up and detained. Is she still a 'victim of trafficking'? Or is she an 'illegal immigrant' working voluntarily in prostitution?

A debt-bonded or indentured prostitute's status as 'unfree' is not necessarily permanent (indeed, the promise that the unfreedoms implied by a contract of indenture are time-limited is one of the things that makes it possible to persuade people to agree to enter such contracts). Even in settings where employment relations in prostitution are most consistently and most profoundly exploitative, and where violence and other forms of abuse by third parties are commonplace, generally the sex trade relies on a mixture of 'free' and unfree labour (see, for example, O'Connell Davidson, 2001c; Uddin et al., 2001; Siden, 2002). This means that individual prostitutes are in many cases able to 'progress' from a contract of indenture or a slavery-like condition to an employment relation from which they can freely withdraw. Some women proceed from here eventually to take on a managerial role and/or to become middle agents or brothel owners.

The point is that although analysis and policy are largely informed by an assumed radical disjuncture between forced and voluntary migration, between forced and free prostitution, between adult and child migrants, and between adult and child prostitutes, in reality these categories do not describe temporally separated, hermetically sealed and permanently fixed groups, nor can they grasp the continuum that exists between each of these poles. Attempts to squeeze the diversity of migrant prostitutes' experience into one of two categories – either 'forced' or 'voluntary' – obscure the complex interplay between structure and human agency in shaping that experience.

## Global Subjects

As noted in the previous chapter, we live in a highly unequal world, and one that is fast becoming more unequal. Both within and between nations, the rich are getting richer and the poor are getting poorer (Castells, 1998). The number of people living on less than US$1 per day rose by almost 18 million between 1987 and 1998, and yet 'The incidence of poverty has increased in the past few years not because the world as a whole is getting poorer, but because the benefits of growth have been unevenly spread. There has been a striking increase in inequality' (UNRISD, 2000, p. 11, cited in Sklair, 2002, p. 48). Not only are there massive disparities of income between rich and poor nations, but also within countries there are often huge gaps 'between regions and districts, especially between urban and rural communities' (Sklair, 2002, p. 49; see also AMC, 2000, p. 116). These inequalities have been a trigger for migration as people from rural areas seek to escape poverty, unemployment and the drab, unchanging routine of their daily lives by moving to more prosperous cities or countries. Often, women and children who migrate are also seeking to escape domestic violence and/or the consequences of family breakdown (Skrobanek et al., 1997; ESCAP, 2000). In some places, economic decline and political and social destabilization have taken place so rapidly and so completely that a majority of the population wish to migrate, and an extremely high percentage manage to do so. For example, out of a total population of 4.3 million, between 600,000 and one million people have left Moldova since national independence in 1991 (UNICEF, 2001, pp. 9–10). During the same period, some 600,000 Albanians, out of a total population of 3 million, migrated (Naegele, 2001).

Some adults and children who seek to migrate to cities or countries where work is more plentiful and better paid are deceived and forced into prostitution in the manner described at the start of this chapter. But it is also possible to openly recruit women and girls into prostitution, for the earnings from sex work can genuinely be very much higher than earnings from any other form of employment open to teenagers and young women (Feingold, 1998, 2000; Zi Teng, 2001). And, if the situation that women and teenagers face at home is bad enough, it is not always necessary even to lie about the working conditions that they will face in prostitution abroad (a recent report by the Institute for Public Policy, Moldova, 2003, suggests that young men and sex workers who recruit in Moldova are sometimes quite open about the very poor deal on offer). Equally, a period of indentured labour in a richer country promises many women and girls an opportunity to earn and save that is unparalleled by any other kind of employment available to them. Research on Thai women who have been taken to Japan as indentured sex workers shows that many are aware of the risks that attend this form of migrant work, but

> The potential for saving makes many women overlook the negative side of this venture. Thus, despite all the stories about harsh treatment, exploitation, and risk, many women still flock to Japan. Some of those who go through the ordeal once wish to return as they believe that their experience will allow them to manage the situation better the second time around. (Phongpaichit, 1999, p. 86)

And as well as migrant women and girls who seek opportunities to work temporarily in a city or country where prostitution is more highly paid, there are those for whom prostitution is entwined in a broader migration project (Andrijasevic, 2003; Agustín, 2004). For them, selling sex may be the fastest way to earn the money to repay debts incurred in the process of migration, or the best or only way to subsist until they are established in the new country. Alternatively, it may be that the only way they can find to migrate is by turning to middle agents or friends with links to the sex trade, or that they turn to prostitution after having migrated through other channels and into other forms of work (for instance, domestic work), and finding themselves poorly paid, cheated or abused. No matter whether they have migrated specifically to work in prostitution in order to save or remit money home, or whether working in prostitution is but one aspect of a migratory project, women and girls can end up in relationships with highly exploitative and abusive third parties. But their vulnerability to abuse and exploitation is not a given or automatic feature of migration – it is politically and socially constructed.

Global political and economic inequalities make it costly and difficult for 'Third World' women and girls to legally travel to richer countries and this increases their dependency on third parties, both within the migratory process and at the point of destination. In some places, immigration policy, policing practice with regard to prostitution, and the employment policies of those who own commercial sex businesses come together as an unholy trinity, making it virtually impossible for migrants to enter the sex trade as independent entrepreneurs (Phongpaichit, 1999; Rodriguez et al., 2001). As global subjects, women and girls from North America, Australia, New Zealand or European Union countries, by contrast, enjoy many privileges. This does not mean that such women and girls are never found in sex work abroad, nor does it *guarantee* them protection from deception and exploitation in the course of migration, or from abuse within the sex industry at the point of destination. However, it does make it a great deal easier for them to work independently in prostitution abroad, and/or to enter into the least exploitative forms of employment relation within the sex industry.

Consider, for example, the not untypical case of one of the British lap dancers in Tenerife interviewed by Esther Bott and me in 2003. 'Tanya' left home and moved to Tenerife at the age of 17. Here she discovered that she could earn more as a lap dancer than in bar jobs or as a promoter (the main forms of employment open to young British migrants without work permits in tourist resorts in Tenerife: see Bott, 2004). She lied to the manager of 'Club X', saying she was 18, and worked there as a lap dancer for several months. Then someone informed the manager that she was underage. The manager fired Tanya immediately but said she could return after her eighteenth birthday. Tanya then worked as a promoter for a bar, earning only 5 euros a day, and hating the job. She returned to Club X as soon as she turned 18, where she earns between 50 and 400 euros per night. In some clubs, lap dancers are encouraged or expected to do 'extras' (i.e. sell sexual services), but Tanya prefers to work in Club X, where the owner and manager enforce a 'no extras' policy.

Though the British girls and women we interviewed generally made positive statements about their experience as lap dancers, the interview data also reveal much ambivalence towards involvement in the sex trade, and contain many contradictory statements about the benefits and risks of migration. Certainly, these data do not add up to an especially rosy picture of life for teenagers and young women as lap dancers in Tenerife. However, as citizens of one European Union country living in another, and as British migrants to tourist resorts where there is a large, well-established and economically successful community of British expatriates, these girls and women cannot properly be described as politically, socially or economically marginalized, even though most are actually working and living in Tenerife illegally (they have not applied for work or residence permits, they do not pay tax or insurance).

The situation for West African migrant women and girls in Tenerife could not be more different. Even if they enter legally, they are unlikely to secure a job as a promoter, waiter or bar tender, or even to be given work in a lap dance club. Employment opportunities for documented African migrants in tourist areas appear to be largely restricted to cleaning jobs in hotels and hair-braiding. And while the authorities pay little attention to the many Britons who live and work illegally on the island, they show a good deal of interest in rounding up and deporting undocumented migrants from Africa. Thus, even if a West African teenager did somehow manage to migrate without the assistance of a third party (thereby avoiding dependency and with it the risk of exploitation), she would not be in the same position as a British teenager like Tanya. When undocumented migrant women and teenagers from Africa turn to the sex trade to survive in Tenerife, they thus have no choice but to enter the cheapest and most vulnerable segment of the industry – street work. And because their status as 'illegal immigrants' compels them to live in a hidden world, they are open to abuse and exploitation by pimps as well as by clients.

'Child migrants' and 'migrant prostitutes' are not a homogeneous group. They are divided by gender, class, race, ethnicity, age, nationality and immigration status, and such divisions make them either more or less vulnerable to abuse and exploitation both within the migratory process and at the point of destination. A migrant woman or child's risk of abuse and exploitation is mediated, at least in part, by the immigration controls that the receiving country applies to people of her nationality. These points are well illustrated by Psimmenos's (2000) research on Albanian children trading sex in Athens. As undocumented migrants from a country that is outside the European Union, and because of widespread xenophobia, Albanians in Athens suffer a high level of political, economic and social exclusion. The problem has been compounded by 'frequent arrests in the streets of Athens and the use of riot police for mass deportations', which further push Albanians into a social space that is hidden from the public eye (Psimmenos, 2000, p. 92). Driven into this clandestine world of poor accommodation, poor work, restricted movement and constant fear, Albanian teenagers are extremely vulnerable to abuse and exploitation by third parties within prostitution.

Furthermore, the hugely negative stigma that is attached to prostitution in Albanian society leaves teenagers feeling that they cannot return home, even if they want to. One of Psimmenos's interviewees stated that, were she to go home, 'my father or brother . . . will kill me with the axe' (2000, p. 96). The attitudes of the Greek authorities are hardly more generous. Albanian women and children working in prostitution in Athens have entered Greece without a visa, often their passports (if they had them) and other legal documents 'have been stolen and destroyed by criminal networks in Athens', and when picked up by the police, minors are either prosecuted or deported (p. 96). Under these conditions, 'children in prostitution become easy targets of exploitation. They constitute a new category of people without the ability to return home or to stay in the country' (p. 96).

Official statistics show that more than 2.5 per cent of the world's population is migrant, and to this figure we must add 'the millions of invisible transnational migrants who are illegal, undocumented, irregular and trafficked' (Sanghera, 2002, p. 2). Sanghera (2002, p. 16) describes these invisible migrants who are attempting to move from poorer to richer countries or regions as 'the *squatters of the new global borderlands*', noting that, as such, they are excluded from political and social entitlements and rights and widely feared as 'undesirable' vagrants and delinquents. Of course, only a small minority of the men, women and children amongst this 'floating' population are involved in prostitution, but this is hardly a situation in which it is possible to protect and promote even the most basic human rights for either children or adults, let alone to ensure that they are free from exploitation within the sex sector (or indeed any other economic sector). Some argue that to prevent people from entering this clandestine, dangerous and unprotected zone, we should strengthen border controls and make more strenuous efforts to discourage and prevent children in particular from migrating. But this is to forget the reasons why adults and children migrate.

**Between Grief and Nothing**

Very few of the world's children are able to remain entirely economically inactive until the age of 18. Even in extremely affluent countries, it is only a privileged minority of children who can depend on their parents to meet their every economic need and want until they are no longer legally minors. Children from families who are struggling to subsist certainly cannot and do not expect this luxury. Nor do children who are brought up in impoverished rural areas, or who live on the streets, or who are placed in institutional care, always simply resign themselves to the privations and misery of their lives until the morning of their eighteenth birthday. Teenagers, and sometimes even younger children, have aspirations and dreams, often also a sense of responsibility towards their families – indeed, many teenage girls already have children of their own for whom they take responsibility – and are capable of actively seeking work. Because persons under the age of 18 are not sheltered from poverty, discrimination and disadvantage simply by virtue of being constructed as 'children' in international laws and conventions, and because they are not passive, incompetent and incapable of independent thought and action until the moment they legally come of age, it follows that migratory pressures can operate directly on children. Within this, as has been seen, some are also capable of making a decision (however ill advised) to migrate into sex work, or to start prostituting once they have migrated.

And even in places where the experience of sex work is most consistently harsh and exploitative, where violence by pimps and employers is common, where corrupt police and local officials are not only parasitical on prostitutes but also often rape, rob and assault them, prostitution can still appear preferable to some children than its alternatives. So, for example, the director of a repatriation facility in a border town in Cambodia observes that migrant children are not always brimming with gratitude towards those who would rescue them, repatriate them and reinsert them back into their own communities: 'Some of the children are ... not happy to be caught and sent home. They tell us they make more money on the streets than on the farms where life is tougher' (Cochrane, 1999). Similarly a report by International Social Service Italy based on analysis of a sample of 256 Albanian children repatriated from Italy to Albania between 1998 and 2000 found that by 2001, 'only 98 of the repatriated children were still in Albania, while 155 had emigrated again' (Rozzi, 2002, p. 19). These children were not necessarily involved in prostitution in Italy, though some may have been, but the report provides a good insight into why even those children who have worked in the poorest conditions in prostitution might resist repatriation. Of the 256 children repatriated, only six found a job in Albania (Rozzi, 2002, p. 19).

Likewise, interviews with sixty Moldovan adolescents who had been returned to Moldova found that almost all, including those who had been involved in prostitution abroad, wished to leave again (indeed, some had been 'trafficked' more than twice before) (Institute for Public Policy, Moldova, 2003; see also Kvinnoforum and Kvinna till Kvinna, 2003). This should not surprise us, given that more than 50 per cent of the Moldovan population lives beneath a poverty threshold set at US$11.50 per month (UNICEF, 2001, p. 8), and that 30 per cent of Moldova's population is aged under 18, and of them around 17,000 live (or rather are held) in grim and inadequately funded institutions for 'social orphans' (i.e. children whose families are simply unable to support them) (UNICEF, 2001, p. 8). In Moldova, for children and adults alike, labour migration is viewed as the only viable way to improve one's life-chances, and remittances from migrants amount to 50 per cent of Moldova's state budget (UNICEF, 2001). Small wonder that Moldovan and Albanian are the top two nationalities of 'trafficking' victims identified by law enforcement officials and NGOs in the Balkan sex trade, and probably amongst sex workers in EU states as well (Task Force on Trafficking in Human Beings, 2003).

I am not arguing that prostitution should be recognized as a legitimate form of work for persons under the age of 18, or suggesting that it is acceptable for children to migrate into sex work. My point, to paraphrase William Faulkner (1961), is that left with a choice between grief and nothing, some people will choose grief, and this is true of children as well as adults. If we want them to make different choices, we had better think how to do something about the nothingness of their alternatives. So long as policy-makers continue to fondly imagine themselves as inhabiting a world that can be neatly encapsulated by forced/voluntary and adult/child dualisms, it seems to me unlikely that they will make much headway in this regard. Indeed, quite the reverse. For many adults and children, the policies that are currently being pursued intensify both the grief that can attend on migration and the nothingness of remaining at home.

# 5 'Paedophilia', Pornography and Prostitution

Until now, this book has focused on the reasons why children enter the sex trade, and their experience within it. But it is also important to ask who buys sex from children and why. As has been seen, dominant liberal understandings of 'the child' and 'the prostitute' make the market for 'child prostitution', 'child sex tourism' and 'child pornography' unthinkable. It follows that when people ask themselves who in the world would use child prostitutes or child pornography, the answer often seems obvious: the unthinkable – 'the paedophile'. Paedophiles have thus occupied a very special and prominent place in popular discourse and policy debate on the commercial sexual exploitation of children (CSEC) over the past decade. But who and what is a 'paedophile'? 'Paedophilia' is a clinical psychiatric diagnostic category with a very specific and limited meaning. According to the American Psychiatric Association's 1995 manual, it refers to a person aged over 16, who 'has had repeated, intense, sexually exciting fantasies for a period of at least six months, has had sexual urges or has carried out behaviours involving sexual acts with one or more children (usually under the age of 13)'. Furthermore, 'the fantasies, the sexual urges or behaviours act as considerable impairments in the individual's ability to function socially, professionally or within other important spheres' (cited in Svensson, 2000, p. 27).

One immediate and obvious problem with the emphasis on paedophiles in discourse on child pornography and prostitution is that it is inconsistent with the definition of 'children' employed in international debate on CSEC. This debate is informed by the UN definition of a child as a person under the age of 18, and although various studies show that children aged below 13 are sometimes involved in prostitution and commercially produced pornography, research generally points to the conclusion that the vast majority of commercially sexually exploited children are aged between 13 and 18. Most are therefore of an age and state of physical development that holds little appeal for those who would be clinically defined as suffering from paedophilia. Meanwhile, research on non-commercial sexual child abuse strongly suggests that only a minority of offenders would either self-identify as paedophiles or fit into the clinical diagnostic category described above (see, for example La Fontaine, 1990; Itzin, 2000). More significantly, it shows that children are most often sexually abused in the homes where they live, 'by the people with whom they live' (La Fontaine, 1990, p. 151). For this reason, some feminists have argued forcefully against the use of the term 'paedophile' in analyses of either sexual child abuse or CSEC on grounds that it deflects attention from the complex and highly gendered power relations that underpin and surround these phenomena. Men's sexual use of children, they argue, is part of a continuum of male sexual violence, and, imagined as such, the whole issue of paedophilia becomes something of a red herring (Kelly, 1996).

Viewed as a whole, the presence of persons under the age of 18 in the sex trade in the contemporary world has very little to do with the phenomenon of paedophilia, and I therefore agree that the ubiquity of this concept in policy and popular discourse on CSEC is unhelpful. And yet I don't think that what is popularly understood as paedophilia can be collapsed under the general heading of 'male sexuality' or 'male sexual violence', or that it is entirely irrelevant to the analysis of CSEC. As this chapter sets out to show, there are certain forms of child sexual exploitation that do appear to be linked to what is generally termed 'paedophilia'. And of equal importance, thinking about paedophilic desire helps to highlight the dangers of the conceptual schema that, through its reproduction of the subject–object binary and its emphasis on children as innately innocent, passive dependants, makes 'child prostitution' and 'child pornography' unthinkable.

## Paedophilia and Sexual Politics

From the mid-nineteenth century on, human sexuality became a focus of scientific inquiry, first within biological and medical science, and then within psychoanalysis. The new sexologists sought, among other things, to identify, define, list and classify sexual 'abnormalities' and the pathologies that gave rise to them (see Weeks, 1985). Through the cataloguing and codification of the 'abnormal' in works such as Krafft-Ebing's (1965 [1891]) *Psychopathia Sexualis*, 'a special group of mankind was invented' – perverts – and then divided into subgroups, each with their own name (Lutzen, 1995, p. 21). Indeed, Krafft-Ebing's compendium of case studies marked, according to Jeffrey Weeks (1991, p. 71), one of the decisive moments in the emergence of modern discourse about 'sexual identity' – 'it represented the eruption into print of the speaking pervert, the individual marked for ever by his or her sexual impulses'. Sex came to be viewed as a property of individuals, something carried in our physiology, genes, hormones, psyches or whatever, something one *is* rather than something one does. In this sense, 'the sexological account of sexual identity can be seen as an imposition, a crude tactic of power designed to obscure a real sexual diversity with the myth of a sexual destiny' (Weeks, 1991, p. 74).

But though such systems of classification and labelling are a precondition for certain forms of social control and surveillance, they also open up possibilities for resistance, or what Foucault terms 'reverse affirmation' (see Weeks, 1985). For where 'identities' are constructed and used as the basis upon which to marginalize people politically and socially, opportunities for group identification and collective action are simultaneously created. Certainly, this dialectic has been played out in relation to 'homosexuality' in Western societies, with the gay liberation movement both reflecting and reinforcing the more general phenomenon of 'identity politics' in North America and Western Europe in the 1970s.

Sexual interest in children featured in the early taxonomies of 'perversion', and 'paedophile' was one of the sexual identities created through the sexological discourse of the late nineteenth and twentieth centuries. Perhaps unsurprisingly, then, paedophiles were amongst those who sought 'reverse affirmation' in the 1970s. In Britain, the Paedophile Information Echange (PIE), established in 1975, was explicitly concerned to normalize paedophilia, and to lobby for paedophiles' sexuality to be recognized as 'natural, harmless and an integral part of their personality' (PIE, 1978, p. 5, cited in Evans, 1993, p. 229). The North American Man Boy Love Association (NAMBLA), founded in 1978, pursued a similar agenda. It is worth looking at the arguments put forward by such groups, since they remain central to the beleaguered few who still advocate on behalf of paedophilia.

Attempts to defend paedophilia generally rest on the propositions that there is nothing intrinsically harmful about adult–child sexual contact, and that children are capable of choosing and freely consenting to sex with adults. To support these claims, it is often asserted that children are naturally sexual: 'All children have sexual feelings already before birth' (DPA, 1999); 'the capacity to have orgasms is present at six months of age and possibly even earlier' (Califia, 1994, p. 68); children spontaneously engage in sexual activities 'for the sake of pleasure and affection' (DPA, 1999). Scientific backing for such assertions, where provided, often comes from Alfred Kinsey et al.'s (1948) *Sexual Behavior in the Human Male*, although much of the material provided in the chapter on 'Early sexual growth and activity' was actually furnished by a man – Kenneth S. Green – whose 'life consisted almost entirely in a highly excited and urgent pursuit of sex with boys and girls, men and women, animals, even mechanical devices', the details of which he obsessively recorded (Gathorne-Hardy, 1999, p. 220). Green's 'information' on babies' 'sexual responses', for example, was gathered by means of him masturbating, or getting mothers to masturbate, 'twenty-eight children from two months to a year, and similar numbers for each year up to the age of fifteen' (Gathorne-Hardy, 1999, p. 222).

Leaving aside questions about the credibility of data gathered in this manner and recorded by such a witness, there is a problem of interpretation. When apologists for paedophilia discuss childhood sexuality, they treat 'sex' as an essence, something that can be detached from any social context and simply experienced. Thus, they describe babies as having 'sexual feelings' in the same way that we might talk about a baby having feelings of thirst or hunger long before she or he would be capable of articulating a desire for drink or food, or of recognizing and reflecting upon her feelings as feelings. But can the genital sensations experienced by babies and small children really be described as 'sexual feelings' in the same way that pangs in the stomach may be described as feelings of hunger? The very powerful critique of essentialism provided by social constructionist theorists of sexuality would suggest not. Such theorists have drawn attention to

> the inter-subjective nature of sexual meanings – their shared, collective quality, not as the property of atomized or isolated individuals, but of social persons integrated within the context of distinct, and diverse, sexual cultures. This emphasis on the social organization of sexual interactions, on the contexts within which sexual practices occur, and on the complex relations between meaning and power in the constitution of sexual experience, has thus increasingly shifted attention from sexual behaviour, in and of itself, to the cultural rules which organize it. (Gagnon and Parker, 1995, p. 11)

Without subjective engagement with these cultural rules and meanings, human beings' bodily responses and behaviours cannot properly be described as expressions of 'sexual feelings'. Erection and even ejaculation can occur when men are executed by hanging, for example, but this does not mean that the execution is 'sex' for the victim. Religious fanatics may flagellate themselves and engage in other behaviours that if practised by a masochist would be experienced as most delightfully erotic. But it does not follow that the penitent pilgrim taking part in a Semana Santa parade is experiencing 'sexual feelings' and would be equally happy to self-flagellate in an S&M club. Likewise, a baby may have a physical response to an adult's touch, an infant may experience physical sensations when it touches its own genitals, just as 6-year-olds may experience physical sensations when they play 'doctors and nurses' and other games deemed by adults to be 'sexual'. But babies and small children are not familiar with the social and cultural rules and meanings that are used to organize and interpret *sexual* experience, and their physical sensations cannot be equated with what adults identify as 'sexual feelings'.

It is presumably out of partial recognition of this fact that those who defend paedophilia often move from the observation that children are capable of experiencing pleasurable sensations when touched by an adult to claims about the 'positive' role that adults can play in *teaching* children to 'enjoy their sexuality'. For example, Gerald Hannon[1] argues that adults introduce children to many of life's pleasures and there is no 'a priori reason why we shouldn't introduce them to sex' (quoted in Freedland, 1996, p. 3). Furthermore, though penetration 'may be of little interest to most children . . . [i]t makes good educational sense to push a child's limits, much as we do in sports or academics, by requiring of them things they might at first feel incapable of doing' (quoted in Freedland, 1996, p. 2). But such arguments only serve to highlight the gulf between the idea of *children's* right to express and enjoy their own 'sexual feelings' and *paedophiles'* rights to express their sexuality. Child liberationists do not normally endorse the practice of pushing children to conform to standards set by adults, or encouraging them to bend to the will of adults 'for their own good' (and in fact, paedophile lobby groups like PIE joined child liberationists in campaigns against corporal punishment in schools: Jeffreys, 1990, p. 205).

Another line of defence is needed, one that can justify adult intervention in children's sexual development and socialization. Thus, those arguing for the acceptance of paedophilia shift from an essentialist to a social constructionist model of sexuality. Social constructionists point out that the historical and cross-cultural variation in human sexual behaviour clearly shows that sexual 'perversion' is, like sexual 'normalcy', very much a social construct. Today, adult sexual contact with small children is almost universally censured, but there have been periods in history when it has been socially acceptable for adults to engage in various forms of sexualized play with children, and there are also known societies where practices which through Western eyes look like child sexual abuse are deemed to be 'normal' (Herdt, 1982; Li et al., 1990, p. 17; Creed, 1994). Even though anthropologists who have studied practices such as boy-insemination rites amongst the Sambia of New Guinea are careful to point out that they are in no way equivalent to the practices of Western paedophiles, those who defend paedophilia often take evidence of cross-cultural variation with regard to adult–child sexual contact as 'proof' that the stigma attaching to it is merely an expression of Western cultural imperialism (DPA, 1999).

I cannot see how adopting a position of moral relativism (arguing that there is no external yardstick against which to judge the rightness or wrongness of practices such as adults masturbating infants in order to pacify them, or initiation rites involving male children fellating adult men or being anally penetrated by them) actually helps the case for paedophilia, however – unless, of course, its apologists wish to go and live amongst, say, the Sambia, not as Western expatriates but as fully assimilated Sambians, obedient to every single cultural rule and code of existence in that society. Indeed, what anthropological research on the complex and variable interrelations between sex and society actually serves to underline is that 'Sexuality cannot be abstracted from its surrounding social layers' (Ross and Rapp, 1981, p. 54, cited in Creed, 1994, p. 92), and this renders paedophilia more, not less, problematic in almost all contemporary societies.

It is precisely because sexuality is embedded in the social, so that the meanings that attach to specific sexual practices have a shared, collective quality, that, in societies where adult–child sexual contact is prohibited, the adult who persistently fantasizes about sex with children or seeks out children for sex cannot escape a sense of him- or herself as 'perverse'. In Western liberal democracies, others who challenge the rules and conventions of the dominant sexual culture (lesbians and gay men, sadomasochists, transvestites, swingers, and so on) are, in principle if not always in practice, able to renegotiate the sexual meanings that attach to practices that are viewed as 'perverse' in mainstream society *with* their sexual partners. Indeed, it is the possibility of such inter-subjective agreement that lends force to the liberal case for tolerance with regard to the sexual practices of consenting adults. This kind of inter-subjective agreement is not a possibility for those who engage in paedophilic sexual activities. The social meanings that attach to sexual behaviours cannot be renegotiated with a baby or a small child who is only dimly aware of such meanings. And even if we recognize – as I would argue we should – that older children are not merely passive subjects of social structures and processes, and that in relation to sexuality, as to other fields of social experience, they can actively construct their own relationships and cultures (James and Prout, 1990; Jenks, 1996), this does not make them adults' equals in terms of knowledge and understanding of the rules and meanings of the dominant sexual culture in which they live. Nor does it place them in a position to jointly renegotiate the meaning of a paedophile relationship.

This feeds into the strongest argument against paedophilia, namely that children cannot give meaningful consent to sexual contact with adults. Paedophilia thus represents a form sexual abuse. Not so, according to its apologists. They hold that in cases of sexual child abuse, there is violence, deception, assault and/or rape, the child is simply used as a sex object. In paedophile relationships, by contrast, there is spontaneity and friendship, 'the adult joins the child in its sexuality', the child is free to withdraw, 'the adult expresses an interest in the child's world', and 'there is common ground even if the contact is only a single event'; 'power is balanced' between the adult and the child (DPA, 1999; see also Bernard, 1987):

> 'pedophilia' means love for children involving erotic feelings. Pedophilia is thus a sexual orientation that, as many other kinds of sexual orientations, is normally connected with loving and caring feelings – in this case towards children. Pedophilia involves respect, true child abuse (i.e. involving physical and/or psychological violence) is seldom committed by pedophiles. (DPA, 1999)

Paedophilia is thus redefined as non-violent, positive and consensual sex between adults and children, a 'sleight of hand' that makes it unnecessary to discuss problems of consent in relation to children 'because if there wasn't consent then it wasn't paedophilia' (Smith, 2000). Avoiding questions about children's capacity and freedom to consent to sex with an adult means that, despite often mentioning the 'fact' that even babies can have 'sexual feelings', to make their case those who write in defence of child-loving typically rely on stories about 13-, 14- and 15-year-olds who supposedly volunteer for sex with paedophiles rather than attempting to support claims about children's sexual interest in adults with examples of babies or very small children in 'relationships' with paedophiles (Califia, 1994; Geraci, 1997; DPA, 1999).

And yet the case for child-loving is not simply a case for lowering age of consent laws – although, as Weeks (1985, p. 230) notes, some paedophile lobbyists do hold that there should be a cut-off point below which a child would be deemed incapable of consent. But paedophiles are also arguing for a very particular and extremely problematic understanding of 'sexual consent' – a notion of 'consent' as something that can be *deciphered* instead of given. Tom O'Carroll, for example, claims that each stage of the sexual relationship between an adult and a child is 'negotiated'

> by hints and signals, verbal and non-verbal, by which each indicates
> to the other what is acceptable and what is not . . . the man might start
> by saying what pretty knickers the girl was wearing, and he would be
> far more likely to proceed to the next stage of negotiation if she seemed
> pleased by the remark than if she coloured up and closed her legs. (1980,
> p. 49)

And whilst O'Carroll concedes that the paedophile may be wrong about the girl's intentional seductiveness, no matter, for he might 'be right in gradually discovering that the child is one who thinks it great fun to be tickled under her knickers' (1980, p. 49). In other words, children who express no desire for sexual contact with adults may none the less have unconscious desires. Thus, all children can be assumed to consent until or unless they actively resist (at which point, back to Hannon, it might 'make educational sense to push them a little' in order that they may discover their true potential). Using this model of 'consent', there is actually no age below which sex could be automatically deemed non-consensual. After all, when a baby smiles and gurgles as the adult wipes its bottom during a nappy change, the adult who 'has a real interest in the sexual feelings of the child' and 'wishes to join at the child's level' (DPA, 1999) might also 'be right in gradually discovering' that this baby is *really* consenting to sex. It is also a construction of consent that obviates the need to consider any of the structural pressures that may prevent a child from resisting or encourage a child to comply with an adult's sexual advances.

The case made for paedophilia is deeply flawed logically, philosophically and morally, and this is one reason why, although paedophile activists sought links with the mainstream gay movement as well as with the libertarian left in the 1970s and early 1980s (and even enjoyed some success in forming alliances with other minority groups),[2] they were never entirely welcome guests at the identity politics party. Many gay papers refused to carry advertisements for paedophile individuals, publications or groups, and a number of major gay events were 'disrupted by conflicts over how much support should be given to boy-lovers and sexually active youth' (Califia, 1994, p. 57). As one US gay lobbyist put it, 'If you attach it [the man/boy love issue] to gay rights, gay rights will never happen' (Steve Endean, quoted in Califia, 1994, p. 58). Liberals and left radicals also remained unconvinced that paedophiles' case was a straightforward rights issue paralleling that of lesbians' and gay men's oppression (see Weeks, 1985, p. 225) and the representation of paedophilia as a harmless life-style choice involving consensual and mutually beneficial sexual exchange was also strongly challenged by many feminists. In the context of 'Second Wave' feminism's emphasis on sexuality as a site in which men's political power over women is played out and reinforced, the issue of sexual consent appeared difficult in relation to adult women (see, for example, Dworkin, 1987), let alone in relation to children. Groups like NAMBLA, PIE and the René Guyon Society were not lobbying for children's rights, feminists argued, but simply for adult men to be granted 'sexual access, without legal hassles, to the territory of children's bodies' (Jeffreys, 1990, p. 189).

For paedophiles, the heady days of even partial inclusion in the new sexual-social political movements were short-lived. In 1979, six members of PIE were charged with conspiracy to corrupt public morals, for example, and the organization was disbanded in 1984 (Evans, 1993, p. 295). Child sexual abuse and then CSEC became the focus of intense public and political concern in the 1980s and 1990s. Far from gaining rights and recognition as an oppressed minority group, paedophiles have been more vigorously rejected and stigmatized over the past twenty years. They are increasingly refused certain civil liberties enjoyed by other citizens (in the UK, for instance, unlike other criminals, child sex offenders can be placed on a register and monitored by the state even after their sentence is spent), and have come to be popularly viewed as icons of evil, monsters posing such an unprecedented threat to society that many would deny them even basic human rights.

The growing moral panic over paedophilia is viewed as a retrogressive development by feminists who work on the issue of violence against women and children. 'How we define those who sexually abuse and exploit children has extensive implications for how we understand the problem, and hence proposed solutions', Kelly and Regan (2000a, p. 21) observe. In the 1980s, feminist researchers had made some headway in terms of revealing the ordinariness of male violence – both domestic and sexual – in societies where men enjoy political, economic and social dominance over women and children. Pathologizing men who sexually abuse children as 'sick' undermines this recognition, for it serves to place them outside the category of 'ordinary' men and to shift the explanatory framework 'away from issues of power and control to notions of sexual deviance, obsession and "addiction"' (Kelly and Regan, 2000a, p. 21).

I fully agree that the public and policy preoccupation with monstrous paedophiles distracts attention from the power relations that underpin both child sexual abuse and CSEC. But for reasons outlined below, I don't think this means that we can simply refuse to talk about paedophilia or to consider the ways in which it does, and does not, intersect with the phenomenon of CSEC.

### The Child, the Paedophile and Subject–Object Troubles

Adults have sex with persons under 18, and even use very small children as sexual objects, for a variety of different reasons. But some of those who have sex with children express very distinct attitudes towards children, childhood and sexuality, and engage in very particular activities. Not all those who have sex with children have a particular and focused sexual interest in children, or experience this sexual desire for children as a force driving them to behave in particular ways, for example. Not all those who have sex with children also have a collection of hundreds or even thousands of photographs of children, or devote great swathes of their waking hours to fantasizing about sexual contact with children, or consciously and carefully construct arguments in defence of adult–child sexual contact, or spend huge amounts of time poring over news reports, scientific journal articles and other literature on paedophilia. But some – albeit almost certainly only a small minority – do. And amongst this small minority, there are people who can be individually responsible for the sexual use and abuse of very large numbers of children.

It is for this reason that I want to hold on to the notion of paedophilia, not as a disease or personality disorder, not as a condition to which anyone is born or even predisposed at birth by his or her genetic inheritance, and certainly not as an excuse for the sexual abuse or exploitation of children, but as a sexual fixation with certain ideas about children. And the ideas that fixate the paedophile cannot be described as the extraordinary or bizarre products of a diseased or disordered mind; they have not been conjured up from some cultural vacuum. Instead, the ideas that obsess paedophiles are central to dominant Western understandings of childhood and sexuality, for, as James Kincaid points out, 'the development of the modern child and modern ideas on sexuality grew up . . . hand-in-hand, and they have remained close friends' (1998, p. 14). For at least the past two hundred years, the definitional base of the imagined binary of Adult and Child has been erotic: 'the child is that species which is free of sexual feeling or response; the adult is that species which has crossed over into sexuality' (Kincaid, 1992, p. 7). And the binaries that accompany the Adult/Child dichotomy ('innocence and experience, ignorance and knowledge, incapacity and competence, empty and full, low and high, weak and powerful', Kincaid, 1992, p. 7) are likewise heavily eroticized.

Kincaid's work draws our attention to the damage wrought by a culture that constructs 'the Child' as asexual and the exemplar of empty innocence, but simultaneously teaches us to regard emptiness as sexually arousing, 'to discover the erotic in that which is most susceptible to inscription, the blank page' (1998, p. 16). Such a culture is necessarily preoccupied by the monstrous perversity of those who have a sexual response to children, he argues, for

> by attributing to the child the central features of desirability in our cul-
> ture – purity, innocence, emptiness, Otherness – we have made absolutely
> essential figures who would enact this desire. Such figures are certainly
> not us, we insist, insist so violently because we must, so violently that we
> come to think that what we are is what these figures are not. They come
> to define us: they are the substance we feed on. The pedophile is thus
> our most important citizen, so long as he stays behind the tree or over in
> the next yard: without him we would have no agreeable explanation for
> the attractions of the empty child. . . . The 'pedophile' . . . is a role and
> position, brought into being by and coordinate with the eroticizing of
> the child. (Kincaid, 1992, p. 5)

Kincaid is primarily concerned with the self-serving hypocrisy of cultural narratives that construct children as vacant and innocent and paedophiles as monsters who defile and rape that innocence. So, for instance, he points out that the furore surrounding the phenomenon of child molesting should not be read as simple testimony to how much 'we-adults-who-are-not-paedophiles' care about the harm done to the individual children affected:

> the cry that child molesting is worse than murder has been heard so often
> it has become a tired slogan, self-evident and vapid. Certainly it is better
> to take the child's life than its virtue, we feel, and we needn't waste time
> saying it. . . . But if we teach ourselves to regard the loss of innocence
> as more calamitous than the loss of life, whose needs are we seeing
> to? Who wants the innocence and who the life? . . . Are we defining the
> child's innocence in the way older societies defined women's virginity?
> (1998, pp. 16–17)

But his work does also shed light on what it is that obsesses those who do actually become sexually fixated by the idea of the Child. There is a literal as well as metaphorical truth to his assertion that in defining the child as an object of desire, 'we create the pedophile as the one who desires, as a complex image of projection and denial: the pedophile acts out the range of attitudes and behaviors made compulsory by the role we have given the child' (1992, p. 5).

The Child/Adult dualism and its associated binaries (innocence/ experience, passivity/activity, powerless/powerful, object/subject) are, Kincaid observes, 'all very wobbly' (1992, p. 7), requiring 'massive bol-stering' precisely because, although central to our psychic, sexual and cultural life, they are so easy to destabilize and therefore potentially easy to transgress. Let me give a non-sexual example of how the instability of these binaries can manifest itself. The idea of children as entirely vacant, passive and object-like rarely matches up with adults' experience of real, live children, and many parents pity themselves as powerless at the very moments when they exercise the most coercive powers over their children, for example – 'she *drove* me to hit her', 'he *knows* how to wind me up', 'you're *asking* for trouble'. Suddenly it seems that the child is refusing to recognize the adult's subjectivity ('Can't you see that I'm tired, stressed, need help, trying my best?'), as well as refusing to comply with her own object-like status (to do as she is told). Parents' sense of bewilderment and resentment at this apparent subject–object reversal seems to me to parallel exactly that of some heterosexual men when they discover (or are reminded) that the man/woman and subject/object binaries do not actually map neatly onto one another. Consider Jean Baudrillard's lament upon the 'supremacy of the object', for example:

> 'Only the subject desires; only the object seduces.' ... In our philosophy of desire, the subject retains an absolute privilege, since it is the subject that desires. But everything is inverted if one passes on to the thought of seduction. There, it's no longer the subject which desires, it's the object which seduces. ... The immemorial privilege of the subject is overthrown. For the subject is fragile and can only desire, whereas the object gets on very well even when desire is absent. (1990, p. 111)

Applying this to heterosexual sexual relationships, Baudrillard then argues that women – because socially imagined as objects – actually enjoy a form of power that is not open to men. 'The woman can demand to be recognized as a subject in her own right.' And yet this demand is ironic:

> What this woman wants, what we all want as objects (and we are objects as much as subjects . . . not passive objects, but passionate objects, with drives that come from the depths of their object-being) is not to be hallucinated and exalted as a subject in her own right, but rather to be taken profoundly as object, just as she is, with her senseless, immoral, supersensual character. ... Once we recognize this fundamental character (this liberty) of the sexual object, the woman is ready for all the games of love and psychology. (1990, pp. 124–5)

The woman – the object – is the powerful party in these games, according to Baudrillard, and 'What makes her power is . . . her triumphal indifference, her triumphal lack of subjectivity' (1990, p. 125). Of course, this argument could be described as but a showy rehearsal of a more ordinary complaint frequently voiced by heterosexual men, namely that gender ideologies dictate that they must do all the running, and yet because the women they fancy don't always fancy them back, this often means experiencing themselves as objects of rejection and ridicule, rather than active, conquering, sovereign subjects. But Baudrillard does none the less direct our attention to what it is that lies at the heart of the ambivalence often felt towards those imagined as objects by those imagined as subjects (the powerful party's anxious suspicion that they are being manipulated or driven – object-like – by the powerless party, and their mournful sense of being denied care, understanding or recognition by the object-turned-subject). And for the purposes of this chapter, his discussion of subject–object inversions in relationships between adults and children is particularly telling:

> The child, deep down, knows he is not a child. And he is not concerned with the affectation of liberty and responsibility with which you wish to dignify him in order better to dignify the pedagogical difference between adult and child. He competes rather on equal terms. He is neither free nor inferior, and leaves it to others to believe that. . . . He can choose to play up difference, to play the fragile child facing the adult; and you then owe it to him to protect him, to valorize him, to attenuate the difference. Or else at any moment he can choose to return you to the absence of difference, real and fundamental (childhood doesn't exist; there is no child). He would be right in both cases. This confers upon him an absolute superiority. (1990, p. 125)

Clearly, to describe the child as enjoying 'absolute superiority' over the adult (or to state that women control the 'game' of heterosexual love) is to abstract the notion of power so far from any basis in material and political reality as to render it virtually meaningless. But the ease with which Baudrillard is able to make this argument, and its appeal to something we all know to be true (for all of us remember ourselves as children, and know that we were not entirely passive, empty innocents, that we were capable of 'playing' adults in certain respects), does serve to underline the instability of the subject–object dualism. There are real, material asymmetries of power between people, but the powerless are not actually objects, even when treated as such. By the same token, the powerful can still experience a sense of weakness and vulnerability even as they exercise their privilege as subjects.

The dynamics of sexual excitement very often hinge on the instability of cultural categories, and more particularly, the instability of the subject–object dualism. Indeed, this binary is central to sexual life as we know it in late-modern Western societies (when and how will you, who imagine yourself as a subject, surrender to your desire to be treated as an object; under what conditions, precisely, will you allow yourself to treat another person as an object in pursuit of your desires as a subject?). Baudrillard moves seamlessly from talk of the woman's 'triumph' as a subject who is simultaneously an object of desire, to that of the child who can play adults both ways, demanding protection at one moment and equality the next, then back to the sexual thrill and mystery of the Other as object. And since Adult and Child, like Man and Woman, are categories constructed in relation to the subject–object dualism, is it really so surprising to discover that some people also eroticize this binary, and take a *sexual* interest in the enigma of the Child as a subject that is an object, an object that is a subject?

The arguments that paedophiles make to justify their sexual behaviour are centrally concerned with this enigma (hence the talk of how the passive, innocent, empty child, i.e. the object, may turn out to be 'one who thinks

it great fun to be tickled under her knickers', O'Carroll, 1980, p.
subject), and it strikes me that such arguments are as much a descrip
of paedophilic desire as a defence of it. Indeed, this confusion between
describing and defending desire appears to be a much more general feature
of paedophile experience, unsurprisingly given the enormous weight of
social and legal pressure *not* to express or even feel such desire. And
this generates a whole new layer of subject–object troubles. To imagine
children as intensely desirable sexual objects who may also be intensely
desiring sexual subjects, but yet to know that society forbids absolutely
any sexual contact with them, is to imagine a world in which children
enjoy 'absolute superiority' over the adults who desire them. The child
as object can seduce (or so it seems to the paedophile), and then choose
between accommodating or refusing the desire s/he has 'provoked'; the
paedophile as subject is made fragile by his or her desire. The paedophile
becomes the victim, driven and controlled by what now appears as an
external force, the seductive child. In this self-referential world, it is hard
to tell who is subject and who is object.

I am asking for paedophilia not to be medicalized as a psychiatric
illness or personality disorder (although I think it worth recognizing that
it is something that people can *believe* they are identified by or 'suffer
from'), but rather to be understood as a focused sexual interest in a set
of culturally constructed ideas about children, childhood and sexuality.
As such, paedophilia appears to be something that people can feel almost
literally consumed by, such that controlling, managing and coping with
their paedophilic desires (and/or other peoples' responses to those desires)
can become an obsession, perhaps even the guiding obsession of their
lives. And focusing upon the strategies that are used to try to control and
manage paedophilic thoughts and desires (as well as strategies used to
manage or manipulate other people's reactions to them) can help us to
understand how paedophilia does (and does not) link to particular forms
of child sexual exploitation.

## Consuming Desire: the Case of Child Pornography

Numerous studies and police investigations have revealed the existence
of people who obsessively collect and store child pornography and 'erotica' (including non-sexually explicit photographs of children, sketches of
children, diaries recording the details of real or imagined sexual contacts
with children, and so on), as well as, in some cases, news cuttings, journal articles and other literature on paedophilia and sexual child abuse,
and/or files of names and addresses of children who have been abused
and like-minded adults who have supplied materials for the collection
(Hartman et al., 1984; Lanning, 1984; Kelly and Regan, 2000a). Obvi-
ously, the propensity of such people to collect and store such materials
is extremely helpful to law enforcers. If the vast majority of convicted

child sex offenders are 'collectors' (Lanning, 1984), this probably reflects the fact that 'collectors' are easier to detect and convict than those who keep no record of their sexual interest in and offences against children. But if a paedophile is understood as someone in the grip of an obsession with controlling and managing paedophilic thoughts and desires, then I think it would be true to say that many paedophiles are collectors. The gathering, filing and storing of the images and ideas that have been invested with the power to invade, haunt and compel them to action (i.e. paedophilic thoughts and desires) is one strategy for turning those desires into manageable, controllable objects.

Moreover, the images themselves can offer a sense of control over otherwise dangerous desires. Speaking of pornography more generally, the psychoanalyst Robert Stoller observed that even in the mildest of heterosexual male pornographies, the actual woman is reduced

> to a two-dimensional, frozen creature helplessly impaled on the page, so that she cannot defend herself or strike back, as she might in the real world. . . . She can be insulted, dirtied, forced to act according to the viewer's will, and remain uncomplaining, smiling, or even phallic – whatever is necessary – but immobile. And she is not only displayed, available for any fantasied sexual hostility, she is also idealized. She does no harm, she brings satisfaction, she is aesthetic perfection (if not, another picture is chosen), she is retouched, she infinitely repairs herself, she demands no revenge, she is absolutely co-operative, she keeps secrets, she costs nothing in money or time, she need not be understood, she has no needs of her own. No wonder she becomes a bore. (1975, p. 133)

For an adult who feels at risk from his or her own paedophilic desires, finding these qualities – frozen, mute, compliant, infinitely self-repairing, infinitely accessible – in the child model may be even more important. To masturbate over a picture of a child carries none of the risk of rejection or discovery that attends on sexual contact with an actual child (indeed, in most countries, providing the adult sticks to masturbating over non-sexual photographs of children, or sketches or drawings or computer-simulated images of children posed in sexual acts, s/he is not committing a sexual offence[3]).

But there are other reasons why paedophiles may be particularly interested in collecting and keeping both sexual and non-sexual photographs and film of children. James Kincaid's (1992) analysis of the relationship between paedophilia and photography is worth quoting at length:

> Pedophile relations exist for a time, a very short time, and then they are not there. They do not develop into any other form, nor do they decay. Now and then some kind of mild friendship develops between the adult and growing adolescent, but that is different, bearing no relation at all to the intensely romantic prior union. That union just goes away. (1992, pp. 225–6)

In paedophilic literature, metaphors of death are sometimes used to capture the meaning of the child's transition to adulthood for the adult who 'loves' him or her, for 'the prosaic fact that children do not stay children takes on enormous psychological and poetic force in the imaginings of child-love' (Kincaid, 1992, p. 226). Looking hard and long at the child, Kincaid argues, is one strategy for guarding against the fact of children's impermanence and so against the sense of loss that the child-lover must by definition repeatedly suffer:

> By turning the world into a permanent object, I become permanent subject, no longer threatened and now completely (if neurotically) in control. With pedophilia, the crucial feature of this fantasy is its promise of constancy, the way it offers up to us the child in a frame, held by our gaze and preserved from time and from running off. Pedophilia seems almost always to be on intimate terms with such possessive looking. The pedophile does not so much want to look in order to imprison the actual child but to imprison the sight. Just as the pedophile does not really want to own the child but the *idea* of the child, so the vision seems to provide permanent access to that idea. But the envisioning is also an end in itself, an erotic world on its own. (1992, p. 227)

Small wonder then, Kincaid concludes, 'that so much pedophile activity . . . has been connected to the camera', and that the need to photograph children 'before they slip away' is felt not just by paedophiles but, 'judging by the television and magazine advertisements of film companies like Kodak and Polaroid, by nearly everyone today' (1992, pp. 227–8).

Kincaid's focus here is on the gentle and romantic images of children 'in bloom' captured by 'child-lovers' like Lewis Carroll and J. M. Barrie, rather than on photographs that graphically depict children's sexual abuse, but even if we stick to what might be considered mild 'erotica' rather than explicit pornography, I think it is important to note that there is a harsh flip-side to the paedophile's 'possessive looking'. If being a child-lover means that one is necessarily caught in a constant, anxious movement back and forth between love and loss, between being first consumed by passion for the child then emptied of it when the child reaches a given age, then, it could be argued, the 'fact of transience and the foreknowledge of it', which Kincaid notes can 'lend to child-love a rather joyless urgency . . . or, more commonly, a form of denial' (1992, pp. 226–7), must surely also lend it a certain hostility. In which case, the impulse to transform the actual child into the permanently accessible idea of a child through photography is, at one level, an impulse to rob the child of its capacity to abandon its 'lover' and escape into adulthood, which is to say, to rob the child of its autonomy and subjectivity.

By focusing on this aspect of paedophilic looking, I think we can also understand the impulse to create and/or store the much more shocking and brutal images that are often found in paedophiles' collections. Here, David Marriott's (2000) analysis of photography, fantasy and race, and, more particularly, his analysis of the photographs of the serial killer Jeffrey Dahmer, is illuminating. Marriott (2000, p. 27) draws attention to the psychoanalyst Otto Fenichel's, (1954 [1935]) discussion of 'scopophilia', in which he notes that when someone gazes intensely at an object, we say that he 'devours it with his eyes'. The eye is an organ that is imagined to 'rob and bite'; 'Wanting to devour, to take something in via the eyes, can run parallel, in Fenichel's view, with the wish to destroy something by looking at it', and Marriott comments:

> To incorporate, to eat, through the eyes; to want to look, and look again, in the name of appreciating and destroying, loving and hating. How do you start to tell the difference between the two? What is Fenichel describing if not the psychical processes which can support, and derange, the act of looking – and, in particular, the act of looking at photographs? (2000, p. 27)

Fenichel further speaks of the camera as a 'devouring eye', one that 'looks at and incorporates the external world and later projects it outward again' in the form of the photograph – an eye that devours, and then spits out, what it looks at (Marriott, 2000, p. 27). The photograph is thus, Marriott argues, an object through which to 'trace the movement of devouring and spitting out' (p. 27). In general, it strikes me that the appeal of pornography, especially that which depicts sexual activities that the user feels ambivalent about, is that it can be devoured and then spat out – discarded or put away until the next time. (A pornographic image that could not be put away, one that hung on the living-room wall, for example, and *had* to be looked at, might inspire disgust without desire, and even if it did not disgust it would almost certainly cease to excite the wish to devour it with one's eyes.) Perhaps there are forms of child pornography that appeal to some paedophiles for the same reason. But I think that there is something more involved in the desire to photograph, tape-record and film acts of sexual abuse and violence against children, and/or to collect photographs, recordings and film graphically documenting such acts. Indeed, to describe the content of some paedophile collections as 'child pornography' somehow seems as inadequate as describing Dahmer's collection of photographs of his victims as mere pornography.

The officers who arrested Dahmer discovered his photographs in a chest of drawers in his bedroom. The photographs 'frame, and focus, a ferocious contact, becoming a type of visual diary that maps bodies naked and abed, ripped open and dismembered, innards exposed, eyes staring out at the camera from decapitated heads' (Marriott, 2000, p. 34). On seeing the pictures, one of the arresting officers, Rolf Mueller, at first thought 'that they were simulations or fakes. As if such indignities could only be inflicted on sculptures or models...as if only an "artificial" camera eye could record such horrendous acts' (Marriott, 2000, p. 35). Similarly, police officers, prosecutors and jurors involved in child pornography cases

report finding it almost impossible first to believe, and then to b
and sounds found in some paedophile collections (tape-record¡
children being tortured, film of babies or toddlers being raped, ρ.
of the mutilated corpses of children killed in road traffic accidents).

Dahmer's obsession was with the black male body; he 'wanted to preserve the looks of the men he desired', in his own words, to make them 'a
permanent part of me', to control completely a person he found attractive,
and to 'keep them with me as long as possible, even if it meant just keeping
a part of them' (cited in Marriott, 2000, p. 35). And as Marriott argues:

> Dahmer took pictures of his victims because he could possess them only
> when they were dead. Dead they offered no resistance to his image of
> them. Dead they became floating zones of desire exactly equivalent to
> their ideal penetrability. At such moments, he could sever and recombine
> them at will, he could even 'fix' them up with someone else. He could
> change their preferred attachments, slice by slice, altering the life as
> originally lived. Only by posthumously possessing – eating – his victims
> could he account for and so narrate how he had been absolutely possessed
> by them. (2000, p. 36)

Necrophiliacs, like paedophiles, must lose what they love. The dead body
eventually decomposes and goes away, just as the child one day ceases
to be a child and the once treasured union vanishes – 'Dahmer turned to
photography to remove – to sublimate – that threat. Photography allowed
him to . . . [convert] his subjects' lives into still lifes, dead fantasies, etched
and fixed on his retina' (Marriott, 2000, pp. 36–7). Photography made it
possible for Dahmer to 'turn life and death into a graspable object – in fact
draining them of any meaning beyond the necrophilic fantasy' (Masters,
1993, p. 146, cited in Marriott, 2000, p. 37). In the same way, storing tape-
recordings, film and photographs of sexual acts of great violence being
perpetrated on small children alongside images of milder molestation,
perhaps also 'ordinary' pictures of children, seems to drain the children
and the adults involved of any meaning beyond the paedophilic fantasy.

These collections make paedophilia – the idea of sex which is unthinkable, impossible, forbidden – into a graspable object, and, as such,
something that can be controlled and managed, ordered, arranged and re-
arranged, devoured and spat out by paedophiles, instead of something that
consumes and then emits them.

## Paedophilia and Commercially Produced Pornography

'Pornography, including both adult and child pornography, is a multi-
billion pound international industry,' Catherine Itzin (2000, p. 426) states,
thereby making it sound as though child pornography is a major segment of a huge commercial industry. Certainly pornography is very big

business – in 1996, 'Americans spent more than $8 billion on X-rated video sales and rentals, live sex shows, adult cable shows, computer pornography, and adult magazines' (Weitzer, 2000, p. 1) – but there has been very little systematic research on children's exploitation in the commercial production of pornography. We do not know how many persons under the age of 18 are employed in the making of pornography for mainstream heterosexual or gay markets, and we do not know the size of the commercial market for what would be immediately recognizable as 'child porn' (see Ennew, 1986).

There is a segment of the mainstream commercial market that is explicitly dedicated to those with a sexual interest in adolescents – magazines like *Teen Hustler*, and internet sites named 'Teen Steam', 'Web's Youngest Women' and 'Live Teen', sites which between them received over 10 million visitors in 1999 (Kelly and Regan, 2000a, p. 55). However, we cannot simply assume that the models and actors used in the production of 'teen' porn are all under the age of 18. The large British and American publishing companies that produce wide-circulation glossy magazines, for example, are now at pains to ensure that the models they use are aged over 18 – whether posing for 'teen' or any other type of pornography. Yet much pornography is produced by small and less easily monitored enterprises, and it is thus probable that persons under 18 are present in some parts of the mainstream international pornography industry. Indeed, many countries' legislation against child pornography offers no protection to children above the age of sexual consent, which may be as young as 14. The fact that pornography for the Western European market appears to be increasingly produced in Eastern Europe and the Newly Independent States is especially troubling in this regard (Lederer, 1996).

It is also worth considering ways in which the mainstream pornography market shades into other forms of commercial and non-commercial sexual exploitation. In Japan, for example, there is a high level of demand for prostitutes dressed in school uniforms (who may or may not be under 18), and various types of pornography depicting the sexual use of adolescent girls. In 1997, 73 per cent of 238 internet websites featuring images of girl children originated in Japan (Kelly and Regan, 2000a, p. 55). But there is also demand for a range of commercial sexual services that fall somewhere between 'teen' prostitution and 'teen' pornography. There is, for example, a club in Tokyo which charges clients Y2000 for a service called 'Ripping pants off a school-girl', and further offers them an opportunity to molest girls as they stand holding onto handles hanging from the ceiling in a room which simulates the environment of a subway train. This latter reflects a reality of women and girls' lives. In the year 2000, 1,854 men were arrested for molesting women and girls on trains, for 'molesters on the subways, or *chikan*, are incredibly common in Tokyo – a survey conducted [the same year] found that 72 per cent of teenage girls had been groped on their way to school' (Wood, 2001, p. 23).

## 'Paedophilia', Pornography and Prostitution

What of pornography involving pre-pubertal children? Un
the general consensus amongst law enforcers working in this fi
such pornography was largely non-commercial. Filmed, phot
audio-taped records of sexual child abuse were produced by
or groups of paedophiles who then swapped them amongst ................
in order to build up their collections. Large amounts of money were not
normally involved (Hartman et al., 1984). Computer and internet technology has greatly enhanced people's ability to record, store, retrieve and
share large collections of child pornography, and has made it easier for
paedophiles to form small but often international networks or 'clubs'. (It
has also facilitated new forms of abuse – for instance, instantaneous transmission of images of a child being sexually abused via webcam, which
allows all the members of a 'paedophiles' club to join together in abuse
on-line.) Such clubs are not normally operated for commercial gain, but
rather serve to provide paedophiles with a source of pornography and a
sense of group belonging and self-esteem.

However, internet technology has also generated new commercial opportunities for pornographers (pay-to-view websites, for example), and
has made it easier to track and measure levels of demand for child pornography. In a recent FBI investigation of two internet membership sites in
the US, which provided access to pay-to-view child pornography websites,
the names of 75,000 repeat users were gathered (*Guardian*, 18.1.2003). A
survey of 40,000 news groups during the first week of January 1998 found
that '0.07% contained major elements of child porn, a total of 6058 images
were recorded, two thirds of which would count as "child erotica"' (Kelly
and Regan, 2000a, p. 55). Meanwhile, UK Customs and Excise officers
report that over recent years, they have increasingly been intercepting
commercially produced child pornography involving pre-pubertal children, much of which is produced in Eastern Europe or Central America.
These materials have typically been advertised over the internet, and ordered by paedophiles with a collector mentality who wish to possess hard
copies of videos or CD-ROMs depicting abuse. Customs officers observe
that whilst there may not be a mass market for this kind of child pornography, the fact that there are over 100,000 people in the UK with convictions for sexual offences against children suggests that the market is not
insignificant either. Considered globally, then, there is certainly room for
individuals to make substantial profits through the production and sale
of child pornography aimed at those with a focused sexual interest in
children.

It would be wrong to suggest that thousands of pre-pubertal children are
daily exploited in a vast and hugely profitable trade in child pornography.
But the fact that child pornography and 'erotica' can play an important role
in the management and expression of paedophilic desire certainly does
contribute to the sexual exploitation of some children for commercial as
well as non-commercial ends.

## Paedophiles and Prostitution

What of the relationship between paedophilia and prostitution? Reliable data on the prostitution of pre-adolescent children are extremely hard to come by. Though cases of children as young as 6 or 7 trading sex either on the streets or in brothels are not unknown, there are very few places in the contemporary world where it is actually commonplace to find pre-adolescent children prostituting. Those who have a specific and focused interest in sex with young children thus cannot expect to find their desires easily or immediately satisfied in brothels, massage parlours, escort agencies and red light areas. Indeed, to the extent that 'paedophile rings' or 'organized networks' of paedophiles can be shown to exist, they would appear to testify to the fact that the mainstream prostitution market in most places does not cater to such tastes. Special contacts are required.[4]

Also interesting in this regard is evidence on Western paedophiles who travel or migrate to poor and developing countries where huge disparities of income and status between themselves and local people make it easier to gain sexual access to children. This evidence (to be considered in more detail in chapter 7) lends further support to the idea that in their home countries such adults cannot simply turn to the established commercial sex trade to fulfil their desires. It also suggests that demand from such people can stimulate the development of a small-scale 'niche market' in particular locations. An infamous example is provided by events in Pagsanjan, the Philippines, in the 1980s. Here, an American named Andrew Mark Harvey who was arrested in 1988 was found not only to have sexually abused large numbers of children himself, but also to have orchestrated their abuse by other Western tourists and expatriates – seventeen other men were arrested in connection with this case. Harvey kept meticulous records of his activities, filing photographs and record cards on each child that described the children's physical appearance and personality, detailed every penny spent on them, and every sexual act performed (Lee-Wright, 1990, p. 229). More than 331 children had passed through his hands. As well as being used for his pleasure and that of his associates, the children were used for the production of pornography, which was distributed internationally (Lee-Wright, 1990, p. 229).

The circulation of this pornography, alongside a gradual spread of knowledge about the activities of men like Harvey in Pagsanjan (mostly by word of mouth, but also by guide-books aimed at tourists seeking sexual experience), encouraged others with paedophilic interests to travel there. This in turn opened up possibilities for locals in poorly paid jobs in the tourist industry to top up their income by procuring children for tourists, which made it yet simpler for paedophile visitors to turn up in Pagsanjan and, without local knowledge, quickly, cheaply and safely satisfy their wants. Following the arrest of Harvey and other Western expatriates in 1988, although older local boys trained as pimps by men like Harvey tried to keep the business going after their 'benefactors' left (Lee-Wright, 1990,

p. 230), the sex trade involving younger children in Pagsanjan diminished, a story of rise and fall that has been repeated in the child sex trade of other 'Third World' tourist areas, such as Sosuá in the Dominican Republic and Pattaya in Thailand.

So far as analysing the relationship between paedophilia and prostitution is concerned, an interesting feature of the Pagsanjan story is that some of the expatriates who set in train the development of this market (even some of those who profited financially from it) appear to have been less than enthusiastic about the town's growing reputation as a sex tourist destination: 'there was always a clash between the passing tourist trade and the resident paedophiles, who wanted to keep the locals for themselves and their friends' (Lee-Wright, 1990, p. 229). One Frenchman even conducted a campaign to have a guide-book that advertised the sexual 'delights' available in Pagsanjan banned 'to protect his adopted town from an anticipated influx of foreign paedophiles. The locals thanked him for his efforts against corruption, unaware that he was one of its agents' (Lee-Wright, 1990, p. 229). The resident paedophiles may also have objected to the tourists because by raising the level of demand for child prostitutes, they encouraged the growth of a much more visibly and explicitly *commercial* trade, and one in which locals began to appear as market actors, rather than passive bystanders or grateful recipients of the expatriates' largesse.

The idea of paying for sex with children who self-identify or are identifiable by others as 'prostitutes' does not always appeal to paedophiles. Indeed, the way in which those who imagine themselves as 'child-lovers' describe their relationships with children suggests that there are some who would definitely *not* wish to arrange their relations with children as straightforward market transactions:

> Pedophiles enjoy the company of children and like to have friendships with children. . . . Such friendships may be quite long lasting and involve strong mutual emotions and sympathy. . . . Often the emotional attachment and sympathy is more important than sex in such relationships. (DPA, 1999)

An illusion of mutuality and emotional closeness is much easier to sustain when the adult does not have to explicitly contract (either with the child or a third party) for commoditized sexual services. In the absence of contract, payment for services rendered can be disguised as sympathetic 'help' (food, clothes, school fees) and/or empathetic indulgence of childish fancies (toys, excursions), and the relationship appears more diffuse – the adult is not interested in the child only for sex, but also wishes to support, educate and care for him or her. Thus Jeremy Seabrook's (2000) collection of histories of Western men who committed sexual offences against children in developing countries provides many examples of paedophiles who used their economic power to draw children into more open-ended and longer-term sexually abusive relationships, rather than to pay for access to child prostitutes.

However, other paedophiles are clearly perfectly happy with the idea of paying for a brief and anonymous sexual encounter with a child who has been forced to prostitute from a brothel or private apartment, or who is selling sex on the streets. Indeed, the fact that the child is 'a prostitute' can help adults to justify and rationalize their sexual use of her or him. As a British tourist in Cambodia told the journalist Daniel Foggo, by the time a 13-year-old girl gets to work in the brothels of Svay Pak, 'she's probably had sex 100 times, maybe 500 times for all I know. You didn't turn her, you didn't make her do that. You're taking advantage of the situation and the opportunity and it's not your fault' (Foggo, 2002, p. 13).

## Beyond Paedophilia

The commercial sex industry does offer some paedophiles a type of sexual access to children that allows them to obtain a sense of control over their paedophilic desires, and there are also ways in which individuals' paedophilic desires generate commercial opportunities for third parties. But whether we are talking about pornography or prostitution, demand for pre-adolescent children appears to be outside the 'norms' of the commercial sex market. Those who have a specific wish to sexually exploit young children thus generally need to use alternative structures to access those children. Whilst such structures are sometimes parasitic on the mainstream commercial sex trade, they can also operate independently of it. Clubs or networks run by paedophiles who 'share' victims of abuse amongst themselves are one instance of such alternatives. Other structures that can be used to secure sexual access to young children include those that allow for the adoption, fostering and institutional care of children.[5] However, there is a need for more research on this subject, since at present there is simply no way of knowing how many such structures exist, or how many children are affected by them (ECPAT UK, 2001; Ariyo, 2003).

The more general point is that children's presence in the global sex trade cannot be reduced to the problem of paedophilia. Although it is important to address the existence of, and harm caused by, those who consistently and consciously seek out young children for sex, and to consider how paedophilic desires articulate with the commercial sex trade, as will be seen in the following chapter, questions about the 'demand side' of CSEC certainly do not begin or end with paedophiles.

# 6 Children in Mainstream Prostitution

## The Problem of Demand

> We must strike at the root of the evil.... Not until it is generally recognised that the man who has wrought a woman's degradation is at least as great an offender against society as the man who has robbed a till or the man who has forged a cheque.... So long as the violation of purity is condoned in the one sex and visited with shame in the other our unrighteousness and unmanliness must continue to work out its own terrible retribution.
>
> Bishop of Durham, 1907, cited in Bartley, *Prostitution* (2000), p. 178

> Penalize the buyers. The least discussed part of the prostitution and trafficking chain has been the men who buy women for sexual exploitation in prostitution, pornography, sex tourism and mail order bride marketing. We cannot shrug our shoulders and say 'men are like this' ... our responsibility is to make men change their behaviour by all means available – educational, cultural, and through legislation that penalizes men for the crime of sexual exploitation.
>
> Raymond, *Guide to the New UN Trafficking Protocol* (2001), p. 9

Both feminist and religiously inspired abolitionists have long viewed, and continue to view, male demand for commercial sex as a root cause of prostitution. For feminist abolitionists, however, the problem of demand is a political matter, rather than a question of 'evil' or 'unrighteousness'. Drawing on radical feminist theory that foregrounds the sexual domination of women by men in the analysis of women's political subordination, contemporary feminist abolitionists hold that the demand for prostitution is, at base, male demand for power over women and girls as objectified bodies. Catharine MacKinnon famously held that 'sexuality is to feminism what work is to marxism' (1988, p. 106). Thus, men's exploitation of women in prostitution is, like capitalists' exploitation of workers in production, not just a means through which to pursue personal advantage, but also a way in which asymmetrical power relations between a dominant and a subordinate class of persons are reproduced. And for feminist abolitionists, commoditized sex is alienated sex, just as for Marx (at least in his earlier writings) commoditized labour 'estranges from man his own body, as well as external nature and his spiritual aspect, his *human* aspect' (1977, p. 69). When a man contracts for the sexual use of a female body in prostitution, he is requiring that the woman or girl estrange her body's sexual capacities from her emotions, her will and her consciousness; in other words, he is demanding that she sever the integrity of body and self (Barry, 1995; Jeffreys, 1997).

Where prostitution is understood as an act of male domination and female submission and twinned with incest, rape, and so on, the demand for commercial sexual services is always morally and politically problematic, for no one can meaningfully consent to be terrorized, raped and dehumanized. Through this lens, whether we are talking about adult or child, or 'free' or forced, prostitution, the client does not buy the prostitute's labour or services. He pays to experience and enjoy violent and coercive power over someone he imagines as his subordinate on a status hierarchy, to exercise personalistic power over 'sexual slaves' (Barry, 1995; Hughes, 2000).

Critics of this line of feminist analysis point out that to speak of alienated forms of sexual expression is to imply that there is such a thing as 'unalienated' sex, some way of arranging sexual relations that allows each person to express their *essential* humanity. This is not only to deny the socially constructed nature of sex, but also to reproduce, albeit with some recasting, the traditional legal and moral binaries of good/bad, normal/abnormal, healthy/unhealthy, pleasurable/dangerous sex (Rubin, 1999). When abolitionists describe prostitution as the 'violation of intimacy' (Abiala, 2003), for example, they implicitly naturalize and privilege 'intimate love-making' over other forms of sexual experience. In so doing, they open the door to some very dubious alliances with those who would more generally be viewed as enemies of feminism and other progressive political movements, namely moral conservatives and religious fundamentalists (see Assiter and Carol, 1993; Rubin, 1993; Chapkis, 1997).

Refusing the proposition that there is one authentic and unalienated form of human sexual expression, 'sex work' feminists also reject the idea that prostitution can be described as intrinsically or essentially degrading. Indeed, under the right circumstances sex work can, according to some, express a form of care or creativity (Chapkis, 1997), and the buying and selling of commercial sex should thus be viewed as legitimate features of 'erotic diversity' (Califia, 1994; Rubin, 1999). Such ideas find endorsement on the website of a newly formed sex workers' union in Britain. Here, it is argued that prostitution can be beneficial to society, and that, far from being 'evil' or power-crazed patriarchs, clients are ordinary men satisfying erotic needs that are not met by their wives or partners, or who

> need to see prostitutes because they have no other sexual outlet. For example, disabled people with weak or short arms may be unable to

masturbate and have no other form of orgasmic release. Prostitutes find that much of their work is of a caring and educational nature, helping people gain confidence and experience, and rid themselves of fears and low self esteem. Most prostitutes say they like their clients, and they are the same kind of people as their friends. (IUSW, 2003)

Where free-choice prostitution is understood as a mutual voluntary exchange, state actions that criminalize or otherwise penalize those adults who make an individual choice to either sell or buy sex appear to be a denial of human rights to self-determination. Furthermore, sex work feminists argue, prohibitionist legislation increases, rather than reduces, prostitutes' vulnerability (Bindman, 1997; Kempadoo and Doezema, 1998). Clampdowns on 'kerb-crawlers', for example, encourage street prostitutes to work in darker, more isolated spots, where the risk of violence is greater, or to turn to indoor forms of prostitution, where they are more likely to be exploited by third parties.

Feminist debate on demand is thus structured around the same binaries (subject/object, free/forced, agent/victim, adult/child) that inform debate on prostitution more generally, and, once again, abolitionist and sex work feminists each find their cause championed by more mainstream politicians and actors – liberals line up with the sex work lobby, conservative and religious thinkers with the abolitionists. The question of how to respond, legally and socially, to the clients of 'free-choice' adult prostitutes is thus as vexed and divisive in international policy debate as the question of how to respond to prostitutes themselves.

In some countries, clients are already penalized (China, most states of the USA, and Sweden, for example, although Sweden is alone in criminalizing the client but *not* the prostitute), and legal penalties are sometimes accompanied by public shaming of men caught buying sex. For instance, Kansas City is now experimenting with 'John TV – a weekly cable TV show displaying the names, addresses and pictures of men arrested for attempting to solicit a prostitute', and in 1995 the Pennsylvania state legislature passed legislation 'requiring courts to publish in the local newspaper the name and sentence of anyone convicted a second time of patronizing a prostitute, in addition to a fine . . . and . . . community service' (Weitzer, 2000, p. 171; see also Bernstein, 2001). Similar tactics have been deployed in China (Ren, 1993), although in a highly selective manner, as is the case in the USA (Bernstein, 2001). In other countries, no legal penalties apply to those who contract for sex, providing they do not contravene what are essentially public nuisance laws (kerb-crawling legislation in the UK, for example).

Once again, however, greater consensus prevails in relation to the clients of child prostitutes. Indeed, one impact of the first and second World Congresses against CSEC is that this policy *is* now widely endorsed, with many countries (including Japan, Canada and the UK) introducing legislation against those who buy sex from persons under the age of 18 (ECPAT,

1999). Though I believe that the market for commercial sexual services is morally and politically problematic, I also want to use this chapter to argue that the relationship between supply and demand is more complex than current debates allow, and that calls for strong and punitive legal responses to those who pay minors for sex are rather less progressive than they may initially appear.

## Who Buys Sex?

Research on the demand for prostitution in general suggests that it comes overwhelmingly (though not exclusively) from men, but surveys reveal much variation between countries as regards how many men admit to prostitute-use. For example, around 9 per cent of men in Britain (Wellings et al., 1993), 13 per cent of men in Finland (Haavio-Mannila and Rotkirch, 2000), 14 per cent of men in Hong Kong (FPA, HK, 2000), 39 per cent of men in Spain (Leridon et al., 1998) and 16 per cent of men in the United States (Monto, 2000) admit to having paid for sex at some time in their life. In some countries, levels of prostitute-use appear to be much higher. Studies suggest that around 75 per cent of Thai men have purchased sex, and that over 60 per cent of Cambodian men visit prostitutes (Brown, 2000, p. 132). Within this, certain subsets of the male population in any given country appear to be more likely than others to buy sex. For example, prostitute-use has historically been and remains common amongst men in the armed forces (Enloe, 1993; Kane, 1993; Sturdevant and Stolzfus, 1996, Moon, 1997; Euler and Welzer-Lang, 2000; Tanaka, 2002; Bickford, 2003; Cheng, 2003; Gill, 2003; Higate, 2003). Seafarers, truckers and male migrant workers who spend long periods working in poor conditions in isolated regions (for instance, those who work in logging and mining) also appear to be particularly likely to provide demand for prostitution (Sutton, 1994; Antonius-Smits et al., 1999; Siden, 2002; Apostolopoulos et al., 2003). In most major cities around the world, sex workers report that foreign and domestic businessmen are amongst their clients (Ren, 1993; Allison, 1994; Lever and Dolnick, 2000; Nencel, 2001). Research also suggests that people are more likely to enter into various forms of sexual-economic exchange whilst on holiday than they are when at home (Kleiber and Wilke, 1995). However, and in most settings, local men (including police officers: see Anderson and O'Connell Davidson, 2003) are amongst those who buy sex. Although the vast majority of those who pay for sex are men, there is also some evidence of demand from women for a variety of sexual-economic exchanges (Meisch, 1995; Nagel, 1997; Haavio-Mannila and Rotkirch 2000, Sánchez Taylor, 2001b).

Existing interview and survey research with men who buy sex reveals that they typically explain their own prostitute-use through reference to one or more of the following motivations: the desire for a particular kind of sexual experience; the desire for particular kinds of sexual partners; the desire for control over when and how to have sex (Hoigard and Finstad, 1992; McKeganey and Barnard, 1996; Faugier and Sargeant, 1997; O'Connell Davidson, 1998; Monto, 2000; Månsson, 2001). Some studies further suggest that there are men who visit prostitutes in search of companionship and what they take to be intimacy (Jordan, 1997; Plumridge et al., 1997). Whatever the motivation, prostitute-users face choices and constraints as consumers. They not only decide what kind of sexual service they want, but also what kind of sex worker and how much they are willing and able to pay; the demand for commercial sexual services is thus highly differentiated.

Though, at the highest level of abstraction, it may be true to say that all clients have a common desire to purchase temporary powers of command over the person of the sex worker (clients pay for the right to instruct prostitutes to act in ways they would not otherwise choose to act), their practices, motivations and subjective perceptions are clearly not identical. The man who pays to be beaten by a 50-year-old female dominatrix would not necessarily (and indeed is rather unlikely to) pick up a 9-year-old boy soliciting at a railway station and pay for penetrative sex with him; the tourist woman who enters into a week-long sexual-economic relationship with a local man or boy in a tourist resort, telling herself that it is a 'holiday romance', is unlikely to enter a brothel and explicitly contract for a specific sexual service from a sex worker; the man who pays for a blow job when out on a stag night with a group of friends will not necessarily go on to provide regular demand for commercial sexual services, and so on.

But though demand is differentiated, the lines of division do not map neatly onto the distinction between adult and child prostitutes. With the possible exception of the market for domination services, where sex workers are invariably older than 18, it is possible to find persons under the age of 18 in virtually every segment of the market for commercial sexual services – street and other forms of outdoor prostitution, hostess club, massage parlour and brothel prostitution, escort agency prostitution, private brothel prostitution (see, for instance, Aggleton, 1999; Kempadoo, 1999b, 1999c; Melrose et al., 1999; Brown, 2000; Kelly and Regan, 2000a; O'Connell Davidson, 2001a; O'Connell Davidson and Sánchez Taylor, 2001; Rodriguez et al., 2001). Even where prostitution is regulated, prohibitions against the employment of minors are not always rigorously enforced, and in any case, persons of 16 and 17 can sometimes obtain false documents in order to secure employment. In other words, children work alongside sex workers aged over 18 in mainstream forms of prostitution, and serve demand from clients in general, rather than (or as well as) clients who are specifically seeking child prostitutes.

Viewed globally, it is almost certainly true to say that only a minority of men are regular or habitual prostitute-users. Nevertheless, those with experience of prostitute-use represent a significant percentage of the world's male population, and in numerical terms, they certainly amount to some millions of men. Because they use or have used prostitutes in a world in which many sex workers are below the age of 18, we can conclude that the numbers of men who have ever paid for sex with a minor are also substantial. This should immediately alert us to problems with any simple binary model of demand that assumes clients of child prostitutes can be neatly demarcated from clients of adult prostitutes and treated as a separate group for analytical or legal purposes.

## Why Consume Commercial Sexual Services?

Why do people buy any good or service? In a study of Latin America's material culture, the historian Arnold Bauer observes that whilst food, clothing and shelter may seem to constitute the basic *needs* of human existence, the processes through which goods are acquired and services consumed in any society cannot readily be explained through simple reference to the idea of 'need': 'Economists are inclined to talk about "wants", which are universal and limitless, rather than "needs", which are in fact almost impossible to define ... from the very beginning, even in the Garden of Eden, people "want" more than they "need"'(Bauer 2001, p. 1). Liberal economists are also inclined to depict markets as the natural and inevitable consequence of people's wants. If there is sufficient demand for any given commodity, then, the theory goes, it will eventually become worthwhile for some self-interested individuals to supply it, and the existence of a market for any good or service is thus taken as proof that there is demand for said product or service.

Against this, it is important to make two observations. First of all, though it may be true that for any market to operate there must be both a supply of and a demand for the commodity in question, commodities do not exist in nature, but come into existence only under very specific social and political circumstances. Things that are today considered as commodities were not viewed as such three or four hundred years ago (in particular, the idea that the human capacity to labour can be treated as a fully alienable commodity is a relatively recent invention and one that only came into existence as a result of an extremely long, complex and bloody historical and political process). Second, whilst people's wants may always have outstripped their needs, the details of what people imagine as their 'needs' and 'wants' is very much a socially, culturally and historically determined matter, and also intimately related to questions about supply or availability. Indeed, we might almost say that supply generates demand rather than vice versa. There is no absolute or given level of demand for mobile phones in any society, or for the services of lap dancers, and before the relatively recent advent of mobile phones and lap dance clubs, no one bemoaned their absence.

Supply may be a necessary condition for demand, but it is not always a sufficient condition. Demand must also be socially constructed in the sense that people have to be taught to imagine that they want or need a given product or service. Human beings are not born wishing to visit lap dance clubs, for instance, any more than they are born with specific desires to use mobile phones, play the lottery or drink coca-cola. They have to *learn* to imagine that these forms of consumption are pleasurable, they have to be taught that consuming such services is a signifier of the fact that they are 'having fun', a marker of their social identity and status. Consumption is, as many sociologists and historians have observed, a form of display both in the sense that it is a marker of identity and social status, and in the sense that it is used to punctuate time, to ritualistically and publicly mark our passage through the day, the week, the year, our lives (Bauer, 2001; Veblen, 1994; [1899]; Ritzer, 2001; Aldridge, 2003).

These points also apply to the consumption of commercial sexual services, for decisions about whether, when, where and how to buy sex are as much, if not more, a public and social matter as a private and personal response to a physical sensation of sexual 'need' or desire. Most societies socialize their members to believe that there are natural and fundamental differences between male and female sexuality. Traditionally, it has been held that men have strong and biologically based sexual 'needs' that cannot be left unmet without harm accruing to the individual concerned, while women are programmed by nature to want less sex, and/or more emotional and 'intimate' sex. This dominant discourse on gender and sexuality naturalizes male prostitute-use, leaving men much more likely than women to imagine themselves as having the kind of sexual 'needs' that could be met by a prostitute, and much better placed to justify their own consumption of commercial sexual services. However, teaching male members of society to imagine themselves as possessed of strong, even uncontrollable, sexual drives does not automatically make them want to buy sex from prostitutes. It is important to reiterate that not all men buy sex (in many places, those who do are in a minority), and it is perfectly possible, probably quite common, for men to hold extremely conservative beliefs about gender, sexuality and prostitution without becoming prostitute-users (Anderson and O'Connell Davidson, 2003).

Why do some make a decision to consume commercial sexual services? As with markets for other goods and personal services, visibility, availability and affordability are clearly important factors. Men appear to be more likely to buy sex in settings where commercial sex is cheaper and more visible, hence the level of demand rises when sexual services are supplied more cheaply. For example, the thriving sex trade that has developed in certain towns in northwest Russia serving Finnish, and to a lesser extent Swedish and Norwegian, clients (IAF, 2001; Rusakova, 2001; Stenvoll, 2002) has not simply won a share of some absolute level of demand for prostitution that was previously met in Finland, Sweden and Norway. The availability and low cost of sexual services has also generated demand and expanded the customer base. And yet the impulse to take advantage of an affordable and visible commercial sex trade is not given in nature. Again, Bauer's (2001) work is useful. He notes that economists are correct to suggest that relative price and supply and demand are important in explaining why people buy what they buy. However, 'embedded in the code we call "price" are several elements that help determine our acquisition of goods' (p. 3). Consumption is a form of display:

> many people acquire goods . . . as markers of identity and a boost to self-esteem. Some people . . . self-consciously consume food, clothing, or live in certain dwellings to express individuality or identity. Even *the way* we consume a certain dish or drink or wear a specific hat or uniform may be designed to produce a sense of uniqueness, or group, or even national, solidarity. (p. 3)

Moreover, the things we buy can provide 'the material substance in rituals that help to create and maintain social relationships – or put another way, goods "fix public meanings"' (p. 5). Certainly, using a prostitute can be part of a 'rite of passage', and/or a ritualized means of consolidating relationships with male friends. Fathers, uncles and older brothers sometimes take or send teenage boys to prostitutes as a way of initiating them into sexual life, and boys and young men will sometimes buy sex to ritually mark their entry into adulthood (Anderson and O'Connell Davidson, 2003). Boys' and young men's initial experiences of prostitution are often prompted by some combination of their own perception of the social demands of masculinity and peer pressure to conform to those demands. Buying sex can represent a way to publicly demonstrate membership of a particular male subgroup, and/or to claim a particular social identity, as 'adult', 'real man' or 'not-gay'. In the words of a 48-year-old Indian client:

> My uncle used to tell me that . . . a real man is one who can lay a woman, because this is what his body is made for. If he does not do it, then people will think he is weak and not a real man. Also, I used to have a lot of wet dreams and I felt very guilty about this. . . . My uncle said my problem would stop if I went to prostitutes. . . . Also I was curious. Some of my friends used to tell me a lot of stories about prostitutes and their affairs with other girls. . . . So it was a good experience for me. My friends had more respect for me once I went to a prostitute. My uncle actually gave me a wristwatch that day![1]

But the consumption of sexual services offers a means through which to claim and display class, race and/or ethnic identity, as well as masculinity, and the 'type' of sex worker and the price paid for services can thus matter a great deal to clients. The perceived link between a client's social status and the racial or ethnic identity of the sex worker whose services he consumes is articulated very explicitly in the following passage taken from an interview with a Thai client:

> I prefer Thai sex workers because I feel more comfortable with them, and I don't feel proud of myself if I go with migrant sex workers. Socially it is looked down on to be with Burmese sex workers because they work in particular types of establishment which are lower, and friends look down on it. In this male society, the place you visit makes you look good

or not. In places where migrants work, the conditions are poor. If you can go to a massage parlour, it makes you look good. Having a university student is good too. Thai women work in different establishments, such as karaoke, and are more expensive. Poorer men have to go to migrant workers because they are cheaper. (Anderson and O'Connell Davidson, 2003, p. 21)

In other words, because migrant Burmese sex workers generally work in cheaper brothels in Thailand, serving demand from migrant men and poorer Thai clients, to buy sex from a Burmese woman or girl marks the client as a person of low social status. This ranking of sex workers according to their racial, ethnic or national identity and the social relations that surround their prostitution is a feature of the market for prostitution in most countries of the world. It is reflected in the prices charged for sexual services, such that those who work in what is viewed as the 'seedy' end of the market (street work, cheap brothels) can command less money for the same service than those who work at the top end of the market. Within this, clients are willing to pay less for sexual access to those who belong to groups that are socially devalued (drug users, the homeless and poor, people from ethnic or racial groups that are deemed to be inferior, etc.), and more for sexual access to those who belong to groups that are socially esteemed (which often means white Europeans in both European and non-European countries).

Though feminist abolitionists are, I believe, right to argue that the consumption of commercial sexual services is a way in which (some) men seek to demonstrate and affirm their 'masculinity' (understood as power over self, others and material objects), attitudes towards gender, sexuality and prostitution are more complex than they allow. Moreover, gender is not the only status hierarchy in any society. Instead, ideas about gender intersect with ideas about class, sexual orientation, caste, ethnicity and race, so that consuming sexual services can be a way in which clients assert their position of dominance in relation to those who are imagined as social inferiors for reasons other than, or as well as, their gender. What does this mean in relation to demand for child prostitutes? As will be seen below, the fact that clients often seek to assert or establish their social identity through their choice of sex worker does not actually lead to any straightforward conclusion about demand for prostitutes under the age of 18, for attitudes towards childhood and commercial sex generate certain contradictions in most societies. Youth may be sexually prized, but children are generally devalued as market actors.

## Choosing Children

As noted above, in virtually every country of the world it is possible to find children working alongside adults in various forms of prostitution. There is clearly a demand for their sexual services in the sense that clients are willing to pay for them. But are there clients who *particularly* want to buy sex from children, and if so, why? The previous chapter considered those who have a focused sexual interest in young children, and who sometimes use prostitution to access such children. It also argued that these individuals, disturbing as their activities may be, are very much in a minority amongst clients of prostitutes aged under 18. There are also some clients who are not paedophiles, but who actively seek out child prostitutes on the basis of myths and misconceptions about sexual health. Recent multi-country pilot research on the demand for commercial sexual services included a survey of 185 men in five countries – Thailand, India, Japan, Italy and Sweden – with experience of buying sex (Anderson and O'Connell Davidson, 2003). Just under 15 per cent of all clients surveyed stated that one of the precautions they took to guard against STDs and AIDS was to seek out younger prostitutes. The majority of those who adopted this 'strategy' were from India (14 out of 26), and of them, more than half were from the group with the lowest level of education. About 7 per cent of all clients (12 people) said that they looked for virgins as a precaution to reduce the risk of STDs. Again, the majority were from India (6), but four were Thai police officers.

It is important to note that the sample used in this survey was not random, and we cannot generalize about Indian or Thai clients as a whole on the basis of these data. But regardless as to how representative they are of the total population of clients in any country, it is deeply disturbing to find even twenty-six individuals who state that they attempt to avoid STDs by selecting younger sex workers, and twelve individuals stating that ideally they prefer to buy sex from virgins. The fact that there is some demand for commercial sex with virgins is further evidenced by cases in which girls have been sold to clients as such for high prices (see, for example, Cochrane, 1999; Johnson, 2000), and in which child prostitutes report having had their vaginas stitched up several times so that clients would believe them to be virgins (*Straits Times*, 2000).

The demand for virgins is often remarked on in the literature on CSEC, where it is generally presented as a peculiar feature of the sex trade in South-East Asian countries and/or a phenomenon that has emerged in African countries as a response to the AIDS pandemic (for instance, O'Grady, 1996; Radda Barnen, 1996; Brown, 2000). However, such assertions need to treated with great caution, since there is no systematic or comparative body of research evidence on which to base claims about the level of this type of demand in any region. But no matter where such demand is found, and whether extremely rare or relatively common, I do believe it merits particular attention and concern, for it points to the existence of demand from clients who are not even interested in constructing a fiction of mutuality or consent around their prostitute-use. The social relations that surround the prostitution of children who are virgins cannot be assumed to be anything other than profoundly abusive, and the man who, having paid a third party, goes on to vaginally penetrate a 12-year-old virgin or a 14-year-old who has had her vagina sewn up five times is hardly likely to be under the impression that she is enjoying the experience.

But what of those who provide demand for children whom they do not believe to be virgins, and who are of an age and state of physical development to be of little interest to most paedophiles, let us say, those aged 15, 16 and 17? In terms of international law, such teenagers are 'children', but even the most ardent defender of their status as such would concede that they have entered a period of life that differs markedly from infancy and early childhood. Certainly, in most societies, older teenagers' participation in sexual and economic life is considered in a different light from that of younger children. It is, for example, often perfectly legal for such teenagers to work in a wide range of jobs, and to make decisions as consumers that are disallowed to younger children. Meanwhile, the age of sexual consent is set below 18 in many countries, and non-commercial sexual relationships between adults and children who are above the age of sexual consent are generally tolerated, even if not actively encouraged. Certainly, sexual desire for older teenagers is not generally socially imagined as pathological. A great deal of sexual and aesthetic value is placed on youth in most societies, while signs of ageing are almost universally deemed unerotic (especially in women). Those who are sexually drawn to 16- or 17-year-olds are not necessarily attracted by their perceived childishness, for the erotic value placed on youth is often so extreme that adolescents may conform more closely to socially constructed ideals of feminine and masculine beauty than do adult women and men. And if we consider that the category 'adult' includes people aged between 18 and 100, the idea of a social consensus on the intolerability of *all* adult–child sexual contact is still harder to sustain. Who really believes that a sexual relationship between a 19-year-old and a 17-year-old should be categorized as a sexual relationship between an 'adult' and a 'child'?

At this point, those who campaign against CSEC would, I think, sharply remind us that the Convention on the Rights of the Child (CRC) is definite and unequivocal about the fact that, for purposes of agreeing to a *commercial* sexual contract, a person below the age of 18 is a 'child'. But none the less, the older teenager's status as such remains ambiguous for most ordinary people, and I would venture to guess that very few clients are familiar with the CRC. Rather than relying on international legal instruments to inform their behaviour as consumers of commercial sex, most people rely on popular ideas about childhood, sexuality and prostitution and their own personal sexual preferences and moral values to make choices between prostitutes of different ages in the same setting. In the pilot study mentioned above, there were widely varying responses to the question 'At what age should a girl be allowed to start work as a prostitute?' But whether interviewees said 15 or 26 was the acceptable age to start trading sex, they justified their answer by saying that this was the age at which a girl became a 'woman', and/or had the physical and emotional maturity to cope with sex work (Anderson and O'Connell Davidson, 2003).

More generally, this research found that although clients attached sexual value to youthful bodies, they did not wish to buy sex from prostitutes they perceived as too young to consent to the sexual encounter. The prostitute had to be young enough to appeal to them sexually, but old enough to be imagined as having sexual agency. This certainly did not mean that clients avoided sex with prostitutes who are children according to the UN definition. Indeed several interviewees, as well as 22 per cent of the 185 clients surveyed, expressed a preference for prostitutes aged 18 or below. But they provided that demand on the basis of a set of ideas about age, gender, sexuality and prostitution that allowed them to construct teenage girls as 'women' who are capable of consenting to the transaction.[2] For some clients at least, an adolescent who has passed puberty, who is of an age to voluntarily enter non-commercial sexual relationships, and who is working in the sex trade is not a 'child' but a prostitute, and as such is morally indistinguishable from prostitutes over the age of 18. When such clients pick out underage prostitutes, it is generally on the basis of price, availability, physical appearance, demeanour, working style, and so on, not on the basis that s/he is a minor.

All of this draws attention to weaknesses in both feminist abolitionist and liberal sex work feminist analyses of demand for prostitution.

### Demand for Embodied Labour

The feminist abolitionist treatment of prostitution as a form of male sexual violence against women produces an extremely thin description of 'the client'. In this account, clients are indistinguishable not only from men who commit acts of rape and incest, but also from each other – all 'are melded together as one homogenous class of penis-wielding colonizers' (O'Connell Davidson, 1998, p. 121). This deflects attention from questions about differences between clients that are actually of enormous significance for women and children who work in prostitution: for example, why it is that some clients rape, beat and cheat the sex workers they use, and some do not; why it is that some clients seek out young and vulnerable prostitutes and others do not; why it is that some clients attempt to assist women and children who have been forced into prostitution and are being subjected to violence by third parties (for instance, by reporting their situation to the police, or by physically helping them to escape: see Siden, 2002; Wolthius, 2002), while others do not? Moreover, when these questions are addressed, some research points to a conclusion that would be unpalatable to feminist abolitionists, namely that clients who view prostitution as a personal service sector (as opposed to a sewer, necessary to society and to individual men as an outlet for excess sexual impulses) may be less likely either to use younger prostitutes or to think that physical violence against sex workers is acceptable (see Anderson and O'Connell Davidson, 2003).

But liberal sex work feminists' approach to the issue of demand is hardly more helpful. Because they are keen to emphasize parallels between prostitution and other forms of employment, they typically pay very little attention to the fact that the 'thing', service or commodity that clients want to buy is not divisible from the person who supplies it. Where the consumer who buys a carpet or an item of clothing has no interest in the identity of the workers whose labour made these commodities available, the worker's age (also gender, race, nationality, caste and/or ethnicity, as well as her/his appearance, demeanour and linguistic capacities) can matter a great deal to those who buy sex. And if clients are interested in the person, as well as the 'service' supplied by the person, then consumer demand is not necessarily entirely irrelevant to the phenomenon of either forced or child prostitution. The fact that many clients favour sex workers who look youthful is certainly one of the factors that makes prostitution a viable (in fact often the best possible) economic strategy for persons under the age of 18, and that provides third parties with an economic incentive to employ children or force them into prostitution.

It is also instructive to think through the logic of the parallels that some sex work feminists seek to draw between prostitution and other therapeutic or caring occupations. If most clients did look to prostitution primarily for some form of 'care and education', then the maturity and experience of the sex worker would presumably be viewed as an advantage. Certainly it should not detract from his or her appeal. Given a choice between a 17-year-old and a 45-year-old therapist, how many people seeking counselling services would choose the teenager? I do not deny the fact that there are some clients who, faced with the same choice, would also pick the 45-year-old. But there are a great many more who would select the 17-year-old. Of course, this does not mean that we can talk of a direct and unmediated link between the demand for and supply of teenage prostitutes. But it does mean that the nature of demand for commercial sexual services is such that the prostitution labour market, unlike the labour market for counsellors (or for psychic healers, aromatherapists, therapeutic masseuses, etc.), can readily accommodate those aged 15, 16 and 17, as well as those above the age of 18.

Thinking about those who buy sex from child prostitutes also highlights another weakness in liberal sex work feminists' approach to questions about demand. Because this perspective focuses on clients as consumers, it does not address the ways in which clients resemble employers. Yet since the 'service' they wish to consume is not divisible from the person, clients do actually face the same problem that employers face in relation to wage-workers. Like employers, clients need the worker's co-operation in order to consume the 'commodity' they have purchased, and the amount of 'value' or satisfaction they get for their money varies according to the 'willingness' or malleability of the worker. Some clients complain about the lack of 'value for money' provided by sex workers who fail to fulfil their every whim – for example, those who will not kiss or cuddle them or who otherwise make it explicit that the transaction is purely commercial, those who refuse to acquiesce to demands for unprotected sex, those who impose time limits on the transaction such that a client will be told his time is up before he has achieved orgasm, or those who will not perform particular sexual acts (Kruhse-Mount Burton, 1995; Bishop and Robinson, 1998; O'Connell Davidson, 1998). This leads some to seek out more vulnerable and inexperienced, and therefore more malleable, prostitutes, as illustrated in the following extract from a German expatriate in South Africa:

> The little girls, ten or twelve years old, I wouldn't describe them as innocent, they're not innocent, but they're fresh. They don't have the attitude of the older whores. The older whores have gone down hill. They use foul language. They drink. They're hardened. The little girls, they're not experienced. They're not hardened, they want to please you, they don't know what to expect, you get a better service from them. (O'Connell Davidson and Sánchez Taylor, 1996b, p. 12)

Finally, we should note that in some settings, it is cheaper to buy sex from a child than from an adult sex worker, and/or to buy sex from an adolescent male than from a female sex worker. Here, demand links to the worthlessness of children, at least those who are not understood to be priceless, which is to say, children who are poor, orphaned, abandoned, runaway and/or who belong to racial, ethnic or caste groups that are deemed in any given society to be 'inferior'. So, for example, Albanian children (boys as well as girls) in Athens are placed on the lowest rung of the prostitution hierarchy, and stereotyped as dirty, cheap and submissive (Psimmenos, 2002, p. 96), and in India, men who cannot afford the services of an adult sex worker may make use of a child like Rafiq (quoted in chapter 3) as a poor but available substitute.

And this links to another 'peculiar' feature of prostitution as a consumer market. Certainly, there are many clients who view prostitution as a personal service sector and behave as consumers behave in other personal service markets (valuing skill and professionalism in sex workers, selecting the most expensive prostitutes they can afford as a way of displaying their own status, and so on). But clients' ideas and beliefs about sexuality, gender, race, age and sex commerce can also intersect in such a way as to make prostitution quite unlike any other personal service sector. It is hard to imagine a person who wanted a hair-cut or a therapeutic massage asking a third party to procure for them a 'dirty and poor' child, or a 'very black, black girl', or an amputee, or actively seeking out a drug-addicted teenager or an alcoholic vagrant woman to provide this service. And yet some clients do precisely this, for they are sexually excited by the idea of sex with a human being they perceive as degraded, worthless or damaged in some way (O'Connell Davidson and Sánchez Taylor, 1996a, 1996b).

## Policy Implications

The idea of reframing and criminalizing all clients of child prostitutes as child sex offenders may sound eminently reasonable when our starting point is the image of a paedophile who pays another adult to rape a 9-year-old. Why should he be treated differently in law from a man who abducts and rapes a 9-year-old, or who rapes his 9-year-old daughter? But matters look more complicated if we recognize that neither child prostitutes nor their clients are homogeneous groups. For instance, adolescent males are amongst those providing demand for prostitution (FPA HK, 2000; Monto, 2000; Anderson and O'Connell Davidson, 2003), and since some boys under 18 are known to buy sex in settings where children aged under 18 are present in prostitution, the possibility that children in prostitution may sometimes be used by child clients cannot be discounted. And when a child who trades sex in order to survive is given money for sex by another child living in exactly the same conditions (as experienced by Rafiq, see chapter 3), it would make little sense to speak of penalizing the child who pays as 'part of the trafficking chain'.

The moral issues raised by men and boys' use of teenage prostitutes also appear more complex if we consider the fact that in many parts of the world there is strong demand for commercial sex from men whose lives are every bit as bleak, violent and hopeless as those of the women and children they buy sex from. Consider, for instance, the 350,000 men who work in gold mines in South Africa (Campbell, 2001). Around 95 per cent of these workers are migrants, the vast majority housed in single-sex hostels, with up to eighteen men sharing a room. Their living conditions are dirty and overcrowded, there is no space for privacy or quiet, there are very limited opportunities for wives or family to visit, and few opportunities for leisure or relaxation. Their working conditions are equally grim, underground in the heat, often working with noisy machinery for eight hours with infrequent breaks, and lack of access to water, in constant fear of fatal, mutilating or disabling accidents. This is hardly an environment in which it is easy for human beings to fulfil their own emotional needs, or indeed even acknowledge that they experience emotions such as fear, loneliness or sorrow. As one miner explained to Catherine Campbell:

> They told me that in this situation you must know now that you are on the mines you are a man and must be able to face anything without fear. . . . To be called a man serves to encourage and console you time and again. . . . You will hear people saying 'a man is a sheep, he does not cry'. . . . no matter how hard you hit a sheep or slaughter it you will not hear it cry. . . . So, that is a comparison that whatever pain you can inflict on a man you will not see him cry. (Campbell, 2001, p. 281)

Sex is viewed as necessary to men's health and well-being, and as a way of demonstrating one's manhood, and it is unsurprising to find that prostitute-use, one of the few possibilities for leisure, is common amongst miners in South Africa (also in parts of Latin America where similar conditions exist: see Sutton, 1994). If some of the men who live and work in these conditions care little about the problems that have driven women and girls into prostitution, or about whether the prostitutes they use are above or below the age of 18, then their indifference merely mirrors the indifference that the rest of world feels towards them.

There are other reasons to exercise caution when discussing sanctions against those who sexually exploit children. Consider, for example, the fact that there are places in the world where it is estimated that between 15 and 30 per cent of those working in prostitution are under the age of 18 and that up to 75 per cent of the male population engage or have engaged in prostitute-use (Brown, 2000; Anderson and O'Connell Davidson, 2003). In such places, proposals to penalize anyone who buys sex from a minor could translate into proposals to incarcerate more than half of the male population. Calls for the universal application of harsh penalties against those who buy sex from children do not necessarily represent either a realistic or a humane response to the problem. More generally, it seems to me dangerous to abstract people's practices as sex buyers from the more general sexual cultures in which they exist, because once the problem is reduced to questions of individual morality, it is all too easy for those who may not use prostitutes, but who are none the less complicit with the daily maintenance and generational reproduction of profoundly oppressive sexual cultures, to wriggle off the hook.

In some settings, dominant attitudes towards gender, sexuality and commercial sex combine in such a way as to almost produce a social expectation that men (at least those of a particular age and class) will engage in prostitute-use. To resist this social pressure is to risk the dishonour of being labelled 'gay' or 'unmanly', something that can carry very serious consequences for the individual concerned. In such contexts, it strikes me as callous (as well as unrealistic) to call for clients to be criminalized. After all, this is rather like calling for them to penalized for an accident of birth, for having been born a male of a particular class, in a particular place, at a particular time. Meanwhile, the 'good' and 'decent' politicians, religious and community leaders, and others in powerful positions who refuse to allow sex education in schools, who tolerate or promote homophobia, institutionalize gender inequalities, enthusiastically perpetuate the Madonna/Whore dichotomy, and so on (in other words, who help to create and sustain a sexual culture in which many boys and men decide to use prostitutes), go without censure.

Recognizing the link between men's prostitute-use and the model of gender and sexuality into which they have been socialized does not force us to adopt a position of moral relativism (i.e. to argue that one culture's traditional practices cannot be condemned for failing to match up to the moral standards of another culture). But it does mean that the *political* nature of challenges to sexual cultures must be acknowledged and debated. Rather than entering into dubious alliances with states and moral conservatives, it seems to me that feminists who want to see the market in commercial sexual services wither away need to devise longer-term and more sophisticated political strategies to win hearts and minds. In many contexts, this means focusing on the common humanity of those who buy and those who sell sex, and recognizing the senses in which they are alike oppressed by the sexual culture in which they live, as well as the senses in which clients contribute to prostitutes' oppression.

The same points apply to those who campaign against CSEC, for whilst they, like feminist abolitionists, may recognize the structural factors that push children into the sex trade, it is actually perfectly possible for governments to act on calls to penalize the buyer without even beginning to address the power relations that lie behind either the supply or the demand side of child prostitution. Indeed, an emphasis on punishing those who buy sex from children helps to discursively construct CSEC as a problem of individual morality, and to deflect attention from the global and national economic, social and political inequalities that underpin it. It is, I believe, hugely telling that the Labour government in Britain *has* managed to introduce legislation criminalizing the clients of prostitutes aged under 18, but *has not* managed to end discrimination in the benefit system and minimum wage legislation against persons aged between 16 and 18.[3] In place of full recognition as economic actors in their own right, children are thus – in theory – offered 'protection' from the morally reprehensible client. And yet what do most clients exploit if not precisely the vulnerability that the state creates through its refusal to accept that not all children are able or willing to remain economically dependent on parents or guardians until their eighteenth birthdays?

Without measures to address the conditions under which children make the decision to sell sex, criminalizing clients looks very much like window-dressing, for no one can seriously imagine that in a year's time, or even in five years' time, all the men who have ever bought or ever would buy sex from a person under the age of 18 will be safely behind bars. The same problem arises in relation to global economic governance. In many cases, children's entry into prostitution is precipitated largely by macro-economic policies being enforced by the IMF to reduce domestic expenditure and increase interest rates, policies that often lead to cuts in social and welfare spending that might otherwise provide a safety net for poor, runaway and/or abandoned children (Kempadoo, 1999a; Mickleson, 2000). In this context, obtaining an international consensus on the need for legal penalties against those who buy sex from persons under the age of 18 looks rather less progressive than it may at first appear.

There is a final, and very important, reason to urge caution about calling for extensions of the state's punitive powers with regard to prostitution – adult or child. In most countries of the world, the civil and human rights of females who work in prostitution are routinely, and often grossly, violated. Prostitutes variously face arbitrary detention, deportation, forcible eviction from their dwellings, enforced health checks, including HIV testing, forcible 'rehabilitation', corporal punishment, even execution; few states offer prostitutes adequate protection from violent crime or abusive employers, and prostitutes are frequently victims of crimes perpetrated by corrupt law enforcement agents, including rape, beatings and extortion. The scale and severity of the human rights violations perpetrated against female prostitutes in the contemporary world was recognized in the 1992 general recommendation made by the Convention for the Elimination of All Forms of Discrimination Against Women (CEDAW) to include prostitutes among those who needed to be offered equal protection under the law (Kempadoo and Ghuma, 1999, p. 293; see also P. Alexander, 1997; Chan, 1999).

Since states are amongst those who most consistently violate prostitutes' rights, it would be naïve to trust that calls for stronger legal controls over those who exploit children within prostitution will automatically produce desirable outcomes for either prostitute women or teenagers. Indeed, crackdowns on CSEC and trafficking have often had extremely negative consequences for both adults and adolescents working in prostitution (see, for instance, O'Connell Davidson and Sánchez Taylor, 2001), and the numbers of people arrested for sexually exploiting children in prostitution generally pale into insignificance next to the numbers of women and teenagers arrested for prostitution and/or immigration offences. There is a great deal of work to be done in terms of changing attitudes towards prostitution and creating legal and social environments which are protective of female prostitutes' human rights before we can be confident that calls for tighter and more extensive criminalization of CSEC will not continue to have these unintended and undesirable consequences.

# 7  Child Sex Tourism

There is a strong historical association between travel, sex, race and political domination (Enloe, 1989; Hyam, 1990; Nagel, 2003). For centuries, Africa, the Americas and Asia 'were figured in European lore as libidinously eroticized ... a *porno-tropics* ... a fantastic magic lantern of the mind onto which Europe projected its forbidden sexual desires and fears' (McClintock, 1995, p. 22), and as Ann Laura Stoler notes: 'Colonial observers and participants in the imperial enterprise expressed unwavering interest in the sexual interface of the colonial encounter. Probably no subject is discussed more than sex in the colonial literature and no subject more frequently invoked to foster the racist stereotypes of European society' (1997, p. 14).

Today, travel is still often associated with a quest for sexual experience with 'exotic' Others, but there is also a more general association between travel and sex. Sex is widely understood to be part of the tourist experience, and whether with other tourists, through local 'holiday romances', or with sex workers, many people expect to have more sex whilst on vacation (Oppermann, 1998; Clift and Carter, 2000; Ryan and Hall, 2001). Within this, the kind of sex they have is, for heterosexuals in particular, often risky. In a survey of British heterosexuals who had had sex with new partners abroad, Hawkes et al. (1994) found that almost two-thirds did not consistently use condoms. The sex is also often more 'casual' and more risqué than the sex they would have at home. There are European holiday destinations that are renowned for the high level of tourist–tourist sexual interaction, and for the overtly sexualized nature of tourism for young people in particular. In Tenerife, for instance, young Britons (female as well as male) pay to go on organized pub crawls that include sexual 'dares' (involving squirty whipped cream and suchlike), and as gangs of young male participants move from one venue to another, they chant 'We're going to make some babies!' to the rhythm of the conga. Commercial sex, including sexual entertainment such as lap dance, strip shows and live sex shows as well as prostitution, is a feature of tourism in many tourist destinations in both affluent and developing countries. The sex sectors of some European and American cities (for instance, Amsterdam,

Copenhagen, Las Vegas) are tourist attractions in and of themselves, just as the Pat Pong district of Bangkok is considered by many tourists to be a 'must see', even if they have no intention of actually buying a sexual service.

If tourism is, to a large extent, sex, what is 'sex tourism'? The term, though widely used, is remarkably difficult to define (Oppermann, 1998; Ryan, 2000). For some, a 'sex tourist' is a person (usually a man) who takes an organized tour, in which the tour operator arranges access to prostitutes along with flights, hotels, airport transfers, and so on. But this definition would exclude vast numbers of men who make their own travel arrangements, or take 'normal' package holidays, and then proceed to avail themselves of the services of prostitutes in the tourist areas they visit. And widening the definition of a 'sex tourist' invariably leads to other problems – does the term only refer to those who travel with the explicit and conscious intention of buying sex, or does it also include those who travel for 'ordinary' reasons, but happen to buy sex one night because they are approached by a sex worker and think, perhaps through the haze of drink or drugs, 'Why not?' And what of those who enter into what they consider to be a holiday romance with a local, but also buy meals for and give gifts to their 'boyfriend' or 'girlfriend'?

Such definitional problems, alongside the fact that prostitution is not universally criminalized, so that prostitution-tourism, organized or otherwise, can be quite legally pursued in some countries, make any blanket condemnation of 'sex tourism' politically controversial. But 'child sex tourism' appears to be another matter entirely. Who could fail to be appalled by the idea of Western paedophiles travelling to poor countries in order to buy experiences that are 'forbidden in their own country' (O'Grady, 1996, p. 10)? Because the campaign against 'child sex tourism' mounted by ECPAT in the 1990s presented the problem largely as one involving sexual deviants ('paedophiles' and 'child molesters') taking advantage of either weak or inadequate child protection laws or poor law enforcement in 'Third World' countries, it was extraordinarily effective in terms of garnering international sympathy and support not just from policy-makers, politicians, journalists and the general public, but also from representatives of the tourist industry and local and national tourism officials. Whilst airline executives and tour operators are hardly likely to wish to involve themselves in a campaign to impose higher moral standards on their customers than those required in law, or to try to police the consensual sexual behaviours of adults who happen to have travelled with them, they are (with some notable exceptions: see O'Grady, 1996) as likely as the next person to want to voice indignation about paedophiles.

Even commentators who in general take a rigorous and critical approach to the analysis of the sex sector have sometimes been happy to go along with sweeping claims about 'child sex tourism'. For example, Lin Lim states that

Child sex tourism – 'tourism organized with the primary purpose of facilitating the effecting of a commercial sexual relationship with a child' (United Nations, 1995, p. 13) – is a particularly serious form of child prostitution, partly because it attracts paedophiles and also because it has been responsible for a palpable increase in the violation of not only young girls but also young boys. (1998, p. 183)

Though perhaps unintended, the implication is that we should view the violation of young boys as *particularly* serious, and consider it somehow worse for a child prostitute to be used by a paedophile client than by a 'normal' adult. And yet Lim, like ECPAT and others who campaign against 'child sex tourism', also follows the United Nations Convention on the Rights of the Child in defining a 'child' as a person under the age of 18. Defined as such, the majority of child prostitutes in the contemporary world are actually too old to be of interest to those who would clinically be defined as 'paedophiles' (they are aged above 13). Moreover, Lim goes on to note that 'ordinary' tourists can become situational child abusers while they are out of their own country, and to observe that the broader tourist industry is partially implicated in the tourist-related sex trade: 'Although reputable travel companies may not intentionally wish to promote sex tourism, their marketing materials often help to sustain the flow, for example, by stressing the attractions of the "nightlife" of certain resorts or by promulgating certain stereotypes of women and children in developing countries' (Lim, 1998, p. 185).

There is thus a tension in her discussion of 'child sex tourism'. At one moment, it appears as a particularly serious form of child prostitution primarily organized by or for paedophiles, but at the next it is enmeshed in and reproduced by the ordinary tourist industry. Such uncertainty is well founded, for it is by no means clear that 'child sex tourism' – whether involving paedophiles or 'ordinary' tourists – can be meaningfully separated from 'sex tourism' or from 'tourism' more generally.

### 'Paedophiles Who Travel Abroad' and Campaigns Against Them

Although the discourse that surrounds it is often emotive, salacious and panicky and the magnitude of the phenomenon grossly exaggerated, 'paedophile tourism' is certainly not a figment of journalists' or campaigners' imagination. It is a reality, and numerous cases have been documented in which Western men travel as tourists, or take up permanent or temporary residence in poor and developing countries, in order to gain sexual access to local children (Ireland, 1993; Seabrook, 2000). The countries/regions targeted include Sri Lanka (Beddoe, 1998; Ratnapala, 1999), Goa (O'Connell Davidson and Sánchez Taylor, 1996c), Thailand (Montgomery, 1998, 2001), Cambodia (Foggo, 2002), the Philippines (Lee-Wright, 1990), the Dominican Republic (Moya and Garcia, 1999) and Costa Rica (Aguilar, 1994). One of the most obvious explanations for this phenomenon is the fact that Westerners know that it is easier, cheaper and safer to obtain sexual access to a child in poor and developing countries than it is back home, and a key objective of campaigns against 'child sex tourism' has been to shift the perception that sex with children in poorer countries is a low-risk crime by raising awareness and encouraging the adoption of laws and policies in both receiving and sending countries that will facilitate the prosecution of foreigners who commit sexual offences against children abroad.

A first step was to put pressure on governments in receiving countries to take the issue seriously. Whilst no country ever actively promoted tourist-related child prostitution, the general phenomenon of prostitution-tourism was viewed by some governments in the 1980s and early 1990s as an inevitable, and fairly unproblematic, by-product of tourist development. Sex tourism in the shape of Kisaeng tours for Japanese tourists formed part of South Korea's planned economic development in the early 1980s, for example. Potential sex workers were lectured on the crucial economic role played by tourism before being granted their prostitution licences, and South Korean politicians praised them for their contribution to the economic development of the fatherland (Mitter, 1986, p. 64). Similarly, some senior officials in China argued that prostitution was an inevitable by-product of an emerging market economy, and coined the slogan 'sacrifice a generation of women to obtain economic development' (*Hong Kong Economic Times*, 1993). In Fujian, the provincial government even conducted a survey in 1994, asking foreign visitors whether they felt that China's ban on prostitution would hinder the development of tourism (*South China Sunday Morning Post*, 1994). Part of the ECPAT campaign has been to encourage governments to recognize and condemn the sexual exploitation of children within prostitution-tourism. So, for example, in 1993, a number of political and community leaders from Thailand, Vietnam, the Philippines and other countries were asked by ECPAT to sign a statement saying: 'I oppose the prostitution of children and view with concern the growing incidence of this practice. The sexual abuse of children by foreign tourists must be ended' (O'Grady, 1996, p. 50).

Campaigners against 'child sex tourism' have also sought to identify and counteract other factors behind the relatively low risk of prosecution associated with child abuse in poor and developing countries (see Roujanavong, 1994), and have drawn attention to a lack of will to combat the problem on the part of the governments of affluent countries which send 'child sex tourists'. Campaigners pointed out, for example, that Western governments' lack of interest in crimes against 'Other' children led many sex tourist receiving countries to pursue a policy of deporting foreign nationals accused of child sexual offences rather than prosecuting them, and this, combined with the fact that offenders could often bribe their way out of trouble, meant that people who had been caught abusing children abroad could return home and continue their lives without fear of prosecution. ECPAT therefore lobbied hard and with a good deal of success for sending countries to introduce extraterritorial criminal laws that would allow states to 'penalize the sexual crimes of their nationals or residents when perpetrated against children in other countries' (Muntarbhorn, 1998, p. 7). Such laws were not to be seen as a substitute for, but as a complement to, 'effective laws, policies, and law/policy enforcement in the destination countries of such exploiters' (Muntarbhorn, 1998, p. 7). By 1998, twenty countries had introduced extraterritorial laws pertaining to child sex offences committed abroad, but in many of these countries, no court cases had yet been initiated. Germany, the country where most cases had been pursued, had only prosecuted thirty-seven people under these laws, and only six of these cases led to conviction (Muntarbhorn, 1998, p. 19).

Individuals believed to profit by organizing 'child sex tours' to countries where child prostitutes are more cheaply and readily available were another focus of concern in campaigns against 'child sex tourism'. Again, lobbyists often met with success. The British government enacted legislation in 1996 – Sexual Offences (Conspiracy and Incitement) – designed to 'strengthen action against those in the UK who organise sex tours or who encourage others to travel abroad for the purpose of sexually exploiting children' (Home Office, 1996, p. 10). In Australia, the Crimes (Child Sex Tourism) Amendment Act came into effect in 1994, and covered, among other things, 'those responsible for organizing overseas tours for the purpose of engaging in sexual relations or activities with minors' (Hall, 1998, p. 90).

Yet the term 'organized sex tour' is somewhat misleading. There are no 'paedophile package tour operators', garnering huge profits by chartering planes and block-booking hotels in 'child sex capitals' for large numbers of individuals intent on sexually abusing small children. Although there is some evidence to suggest that organizations that support and champion paedophilia have facilitated their members' travel to poor and developing countries in order to gain sexual access to children, either by providing information and advice or occasionally by more direct means,[1] these organizations are few and far between, and in any case operate more as collectives than as large-scale business enterprises. Such organization as is involved in 'paedophile sex tourism' is generally either through informal (and non-profit-making) networks, or parasitic on more mainstream forms of sex tourism. So far as the former are concerned, an extract from a letter written to me by a man who self-identifies as a paedophile is instructive. He describes how he came to travel to the Dominican Republic in the mid-1980s:

Through a meeting in Philadelphia of the NAMBLA organisation, I came to know a school teacher named Ted. . . . He knew an expat German named Dieter who had had problems in Germany and relocated to Santo Domingo. . . . He had a small house in the capital. I was working as a teacher at the time. One spring.... Ted suggested to me that I and he and a third teacher who was from Canada fly down to the Dominican Republic, rent a car, stay with Dieter and look for boys. I was very involved in my photography at that time and wanted to add to my foto files. My intent was not to pick up boys. Ted enjoyed sex with black or Hispanic or white mid to older teens and the Canadian was interested in sex with white and Hispanic boys. None of us had been there before and we went on the information of the German.... The information we got from Dieter was that the easiest boy to pick up would be one of the shoe shine boys.... Ted and the Canadian both 'scored' with boys the first night. The Canadian took 'his boy' to a cheap hotel he had been told about by Dieter. It was dangerous because the boy was black and young and the Canadian was white. But with enough money, the desk clerk would turn his eye. Ted picked up an older mulatto boy and arranged to take him back to the house of the German.

But not all 'paedophiles who travel abroad' rely on others like themselves to provide them with access to children. Some make use of facilities that are primarily geared towards the interests of 'ordinary' sex tourists, and this draws attention to a key weakness in analyses that assume a clear line of demarcation between 'child sex tourism' and 'sex tourism' more generally.

### Blurring the Boundary

Travel and the Single Male (TSM) is an American-based organization run by and for sex tourists and boasts some 5,000 members. It publishes a guide-book and sells club membership for US$50 per annum. Members receive a quarterly newsletter, discounts in some hotels and brothels, and, most importantly, are provided with access to the TSM internet site. This provides information on travel and prostitution in various countries around the world, access to soft-core pornographic photographs of female sex workers from those countries, two message boards and a chat room for members to swap 'sexperiences', views, 'news' and handy travel tips. The worldview of TSM members typifies that of Western heterosexual men who habitually practise sex tourism to poor and developing countries, which is to say that it is profoundly misogynist, homophobic and racist (O'Connell Davidson, 1995, 1998, 2001b; Seabrook, 1996; O'Connell Davidson and Sánchez Taylor, 1999).

    In 1998, Jacqueline Sánchez Taylor and I interviewed several American TSM members in Boca Chica, the Dominican Republic, as well as two expatriates whose bars feature in the information provided on the Dominican Republic on TSM's website alongside photographs of their female bar staff, and other expatriates whose names also feature in the 'chat' between members posted on the website. A group of American expatriates and sex tourists linked to TSM (one of whom was a New Jersey police officer) identified one of their cronies as having 'an obsession with virgins'. They told us that the man concerned had paid the families of eight Dominican girl children aged around 11 in order to rape them, and had shown them pornographic photographs of one his victims. In telling us of this man's exploits, one expatriate described him as a 'paedophile', and remarked that many American paedophiles come to the Dominican Republic. 'This one we put up with,' he said, 'but the rest of them we don't want nothing to do with.' The conversation continued as follows:

*JOD:* Why do you put up with him?
*Expatriate 1:* He's a character...
*Expatriate 2:* He's not a paedophile. You're talking 8, 9, 10 years old. That's a paedophile...He's not a paedophile...you can't say that about him.
*Expatriate 1:* Well, what's a guy that fucks an 11-year-old girl?
*Expatriate 2:* He doesn't. He doesn't...No.
*Expatriate 1:* Oh? I've seen the pictures.
*Expatriate 2:* Paedophiles will go right down to 2, 3 years old.
*JOD:* You get people like that coming down here?
*Expatriate 1:* Yeah.
*Expatriate 2* [to sex tourist friend]: You're a policeman, what's a paedophile?
*US police officer:* I don't know...Like 5, 6, 7.
*Expatriate 1:* An 11-year-old?
*US police officer:* I don't know.
*Expatriate 2:* No, no, he's not a paedophile, you shouldn't call him a paedophile, you can get folks in trouble talking about them that way.

Subsequent interviews with a range of informants led us to believe that the man with 'a thing for virgins' secured access to children through an American expatriate and his Dominican wife who together run a brothel in Boca Chica catering to demand from tourist men, including TSM members (O'Connell Davidson and Sánchez Taylor, 2001). Further evidence of a link between TSM and child sexual exploitation comes from postings on the message board about a man who, Ministry of Tourism officials informed us, had been deported in 1997. During a police clampdown on child prostitution that year, 'Mr D', a French Canadian, was found to be organizing the prostitution of minors from his hotel in Boca Chica. A posting from TSM's message board describes Mr D's hotel prior to its closure and his deportation:

many of the male guests and others from outside the hotel hang out [in the hotel bar] drinking. This as you can guess also draws the attention of the *chicas* and a number of them hang about as well. D. does not in any way discourage this as he has correctly concluded that having the girls there also keep the guys there longer and keeps the drinks flowing.... A girl...was knocking on my door literally 2 minutes after my checking in, asking if I wanted a blow job.... I enjoyed my stay completely.... A few girls were also staying at the hotel.... They are often available for entertainment as you might expect. (posted 4.9.97)

TSM is not unique, for there are many other clubs, guides and businesses catering to demand from 'normal' sex tourists (on whom more will be said below) that also facilitate paedophile tourists' sexual access to younger local children, even if those who run them are normally careful to make disclaimers about child prostitution and to ensure that their published materials contain no reference to or photographs of those under 18 (see, for instance, Cassirer, 1992; Hammer, 1997; Wilson, 1998). Indeed, one often cited example of the successful prosecution of a 'child sex tour' operator actually involved a British man, Michael Clarke, whose business ('Paradise Express' holidays to the Philippines) was geared to the desires of 'ordinary' sex tourists rather than paedophiles. In something of a 'sting' operation, Clarke agreed to the request of an investigative journalist and a Christian Aid worker, who were posing as paedophile tourists, for underage girls for sex. His actions were secretly filmed, which led to Clarke's arrest and trial for procuring child prostitutes and inducing others to be clients of child prostitutes. He was sentenced to sixteen years in jail, followed by deportation from the Philippines (Kane, 1998).

Though Clarke's actions are not defensible in any way, I do not think that on the basis of the evidence available he can properly be described as an organizer of 'child sex tours'. He was a man attempting (and some say rather unsuccessfully) to operate a business catering to sex tourists in general, but who was apparently willing to accommodate the tastes of paedophiles when approached and asked to do so. The distinction is important if we are to see, rather than turn a blind eye to, the ways in which 'sex tourism' and 'child sex tourism' are bound up in each other, and how both are bound up in tourism more generally. And once the interconnections between 'child sex tourism', 'sex tourism' and 'tourism' are acknowledged, it becomes clear that the impact of campaigns against 'child sex tourism' may be more limited, and more ambiguous, than might at first be assumed.

### Travel, Sex and Inequality

Tourists have sex – commercial and non-commercial – in holiday destinations in affluent as well as poor countries. However, sites of sex tourism in developing countries can be distinguished from those in affluent countries not necessarily by the existence of a large, diverse, formally organized sex industry serving demand from tourist clients, but more particularly by the existence of a busy informal sex sector. In this latter sector, local/migrant people (both adult and child) enter into a wide range of sexual-economic exchanges with tourists. For instance, there are adult and child prostitutes working either independently or under the control of a third party, soliciting custom from beaches, parks and ordinary tourist bars; there are pimps and hustlers (both adult and child) offering to procure all manner of sexual experiences for tourists; and there are individuals who may not define themselves as 'prostitutes' or 'sex workers', but who seek sexual relationships with tourists either as a means of accessing a life-style they cannot afford, or in the hope of receiving gifts that will supplement their very low income from hotel or bar work, or because they wish to migrate to a richer country and hope to find a sponsor or marriage partner who will facilitate their migration.

Prostitute–client exchanges in the informal sector are often more open-ended and loosely specified than those which take place in the formal sector. Prices and limits to the contract are not always negotiated in advance, and prostitutes may provide anything from two hours to two weeks of full access to their persons, performing non-sexual labour for the client (shopping, tidying, washing, translation, and so on) as well as sexual labour. They will also often act in ways that are taken to signify genuine affection, for instance holding hands, kissing, walking arm in arm, sharing a bed (all things that few experienced sex workers in Western countries would do with a client). Taken together, all this means that sex tourist destinations in poor countries or regions offer the tourist not just extensive and cheap opportunities for sexual experience, but also opportunities for types of sexual experience that would not be readily available either back home or in tourist destinations in more affluent countries. This wealth of sexual opportunity leads both male and female tourists to describe such places as 'sexual paradise', 'Fantasy Island' and 'Disneyland' (O'Connell Davidson and Sánchez Taylor, 1999). But sexual Disneylands do not exist in nature. They have to be created.

There is some national and regional variation in terms of the history of such creations. In Thailand, as in several other South-East Asian countries, a period of 'economic colonialism and militarization in which prostitution is a formalized mechanism of dominance' has been a key stage in the development of sex tourism (Hall, 1994, p. 151; see also Truong, 1990; Bishop and Robinson, 1998). But sex tourism does not always or only involve the maintenance and development of existing large-scale, highly commoditized sex industries serving foreign military personnel. It has also emerged in locations where no such sex industry existed, for instance the Gambia (Morris-Jara, 1996) and Cuba (Fernandez, 1999).

In general, sexual Disneylands are the product of a complex set of linkages between international debt, price fluctuations in global commodity markets, economic development policy and prostitution (Kempadoo, 1999a; Bishop and Robinson, 1998; Chant and McIlwaine, 1995), as well as laws and social policies adopted by individual countries (see, for example, M. Alexander, 1997). The International Monetary Fund agreements and World Bank structural adjustment loans, sector adjustment loans and programme loans that governments of developing countries have had little choice but to enter serve to swell the prostitution labour market, for the policy packages tied to these loans have had a devastating impact on the poor. Structural adjustment processes are widely reported to have undermined traditional forms of subsistence economies, led to high levels of unemployment, redirected subsidies away from social spending and basic commodities towards debt servicing, and often to have encouraged massive currency depreciations leading to a concomitant drop in the price of labour (Anderson and Witter, 1994; NACLA, 1997; Beddoe, 1998; Kempadoo, 1999a).

Structural adjustment has created a 'surplus' labouring population, as well as driving down the wages of those in work, and has thus been associated with the growth of the informal economic sector in a number of countries as ordinary people (both above and below the age of 18) desperately seek ways in which to earn a living, or supplement or substitute for impossibly low waged employment (see, for instance, Witter and Kirton, 1990; LeFranc, 1994; Black, 1995; Safa, 1997). Though sex tourism involves only a minority of local and migrant persons, expatriates and tourists in any given setting, prostitution and other forms of tourist–local sexual-economic exchange are, none the less, amongst the wide range of activities that take place in the informal tourism economy in developing countries (for instance, Meisch, 1995; Cabezas, 1999; Williams, 1999; Phillips, 1999; Ford and Wirawan, 2000; Sánchez Taylor, 2000, 2001b).

The economic and political position of tourists could not be more different from that of locals with whom they come into contact in developing countries. Even the working-class budget tourist from Britain or Germany, for instance, is in a position to spend about as much on a package holiday in Thailand or the Caribbean as most ordinary local and migrant people working in the formal or informal tourism economy will earn in a year. This means that tourists, as well as being able to afford to consume sexual services if they so choose, are in a position to freely dispense gifts and sums of money which, though negligible to them, represent significant benefits to the average local person. Even the half-empty shampoo bottles, unused medicines and uneaten foodstuffs that the tourist would throw away at the end of a holiday can make an important contribution to a household that is struggling to subsist. Small wonder, then, that many locals, both adult and child, seek to befriend tourists and/or to enter into sexual relationships with them.

Moreover, tourists' citizenship of politically powerful nations and their relative affluence combine to bestow upon them rights and freedoms that are denied to most of the locals and migrants they meet on their 'Third World' travels. Their passports allow them to cross national borders virtually at whim, and they also enjoy a range of social, economic and cultural benefits that effectively amount to a degree of substantive citizenship far greater than that enjoyed by ordinary working-class citizens of the countries they visit. A tourist can, for example, expect to be housed in accommodation that is connected to a water supply, as well as to find a range of leisure facilities geared towards his or her interests, shopping facilities to meet his or her desires as a consumer, and so on. This is more than can be said of the average working-class Jamaican, Thai or Kenyan, for example. But tourists' privilege is not merely a reflection of their greater individual spending power; it results in large part from *government* spending on infrastructural development to support tourism (airports, roads, water supply, sewage disposal, electricity and telephones), something which actually diverts money from projects that might help ordinary local people to enjoy basic social, economic and cultural rights of citizenship (Patullo, 1996; Howard, 1999). Again, sexual relationships with tourists represent one of the few ways in which ordinary local adults and children can tap into privileges reserved for tourists and elite locals.

The tourist and the local are simultaneously brought together and separated by global inequality. Were it not for the huge disparity in terms of political and economic power between affluent and developing nations, the average Western tourist would not be in a position to take long-haul holidays to 'exotic' destinations, and those who did venture to Thailand or Sri Lanka or the Dominican Republic would not find themselves automatically positioned as the local's superior in terms of social, political and economic rights and freedoms. In a different and more equal world, long-haul tourists would find it no harder and no easier to make contact (sexual or otherwise) with local people than they find it to strike up such acquaintances with locals when they visit tourist resorts in their own country or an equally affluent country. Travel between and within affluent countries does not equip the tourist with the power to 'harm or help' the local people with whom they come into contact, but travel from rich to poor countries does (see Brace and O'Connell Davidson, 1996). In the 'Third World', even 'third-rate' American/European tourists are kings or queens, and whether they dream of holiday romance, or of ready opportunities for anonymous sex, or of affordable commercial sex, or of raping 11-year-old girls, or just of being sweet-talked by a series of 'dusky' strangers, they are in a position to make their dreams come true. That's Disneyland.

But the global processes and national social and economic policies which bring tourists and locals face to face as profoundly unequal parties are not enough, on their own, to create the phenomenon of sex tourism. Back home, the same people often could and do find themselves face to face with individuals who are structurally positioned and socially constructed as their unequals, and yet do not necessarily feel the urge to pursue sexual contact with them. In London, Hamburg or San Francisco, for example, we rarely see ordinary, middle-aged men and women flirting with homeless teenagers who sit on the pavements begging for spare change, or inviting them out to dinner and then back home to bed. Understanding Disneyland also requires us to think about the connections between travel, sex and race, and to consider what is being consumed within tourism more generally.

### The Scene and the Obscene

In a survey of 661 German men who had had sex with one or more local women or girls in Thailand, the Philippines, Kenya, Brazil and the Dominican Republic, for example, Kleiber and Wilke (1995) found that only a minority, 22 per cent, described themselves as 'sex tourists'. As Günther observes, the curious phenomenon of sex tourism without sex tourists rests on the fact that many settings of tourism-oriented prostitution allow 'for a personal, noneconomic and self-serving "framing" . . . of the tourist–prostitute relationship' (1998, p. 71). Similarly, Sánchez Taylor's (2001b) survey of 240 female tourists in the Caribbean found that almost a third had had sex with one or more local men in the course of their holiday. Of these, 57 per cent acknowledged that they had 'helped' their partner out financially or materially. Asked if they had ever used a gigolo or male prostitute, all of them said 'No'. Such findings are partly accounted for by the fact that the open-ended and non-contractual nature of informal-sector prostitution allows tourists to delude themselves about the commercial basis of their sexual interactions.

But fantasies about the sexuality of the Other also play an important role in the 'framing' of such encounters as 'not-prostitution'. Rather than being confronted by what they understand and recognize as prostitution, Western tourists see local women, men and children dancing, drinking and smooching with tourists, and interpret this as validating racist fantasies of the hypersexual Other (Kempadoo, 1994). The scenes they witness in sex tourist resorts are taken as proof that different meanings attach to sexual behaviour in the host country, that sex is more 'natural' and 'free' amongst local people. Thus, 'open-ended' forms of prostitution in South-East Asian or Latin American/Caribbean countries can be (mis)interpreted in such a way as to make tourists feel chosen and desired for themselves, rather than for the contents of their wallets (Seabrook, 1996; Bishop and Robinson, 1998; O'Connell Davidson and Sánchez Taylor, 1999).

Awareness that local people are actually prostituting does not necessarily prompt the reappraisal of such ideas. Instead, sex tourists tell themselves that there are 'cultural' differences as regards prostitution, and/or that they are not paying for sex when they give money to a local sexual partner, but rather 'helping' her or him out. Take, for example, the following extract from a guide-book for gay male sex tourists to Thailand: 'Many Westerners are troubled about the idea of paying a young man for his time or sex, seeing it as pure prostitution, but this is an oversimplification. In Thailand, as in other less-developed countries, you will be considered a higher-status person . . . with obligations to those less fortunate than yourself' (Hammer, 1997, p. 18). Jean Baudrillard's discussion of the scene and the obscene is useful here:

> More visible than the visible – this is the obscene. More invisible than the invisible – this is the secret. The scene is in the order of the visible. But . . . [t]he obscene is the end of any scene . . . [the] hypervisibility of things is also the imminence of their end, the sign of the apocalypse. . . . If all enigmas are resolved, the stars go out. If everything secret is returned to the visible (and more than to the visible: to obscene obviousness), if all illusion is returned to transparence, then heaven becomes indifferent to the earth. (1990, p. 55)

Set in particular scenes, prostitution can appear to the tourist as quite heavenly. As has been noted, in the informal prostitution scene, the commercial basis of sexual interactions between tourists and local or migrant persons is invisible. But more than this, the gulf between each party in terms of life chances, material security and even age is concealed. Age means something different in a strange and 'exotic' land where children, like tropical plants, grow fast, and girls of 13 can be attracted to men of 60: 'Here a man has no age', as one expatriate in Costa Rica put it (O'Connell Davidson and Sánchez Taylor, 1996d). And last but not least, the local or migrant persons' sexual behaviour is mysterious. Even for tourists who buy explicitly commoditized sex, and who recognize their behaviour as prostitute-use, the discursive construction of racial, ethnic or national difference as sexual difference means that prostitution can retain an enigmatic quality. There is something mysterious about the Other sex worker. Thus, for example, European, North American and Australian tourists marvel at Thai sex workers (unlike junkie street prostitutes or cold, hard-bitten professionals back home, they seem to be 'nice girls' who 'do it for their families' and are truly 'warm and caring') and at Brazilian and Dominican sex workers who 'seem to really enjoy the sex' (Cohen, 1982; Kruhse-Mount Burton, 1995; O'Connell Davidson, 1995, 1998).

But racism and ethnic Othering take many forms, and their relation to sex is not always one of magical illusion, nor do all those who use prostitutes want such illusions. For some clients, the obscene is not the end but the beginning of sexual pleasure. They *want* to enter a pornutopia (see Hartsock, 1983, p. 175), where women and girls are paid 'fucking machines'; or they want cheap sex, or 'dirty' sex, sex with someone they view as low and debased – sex with someone to be 'immediately devoured' rather than 'seduced', to paraphrase Baudrillard (1990, p. 59). Who better to fulfil such desires than sex workers belonging to groups that are in general socially devalued on grounds of race, ethnicity or 'caste'? All of these points hold good in relation to both paedophile and 'normal' sex tourists.

Tourists' sexual behaviour is also shaped by the discursive construction of tourist destinations as liminal spaces in which it is both possible and desirable to suspend normal routines and transgress the rules that govern daily life. This means that it is not only inexpensive and convenient to engage in what Joane Nagel (2003, p. 17) terms 'ethnosexual adventuring' and 'ethnosexual invasion' (that is, recreational sex with, or sexual abuse of, members of other ethnic groups) in tourist centres in developing countries, but also guilt-free. No matter where they come from, a great many tourists share the sentiment behind the Japanese adage 'shameless behaviour during a trip is to be scraped off one's mind' (Allison 1994, p. 140).

## Saying 'No to Child Sex Tourism!'

If 'children' are to be defined as persons under the age of 18, then it is extraordinarily difficult to sustain the idea of a clear, sharp boundary between 'child sex tourism', on the one hand, and 'sex tourism' and 'tourism', on the other. 'Ordinary' tourists who visit brothels or use street prostitutes, like 'ordinary' clients in other settings, do not necessarily care very much whether the prostitute they use is 15 or 16 or 20 or older, providing they fancy the look of her or him. The same point holds good for those tourists who find sexual partners in the informal tourist-related prostitution sector, where the bulk of child prostitution often takes place. For how are tourists to tell the exact age of the locals who proposition them, especially given that many are drunk by the time they 'pull'?

The main ambition of many tourists – male and female – whom Jacqueline Sánchez Taylor and I interviewed in Latin America and the Caribbean was to 'party' and enjoy the novel experience of going out to bars and clubs and being surrounded by a bevy of 'lovely young ladies' or 'gorgeous young guys', all miraculously 'up for it' (O'Connell Davidson and Sánchez Taylor, 1996a, 1996d, 2001). Such people are not paedophiles, nor do they conform to the dominant stereotype of the 'sex tourist'. They do not go to seedy brothels where women and children are visibly brutalized by brothel keepers. But they will have sex with a lo-cal 15-year-old if she or he approaches them in a disco, smiles, flirts and dances with them, and offers to come back to their room. And in the morn-ing, if she or he asks for US$10 for the taxi fare home, they will give it, maybe with a little extra, just to be kind. They will feel no worse about this interaction, possibly better even, than they will feel about their other inter-actions with locals – the boy who shines their shoes, the woman or teenager who cleans their room, the small child who washes sand from their feet as they lie on a sun lounger on the beach in exchange for a few coins, the old woman who pleads with them to buy fruit from her, the little beggar child sitting on the pavement outside their hotel. The sex, like the sun, the sand, the drinking, the excess and above all the conspicuous waste (of food, energy, natural resources and time) in places where local people cannot af-ford to waste anything at all is all part of the tourist experience. It is all part of the 'local colour', the 'party atmosphere', the 'exotic beach resort with a great nightlife' that tourists have been sold, not by 'organized child sex tour operators', but by big, respectable, mainstream tourism companies.

Because campaigns against 'child sex tourism' focus attention on the minority of 'deviant' tourists who travel in pursuit of sex with young children, they actually ask very little of the tourist industry. The industry can be loudly applauded for assisting with the distribution of baggage tags emblazoned with the logo 'No to child sex tourism!', for agreeing to monitor accredited members of travel agents' associations to ensure they are not advertising 'child sex tours', for being willing to show in-flight videos telling people that it is illegal and wrong to have sex with 6-year-olds. But very few campaigners insist that the industry address questions about the derisory wages paid to hotel workers, or think about how this might contribute to their willingness to accept 'bribes' and 'tips' for turning a blind eye to the activities of tourists. Nor are we called upon to think about the social costs of tourism, or the fact that profits from tourism are largely repatriated to affluent sending countries and so will never 'trickle down' to those who pick up tourists' litter, clean their toilets, make their beds, serve their food, and fulfil their sexual fantasies.

Saying 'No to child sex tourism!' also deflects attention from the exploitation of child labour in the tourist industry more generally. As Maggie Black comments, 'sexual exploitation is not the only hazard relating to the employment of young people' within the tourist economy, and yet 'it is the only one on which attention appears to focus' (1995, p. 9). Furthermore, as Kempadoo and Ghuma observe, 'the emphasis on child prostitution as the main problem in sex tourism can be seen to quietly allow other forms of prostitution to continue to take place without hindrance, scrutiny, or attention to the human rights of women and men who provide sexual services in the tourist industry' (1999, p. 292). Worse still, it lends the cloak of legitimacy to violations of sex workers' rights (both adult and child) by police and other state actors, who have in many places responded to international pressure to end 'child sex tourism' by simply clamping down on those working in informal-sector prostitution. In the Dominican Republic, for example, women and teenagers in tourist resorts were frequently rounded up by police as a response to international pressure to address the problem of 'child sex tourism' (to give an idea of the scale, 170 were arrested in a single night in a single tourist resort during one raid in 1998). Once remanded in police custody, there were no beds to sleep on, and the women and girls had no entitlement to food until such time as they were convicted. After being held in these conditions for between one and four days, they were taken to court, where they were required to pay a fine in order to be released. Haitian women and teenagers were deported. Women also report having been beaten or raped by the police, as well as subject to extortion (Cabezas, 1999). This situation is not unique to the Dominican Republic. The number of women and teenagers who have ended up deported, or behind bars, or in 're-education', 'rehabilitation' or whatever euphemism is preferred, as a result of international concern about 'child sex tourism' far outstrips the number of Western paedophiles or men like Michael Clarke who have been similarly treated. It strikes me that this fact should give campaigners pause for thought.

# 8 Beyond Binaries?

> If the best thing we do is look after each other, then the worst thing we do is pretend to look after each other when in fact we are doing something else.
>
> Phillips, *Equals* (2002), p. xi

In asking us to look after children, campaigns against CSEC could be said to make an appeal to the best in us. But such campaigns also rest crucially on the assumption that commercially sexually exploited children represent a distinct and unitary group that stands in particular need of looking after. One of the aims of this book has been to show that there is no clear, firm or absolute line of demarcation between commercial sex involving adults and that involving children. Though the commercial sex market is partially segmented by age, the vast majority of child prostitutes around the world work alongside adults in similar or identical conditions, sometimes for the same employer or pimp, and usually serving the same client base. Children are rarely *uniquely* abused and exploited in the sex trade – where children are subject to slavery-like conditions within prostitution, so too are adults; where there are children who sell sex because they will starve unless they do so, there are also people aged over 18 who face the same stark choice. The structural factors that precipitate children's and adults' entry into the sex trade and make it difficult for them to exit it are also often identical. And since children do not actually inhabit a separate social, political or economic universe from adults, their destinies are intertwined with those of adults in their community, so that where adult populations are unable to secure basic economic, social and cultural rights, children are vulnerable to sexual as well as other forms of exploitation.

Moreover, because persons under the age of 18 are never just 'children', but are also socially marked in other ways (male or female, black or white, 'upper caste' or 'lower caste', members of socially and politically marginalized groups or of socially privileged groups, and so on), their vulnerability to sexual exploitation and sexual violence largely tracks that of their adult counterparts. So, for example, an estimated 15,700 women and girls were raped during the civil war in Rwanda (Turshen, 2001), with the fate of victims aged below 18 being determined by their gender and ethnicity, in other words, by the social identity they *shared* with adults, not by their age and so their difference from adult women. Equally, where the 'whore' stigma is applied to those who transgress strictures used to control female sexuality, girls are made vulnerable to rights violations by the gender identity they share with adult women, not merely by their age. And in contexts where prostitute women are most profoundly stigmatized, refused basic civil and human rights, and forced to live and work in isolated brothel communities, their children are viewed and treated not simply as 'children', but as members of a dishonoured community of outcasts (INSAF, 1995; Uddin et al., 2001).

Those who campaign against CSEC insist that children should not be stigmatized for their involvement in the commercial sex trade (Muntarbhorn, 1996; ECPAT, 1999). But how can we say 'No!' to the stigmatization of child prostitutes whilst simultaneously either saying 'Yes!' to, or remaining mute about, the stigmatization of adult women in prostitution? Likewise, when societies tolerate or endorse the stigmatization and persecution of homosexuals, those below as well as above the age of 18 are socially and culturally isolated as well as often economically marginalized. As a result, gay children, as well as adults, sometimes turn to the sex trade in order to subsist, where they are often vulnerable to homophobic violence from clients, non-clients and police, as well as to arrest and imprisonment. Can we combat these violations of children's rights without also joining more general calls for lesbian and gay rights? Is it realistic to suppose that we can leave profoundly conservative gender and sexual ideologies intact, yet secure some kind of 'stay of execution' for those aged under 18? Calling for the de-stigmatization of commercially sexually exploited *children* seems as morally dubious and logistically flawed as calls to fight 'child apartheid' would have been in the old South Africa.

Attempts to draw a boundary between adults' and children's involvement in the sex trade through reference to the degree of harm it implies for the individuals concerned are also unsatisfactory. Lim, for example, claims that children's vulnerability 'is one of the crucial factors distinguishing child prostitution from adult prostitution' (1998, p. 174), and yet it is hard to see how such an assertion could be empirically validated. The problem here is not simply that some adults are also very vulnerable within prostitution and other forms of sex commerce (for example, adults with mental health problems and/or high levels of drug or alcohol dependency, adults who are subject to slavery-like conditions), but also that people under the age of 18 are clearly not all *equally* vulnerable within the sex trade or uniformly harmed by their involvement in it. The experience of a 17-year-old British girl who sells sexual services in a lap dance club in Tenerife is not identical to that of a 10-year-old child who trades sex in order to survive on the streets of Lagos, and neither child's experience is the same as that of a 2-year-old who is sexually abused by an adult guardian for purposes of producing pornography.

Nor is it always clear that CSEC represents *the* central or most significant aspect of a child's oppression. If children trade sex because they will starve if they do not, or use prostitution as part of a strategy to escape a life in which they are hungry and barefoot and/or experiencing physical or sexual violence, for example, then to identify their commercial sexual exploitation as *the* factor threatening their 'physical, psychological, spiritual, moral and social development' (ECPAT, 1999, p. 8) seems rather to put the cart before the horse. Moreover, there are contexts in which children's sexual exploitation is but one horrible motif in an experience more violent and terrifying than most of us can even imagine. A 14-year-old girl abducted by the Revolutionary United Front in Sierra Leone to serve as a soldier's 'wife' states that 'I've seen people get their hands cut off, a ten year old girl raped and then die, and so many men and women burned alive' (HRW, 2003); girls kidnapped by rebel forces in Uganda speak of being forced to beat other children to death and to participate in massacres, as well as of being raped and compelled to provide sexual services to rebel soldiers (Prosser, 1999). ECPAT comments that though money is not part of the transaction when children involved in armed conflicts are 'expected to perform sexual and other services in return for protection and staying alive', this is none the less 'commercial sexual abuse' (1999, p. 11). I would not dispute the fact that such children are victims of sexual violence and exploitation, but their 'commercial sexual abuse' is hardly the sole or defining feature of the harm inflicted upon them.

It would be wrong to suggest that those who campaign against CSEC all fail or refuse to see the complex intersections between children's and adults' sexual victimization and exploitation, and between children's sexual exploitation and other children's and human rights violations. However, they do none the less insist that children are uniquely vulnerable within and uniquely harmed by the sex trade, and that it is therefore justifiable and necessary to approach commercially sexually exploited children as a separate group, and to treat CSEC as a *particularly* disturbing form of children's rights violation. Thus, rather than inviting us to consider the nature, causes and meanings of diversity in children's experiences of sexual oppression, abuse and exploitation in the contemporary world, anti-CSEC campaigners are at pains to establish that the commercial sexual abuse of a child amounts to forced labour and a contemporary form of slavery whenever, wherever and however it occurs. In this way, they have popularized a discourse that simultaneously encourages us to draw a boundary between adults and children subject to exactly the same unfreedoms within the sex trade, and lumps together as one homogeneous group persons aged from 0 to 17 with disparate experiences of sexual exploitation in entirely different social, economic and political contexts.

This takes us back to the questions posed at the start of the book. Why is it so important that we treat children in the global sex trade as a monolithic group? Why do we need to understand 'commercial sexual abuse' as the worst – most serious, defining and damaging – experience a person under the age of 18 could have? Who and what is actually redeemed and protected by the dominant discourse on CSEC? Does this discourse really help us to look after children, or does it allow us to pretend to look after them when in fact we are doing something else? I want to return to these questions by exploring comparisons between representations of children and slavery in contemporary campaigns against CSEC and representations of slavery and race in eighteenth- and nineteenth-century campaigns for the abolition of slavery.

### Redemption Songs

In an analysis of eighteenth- and nineteenth-century abolitionist discourse, Adam Lively observes that: 'The most insistent leitmotif running through white representations of blackness since the eighteenth century is the idea that black people are in some way closer to nature than whites . . . blackness is truth-telling, that it reveals what human beings are really like when stripped of the conventions of culture and civilization' (1999, p. 55). European representations of blackness as an expression of authenticity and connection with natural feelings, Lively argues, were underpinned and reinforced by 'the sentimental view of the African slave promoted by the abolitionists, who – in a twist characteristic of evangelical Christianity – exalted victimhood to a state of masochistic nobility' (pp. 55–6). The images of slavery and slaves promulgated not just in political pamphlets and speeches but also in wider cultural forms (plays, novels, and so on) spoke much more closely to the existence and concerns of a European audience than they did to the experience of the slave (p. 61), for, having been constructed as an empty figure, the black slave became a screen upon which to project and explore European sensibilities. A key element of this exploration concerned the European's reaction to the violence enacted on the slave's body, for 'sensibility is exemplified by the ability to suffer along with the suffering of others. There is a strong physicality to the notion of sympathy as we find it in the sentimental novelists. The reader observes the slave-victim's nerves quivering beneath the lash, and her own nerves tremble in harmony. She dissolves or 'melts' in tears' (p. 75). Furthermore, 'the descriptions of the horrors of the slave trade in abolitionist literature have at times an almost pornographic attention to detail' (p. 75).

It is hard to avoid comparisons with the contemporary literature campaigning against CSEC as modern slavery (also with feminist campaigns for the abolition of prostitution more generally). Though campaigners may select photographs of children in the sex trade and quotations from porno movie copy to illustrate their arguments with the intention of shocking an indifferent world into caring about the commercial sexual exploitation of children, some of the materials that NGOs have produced would (and probably do) make a welcome contribution to any paedophile's collection of child pornography.[1] The 'documentary novel' *Rosario is Dead*, written by Majgull Axelsson (1996) and presented as a gift to all delegates at the First World Congress Against CSEC, may not be pornographic but the details it provides of the physical suffering endured by Rosario Baluyot (a Filipino girl who died at the age of 11 from septicaemia caused by a broken vibrator that had been pushed into her vagina by a tourist client and left in her body for months) are certainly so graphic as to appear somehow gratuitous. Does anyone really need to be told about the colour and odour of the discharge emanating from her dying body, for example, in order to be convinced of the horror of her case? And what is added to our understanding of CSEC by Axelsson's reconstruction of the girl's thoughts and feelings on her deathbed ('"Water. Give me water!" She took a firm grip of Sister Eva's habit and begged for the last time', p. 110)?

Such details are often relished by campaigners. '*Rosario is Dead* is a unique book,' Helena Karlen of ECPAT Sweden announces in the fore-word; 'The reader cannot escape Rosario's humiliation and suffering, one is compelled to share it. It is a painful, yet vitally important, book which should be compulsory reading for all adults' (1996, pp. 5–6). There is no discussion of questions about consent and dignity in relation to the publication of such details, or, indeed, the use of a photograph of Rosario Baluyot laid out in her coffin on the back of the book. Instead, the author is thanked for having documented 'this horrifying and gripping story' with 'empathy and respect for the exploited child' (Karlen, 1996, p. 6). But would any of *us* want the world to know so precisely the manner of our death, or to have the image of our corpse adorn the cover of a novel, or to be granted posthumous fame only as an emblem of suffering? If the answer is 'no', then where is the empathy and respect?

The impulse to go into such detail comes, I think, largely from the author's own sense of horror at what he or she has witnessed or read about, and his or her hope for some catharsis through recounting that horror in every gory detail. It is an impulse that I find perfectly understandable since I struggle with it myself (how successfully is for others to judge), but it none the less reflects a preoccupation with the humanity and sensibilities of the author and audience, one that often overrides a concern to understand the subjective lived experience of actual children working in prostitution. Thus, the anti-CSEC campaign literature is often prefaced with commentary on the author's own emotional response to the suffering of children:

> Four years ago I began teaching at the Government Rehabilitation Center for teenage girls arrested for prostitution.... My first encounter at the Center was with an eleven-year-old girl which nearly broke my heart. I could hardly bear the thoughts of what that little girl had experienced.

> At this point I began to feel for this work. The closer I came to know the girls, the stronger the feeling. It was so strong at times that I could hardly bear to go teach my class because I would see their faces and start imagining their pain. (Golman, 1996, pp. 9–10)

And discovering one's own capacity to suffer with the suffering of children is redemptive of one's own humanity:

> I had thought that during my twenty years working in Asia I had become immune to the suffering of people but here I was faced with the factual account of young children being systematically enslaved and used as sexual objects by adults. (O'Grady, 1996, p. 6)

This newly recovered humanity can then be expressed through working with, or campaigning for, the suffering slave children. The same possibilities exist at societal level:

> how many Rosarios will it take for us to realise that for each boy or girl who gets sucked into the sex trade, who perishes at the hands of perverts, we allow an important piece of ourselves to be destroyed as well? A society that is unable to guarantee the safety and well-being of its most vulnerable members – the young – is a society that is on the verge of disintegration. Rosario died as she had lived. Ignored. Uncared for. Traded like any other commodity in the market. The victim of a society that has become as spiritually impoverished as it is materially poor. (Editorial, *Philippines Daily Enquirer*, 22 December 1987, cited in Kane, 1998, pp. 91–2)

Thus, Rosario Baluyot, like Tom in Harriet Beecher Stowe's *Uncle Tom's Cabin*, becomes 'a Christ figure' (Lively, 1999, p. 87). Her humiliation, suffering and death are held up as promising us redemption, if only we will realize and repent our own spiritual impoverishment and commit ourselves to the mission.

The strong similarities between representations of blackness in eighteenth- and nineteenth-century abolitionist discourse and representations of children in contemporary campaigns against CSEC as modern slavery should not surprise us, since black people (and other non-Europeans) have, as was noted in chapter 2, often been regarded as 'childlike', as moral and political 'infants'. But the parallels are striking, none the less. In eighteenth- and nineteenth-century Western societies, the 'child', like the 'savage', increasingly appeared as 'everything the sophisticated adult was not, everything the rational man of the Enlightenment was not' (Kincaid, 1998, p. 15), 'innocent' and 'pure' in the sense of being uncorrupted by knowledge and worldly experience. This vision of the child persists: 'a dominant modern discourse of childhood continues to mark out "the child" as innately innocent, confirming its cultural identity as a passive and unknowing dependent, and therefore as a member of a social group utterly disempowered – but for good, altruistic reasons' (Jenks, 1996, p. 124). It is precisely because 'children' are imagined as vacant and untouched by knowledge or civilization that they too can serve as an empty screen upon which to project and explore our own sensibilities.[2]

At this point, it might objected that those campaigning for political change have to win hearts and minds, and so necessarily rely on rhetoric and the use of sensational individual cases to highlight a given problem. If we sympathize with the ultimate goal of their campaigns (the abolition of slavery, the elimination of CSEC), we should not be too critical of the methods they employ to garner popular support. However, I do not think that the means and the ends can be so neatly separated in any political struggle. The emancipatory potential of the campaign against CSEC is severely limited by its reliance upon and reproduction of Adult and Child as oppositional social categories (as well as other key binaries of Western liberal thought), just as the abolitionist movement's potential to contribute to a struggle for full equality was restricted by its dependence upon notions of racial difference, and, increasingly through the nineteenth century, its acceptance of the concept of a biologically based racial hierarchy (Midgley, 1998, p. 165). But perhaps the most significant aspect of Lively's commentary on abolitionism and the sentimental imagination for late-modern discourse on CSEC as a contemporary form of slavery is found in the following passage:

> the European imaginative literature on slavery and the Negro is strikingly homogeneous. There are some differences of emphasis and inflection, but en masse it presents a common idealization of the African. He (and for the most part the slave figure is male) is defined above all by his enslaved condition, his suffering. To the extent that he is thought to have any existence at all anterior to his being a slave, it is as the expression of a philosophically imagined Nature. He has, of course, no independent culture or history. Before slavery there is only the state of nature, a *tabula rasa*. And in slavery, too, there is no culture, no economics, no shades of collaboration, no daily, covert acts of resistance. There is only the individual master confronting the individual slave. And hovering above them, moral absolutes. (1999, p. 83)

In materials produced by those campaigning against CSEC, child prostitutes are also homogenized and defined by their enslavement and suffering. Even in the wider research literature on child prostitution, it is extremely rare for attention to be paid to children's independent culture or the strategies they use to cope with or resist oppression – Heather Montgomery's (1998, 2001) research with children involved in tourist-related prostitution in Thailand is a notable and extremely valuable exception. And because the representation of CSEC as a 'contemporary form of slavery' deflects attention from the variability of children's involvement in the sex trade in terms of its social organization and the social relations that surround it, it detaches it from its social and political context, leaving only an image of the individual brothel owner, client, pimp or pornographer (cruel sinner) confronting the individual child (pitiful innocent).

I hope this book has shown that these absolute categories and dualisms do not begin to grasp the complexities of children's presence in the global sex trade (not even the complexities of the experience of those who actually are subject to slavery-like practices within prostitution). But they *do* make it possible to draw a bright line between commercial sex involving adults and commercial sex involving children, and so to cling to 'the child' as a monolithic, undifferentiated social category. The discourse that constructs CSEC as 'modern slavery' and the 'rape of innocence' implicitly assumes and universalizes a totalizing model of 'childhood' within which *all* children (whether babies or teenagers, rich or poor, black or white, male or female, straight or gay, orphaned or with parents, living in an affluent suburb in a politically stable country or a refugee camp in a war-torn region) are, or are entitled to be, innocent, dependent, incompetent and vulnerable. In this sense, it redeems a cultural category that comforts *us* (as opposed to any child who trades sex) and protects *us* from having to question other key binaries of liberal thought (consent/force, freedom/slavery, subject/object). Back to Adam Phillips, quoted at the start of this chapter:

> If the best thing we do is look after each other, then the worst thing we do is pretend to look after each other when in fact we are doing something else. One of the many disturbing things about psychoanalysis . . . is that it shows us why it is often so difficult to tell these things apart. Or rather, it shows us that this distinction, upon which most of our morality depends, is often spurious because we are always likely to be doing both things at once (and several more). . . . It is to what is being taken when we take care of another person that Freud drew our attention. . . . What psychoanalysis suggests is that the whole notion of helping people is one of our favourite cover-stories for the moral complexity of exchange. (2002, p. xi)

Certainly, anti-CSEC campaigners want to help children. But in dominant discourse on CSEC (and indeed on childhood more generally) the relationship between taking care of children and taking care of ourselves is reduced to simplistic formulations to the effect that 'children are our future'. Yet in truth, there is a great deal more to the relationship than that. What is given and taken (and by whom) in the exchange between adults and children is nothing if not morally complex. As argued in chapter 1, 'children', when understood as a unitary category of persons defined by their innocence, vulnerability and lack of agency, provide a bulwark against the disruptive forces of modernity. So long as 'children' are defined by their difference from 'adults', constructed as beyond contract, as objects not subjects, then they can connect us to each other and anchor us in fixed and certain moral terrain, protecting us from the miserable spectre of a world in which 'the private' sphere is governed by the same principles of contract as 'the public' realm. 'Children' are our present as much as our future, and we are thus heavily invested in structures and ideas that serve to keep them innocent, vulnerable and dependent. For as Jenks observes:

> To abandon a shared category of the child is to confront a daunting paradox. If as adults we do just that, what happens to the concept of 'childhood' through which we, as adults, see ourselves and our society's past and future? If... the concept of 'childhood' serves to articulate not just the experience and status of the young within modern society but also the projections, aspirations, longings and altruism contained within the adult experience, then to abandon such a conception is to erase our final point of stability and attachment to the social bond. (1996, p. 136)

Few people wish to confront this daunting paradox, hence opportunities to tie children into 'a narrative of rescue and salvation' are seized upon with great enthusiasm (Brace, 2003, p. 6). CSEC provides such an opportunity.

Is there another way to tell the story, one that recognizes both the very real differences between human beings in terms of their capacity for self-protection and autonomy, and the extent and severity of the abuse and exploitation to which people (adult as well as child) can be subject within the global sex trade, but that does not insist on a cast-list consisting only of victims, sinners and saviours, or reinforce children's politically constructed subordination to adults? I believe that there is, but only if we are willing to refuse the comforting certainty offered by the binaries of Western liberal thought (including the Adult/Child dichotomy), and find other ways of imagining our connections with each other.

### Re-imagining the Subject and the Social Bond

Norman Geras observes that liberal legal and moral culture 'is largely structured around the notion that one should refrain from harming others, but that helping or not helping them is a matter of individual inclination' (1998, p. 58). In modern liberal democracies, people who help others are often admired and praised, but those who make no attempt to mitigate or end 'the calamities and sufferings of others', who are bystanders to injustice, injury and distress, are not considered to be morally wanting. Thus, 'A liberal culture underwrites moral indifference' (Geras, 1998, p. 59), and this should not surprise us, he continues, for

> the principal economic formation historically associated with liberalism, defended by liberals – whether confidently or apologetically – today as much as ever, is one in which it has been the norm for the wealth and comfort of some to be obtained through the hardship and poverty of others, and to stand right alongside these. It is a whole mode of collective existence. Not only an economy. A world, a culture, a set of everyday practices. (p. 59)

Through the lens of liberalism, society appears to be comprised of a multitude of individual rights-holders who manage their social, political and economic relations through contract. The principal of contract restrains people from interfering with or harming others – no individual can *force* another to part with her or his property or labour, or *demand* her or his loyalty, obedience, affection or assistance; he or she can only invite others to voluntarily enter into contractual arrangements. Contract is also presented as the mechanism by which individuals can make connections with each other – by entering into either implicit or explicit contracts, they can 'belong' to a nation, a political party, a firm, a club, a trade union, a friendship network, and so on, without fear of being invaded or engulfed by other members of such collectives. Contract seemingly makes it possible to reconcile a radically individualistic model of humanity with the notion of a social bond. But the kind of social bond it implies is very particular and very limited, which is why it can underwrite moral indifference. It is also why even those who defend it most vigorously secretly know that it provides a frail and precarious basis for human sociality and have therefore always sought to sustain a parallel 'private' realm in which human connections are fixed, permanent and sacred.

The classical liberal conception of the individual as an autonomous rational rights-holder, and of a just society as one in which such individuals are granted the freedom to make whatever contracts they wish to with each other, cannot be lightly dismissed since it is a model that has undoubtedly helped (certain) people to resist (certain) forms of political oppression. But because it rests on the subject/object binary, assuming that subjects are constituted in splendid isolation from their material circumstances and defined by their capacity to claim and exercise rights and to act autonomously, it is also a model that allows other forms of oppression (political, social and economic) to persist unchecked. It divides the world into 'agents' and 'victims', but sets the threshold for unfreedom so high that any element of choice – even the choice between grief and nothing – is deemed to represent freedom. To rescue ourselves from the miserable and soulless world this implies, we construct categories of persons as victims and objects, defined by their supposed lack rational autonomy and/or capacity to make choices – the slave, the trafficked woman, the disabled person, the child – and congratulate ourselves on our willingness to look after them.

And yet the idea that human beings can be neatly divided into fixed, impermeable groupings defined by their difference from one another – Adult and Child, free worker and slave, voluntary migrant and trafficked person, agent and victim, subject and object – is just that, an *idea*. In reality, the lines between tyranny and consent, domination and freedom, objectification and moral agency, childhood and adulthood, are not and never have been clear-cut, nor do they map neatly onto one another. Those who are tyrannized and treated as objects are still subjects, still feel their dishonour as keenly as those who are treated as fully autonomous human beings. Indeed, one of the reasons why poverty, racism, sexism, ageism and homophobia carry such profoundly destructive signatures is because they each, in their own way, compel people to 'assume the status of the Other' (Beauvoir, 1972 [1949], p. 29), defined by what they are *not*, do *not* have, can *not* do or be, in short, by their powerlessness relative to other people. In this sense, they force people to experience themselves as objects rather than subjects. But when people experience themselves as objects, it is painful, humiliating and destructive precisely because they are aware of their own consciousness or subjectivity.

Campaigns to highlight the plight of victims of tyranny and discrimination, and organizations and individuals who attempt to assist those who are harmed, abused and victimized, always tread a difficult line between exposing and ameliorating injustice and reinforcing the objectification of the Other. To be recognized and cared about as a victim often means being viewed as an object, and so unable to claim social honour and esteem. But simply inverting the discourse by insisting that those who are objectified and victimized should be treated as fully autonomous subjects is to side-step the problem posed by the significant differences between human beings in terms of their capacity to independently pursue their own interests as subjects. For example, to expect a baby, a small child, a person with Alzheimer's disease or a very serious learning disability, to manage their needs by entering into a series of implicit and explicit contracts would clearly be to leave them in a wretched, even life-threatening, condition. But drug addiction, alcoholism, mental health problems, as well as poverty and other forms of structural oppression, also operate to severely constrain people's capacity to assume full moral agency. How are we to care for and about them without treating them as victims and objects?

I think we have to question the classical liberal conception of rights-holders as autonomous rational individuals with the capacity to exercise their right. This view of the rights-holder overlooks the fact that, as human beings, we are all simultaneously objects and subjects, which is to say, it rests upon a false opposition between reason and emotion, mind and body, rationality and physicality, and so disregards what all human beings have in common. 'Sovereign selves' are also actually imprisoned in a human body that is needy and potentially frail. All of us either are, or were once and will one day again become, fragile and physically vulnerable. Even for the lucky able-bodied ones, there is but a short span of time in which the subject-self can hope to dominate the object-self. And even in this short span of time, there are limits to how completely we can control our physicality, contain the passions of our object-selves, or restrict our dependence on other human beings. Everybody needs somebody, as the saying goes. It follows that there are limits to how far any of us are able to manage without care or to function merely as autonomous, rational individuals, and so there are limits to the benefits we derive from being constructed as rights-holders in the classical liberal sense.

If nothing else, the unpleasant spectre of infantilization in sickness and old age should alert us to the dangers of constructing those who need care as objects and victims, rather than as simultaneously subjects *and* objects, and make us question the worth of a social and political order in which human beings imagine themselves as bound together only by contract. Joan Tronto has observed that as a moral phenomenon, caring is incompatible with market relations of exchange, 'the paradigmatic relationship of modern society', a paradigm that 'involves putting one's own interests first... [asserting] one knows one's own interests best... [and reducing] complex relationships into terms that can be made equivalent' (1989, pp. 178–9). And caring also 'raises questions that cannot easily be accommodated by the starting assumption in most contemporary moral philosophy that we are rational, autonomous actors' (p. 179). Thinking seriously about caring allows us to recognize 'autonomy as a problem that people must deal with all the time, in their relations with both equals and those who either help them or depend on them' (p. 180).

At present, stories that are attentive to the nature, causes and meanings of diversity in children's experiences of sexual oppression, abuse and exploitation, and that recognize the commonalities between some adults' and some children's experience in the global sex trade, have little popular currency. It is more difficult and more painful to listen to and care about children in the global sex trade as simultaneously subjects and objects than it is to approach them merely as victims and objects, not least because to do so is to diminish the difference and so the distance between 'us' as adults and 'them' as children. As this distance shrinks, so we are forced not just to acknowledge the bleakness of the options open to many of the world's children, but also to confront the limits of our own autonomy, to see ourselves as objects as well as subjects, to admit our own – often unmet – need for care, and to critically reflect on our refusal to care about the oppression and suffering of other adults. For this reason, I believe that telling more complicated stories about children's presence in the sex trade not only is vital to the formulation of effective, context-appropriate policies and interventions with regard to specific groups of children, but can and must also contribute to a broader political project.

We should not accept a world in which the dominant legal and moral culture is one of moral indifference, but attempt to protect children from it by insisting that they alone are beyond contract. And we cannot move towards a world in which 'caring for others is... a more central part of the everyday lives of everyone in society' (Tronto, 1989, p. 184) without a more complex vision of autonomy, moral agency and human sociality than that provided by liberalism.

# Notes

1 I wrote a series of research reports for End Child Prostitution in Asian Tourism (ECPAT) in 1996, was commissioned to write theme papers on 'The Sex Exploiter' for both the First and Second World Congress against the Commercial Sexual Exploitation of Children (O'Connell Davidson, 1996, 2001a), and have spoken at a number of conferences on CSEC organized by governmental and non-governmental organizations.

### Chapter 1 Beyond Contract? Dualist Legacies, Late-Modern Anxieties and the Sanctity of the Child

1 In 2001, an estimated 685,000 children aged below 15 were killed by unintentional injuries worldwide, and 21 per cent of these deaths were a result of road traffic injuries (WHO, 2003).
2 The 'woman question' was a focus of debate within liberalism in the nineteenth and early twentieth centuries (as well as between liberals and Marxists; see Bebel, 1997 [1883], for example), and, in fact, men's authority over women was perceived as posing something of a quandary even by the early social contract theorists (Pateman, 1988; MacInnes, 1998).
3 Hence, stories about successful women giving up a high-flying career in merchant banking or stockbroking in order to look after their children at home have provoked much debate, as have calls from a number of women Labour MPs – 'Blair's babes' – for the 'modernization' of parliamentary procedures.
4 I am thinking here of things like membership of 'Mother & Toddler' groups and Parent–Teacher Associations, and milling about with other parents at football practice, dance classes, school parents' evenings, which directly generate social interaction; also of the collective experience parents acquire through their conformity to prevailing norms of child-rearing, including norms governing consumer spending on children. Knowing who Harry Potter is, whether or not Pokemon cards are still popular, how much a trip to Disneyland costs, etc., contribute to a sense of community belonging and connection.
5 Gayle Rubin (1997) uses this term in her discussion of marriage as a gift exchange in which women are conduits to relationships between men, rather than partners to such relationships.

6  See Orlando Patterson's (1982) discussion of the idiomatic handling of power, in which he distinguishes between 'personalistic' and 'materialistic' idioms.

## Chapter 2   Prostitutes, Children and Slaves

1  For example, in London, prostitution is believed to generate around £200 million annually (Matthews, 1997); the turnover of Nevada's thirty-five licensed brothels is claimed to be $40 million a year (Hausbeck and Brents 2000); and in Thailand, the Philippines, Malaysia and Indonesia, the sex sector is estimated to account for between 2 and 14 per cent of gross domestic product (Lim, 1998).

## Chapter 3   On Child Prostitutes as Objects, Victims and Subjects

1  This can apply to sexual-economic exchanges with men as well as with women, because in some cultural contexts, it is primarily the anal receptive role that is stigmatized as 'homosexual', with the male who takes the insertive role in anal or oral sex remaining 'masculine'. In such settings, boys can demonstrate themselves to be manly and 'not gay' by having sex with receptive 'homosexual' men in exchange for money (see, for instance, Moya and Garcia, 1999).
2  In research on street prostitution in Britain, Joanna Phoenix found that seventeen out of twenty-one interviewees mentioned 'Sugar Daddies', regular clients who, 'in addition to buying sex, give prostitutes extra money' (1999, p. 138). Their accounts of relationships with such men further complicate the boundary between commercial and non-commercial sex.
3  In ECPAT's Model National Plan for governments committed to implementing the Agenda for Action against CSEC, for example, only one out of fourteen objectives listed refers to child participation (ECPAT, 1999).

## Chapter 4   Child Migration and 'Trafficking'

1  Some women who have been 'rescued' in Bosnia-Herzegovina and repatriated as 'victims of trafficking' have had their travel papers stamped with a 'deny entry' stamp by the State Border Service, on grounds that this will prevent them from being 'trafficked' again (Kvinnoforum and Kvinna till Kvinna, 2003, p. 102).
2  In Britain, the case of Victoria Climbié recently drew attention to the fact that African children who have been sent to live with kin in the UK can find themselves 'at risk to extreme forms of exploitation' (Ariyo, 2003). Victoria was sent from the Ivory Coast to live with her aunt in the hope of a better life in Europe, but died in February 2000 following horrific abuse at the hands of her aunt and her aunt's boyfriend and neglect by the professionals who should have offered her protection. However, there are also documented cases in which British children have been subject to the same kind of horrific treatment by British parents and foster carers, but newspaper reports rarely move from individual cases of neglect or abuse to statistics on how many British children live with their natural parents or in foster care and so, by implication, are open to the same kind of abuse. In other words, British childcare arrangements and fostering practices are not pathologized in the same way.

### Chapter 5  'Paedophilia', Pornography and Prostitution

1 A Canadian university professor whose views on 'boy-loving' caused a furore in the 1990s.
2 For example, Britain's Gay Youth Movement's Charter of the late 1970s stated that the liberation of lesbians and gay men requires the liberation of women and 'all other oppressed groups, including sexual minorities such as transsexuals, transvestites, and paedophiles' (cited in Jeffreys, 1990, p. 188).
3 In 2002, the US Supreme Court overthrew a congressional ban on virtual paedophilia, for example (*Ananova*, 2002).
4 For instance, a trial in Draguignan, France, in 1997 involved seven men who had grouped together to pursue a common interest in sex with children. The 'president' of the organization, a 73-year-old man, had twelve previous convictions for sexual offences against children. In 1994, three of the men travelled together to Romania, where they paid for sex with children. They then brought two Romanian children to France in 1995, and prostituted them to the others (ACPE, 2001). If younger children were readily available in the prostitution market in France, why bother to travel to Romania or to bring Romanian children back to France?
5 The chairman of the passport and visa service of the Chelyabinsk region of the former USSR recently stated: 'I am rather concerned about orphans, About 800 children from the Chelyabinsk region were adopted by foreign citizens during the period 1999–2003. We can trace those children's lives for three years. No one knows what happens to them next' (*Pravda*, 2003).

### Chapter 6  Children in Mainstream Prostitution: the Problem of Demand

1 Taken from transcripts of interviews conducted by Abha Dayal as part of multi-country pilot research on demand for the labour/services of domestic and sex workers (Anderson and O'Connell Davidson, 2003).
2 There is also clearly demand for youthful-looking male prostitutes (see, for example, Connell and Hart, 2003), and whilst there has been less research on such demand, I see no reason to suppose that men who buy sex from 16- and 17-year-old males differ much from those who buy sex from teenage girls in terms of their attitudes and motivations.
3 In Britain, people aged 16 and 17 are only eligible for means-tested benefits in certain limited circumstances: for instance, if they are unable to work as a result of ill health or disability, pregnancy or the care of dependants. They may also be entitled to income-based job-seeker's allowance, but in practice often find it difficult to demonstrate eligibility. In general, it is expected that 16- and 17-year-olds will be supported by parents, or be in education, full-time employment or Work-Based Training for Young People (WBTYP). The minimum allowance for those on training schemes is just £40 a week. In October 2004, the government introduced a minimum wage for 16- and 17-year olds of £3 an hour, less than the minimum wage for persons aged 18–21, and guaranteeing young people only £105 for a 35-hour week, a sum that children's charities consider to be insufficient to lift above poverty levels those young people who live independently and have to work full-time (see Liberty, 2002; Barnardos, 2004).

### Chapter 7    Child Sex Tourism

1  For example, a Danish television documentary investigated the Danish Pedophile Association (DPA) and found evidence that members of the DPA were involved in organizing tours to India that included sex with child prostitutes (personal correspondence with Vernon Jones of Save the Children Denmark).

### Chapter 8    Beyond Binaries?

1  See, for example, the photographs of child prostitutes and their clients in Radda Barnen's special issue of *Barnen Och Vi* (1996), or the pamphlet produced by Folkaktionen mot Pornagrafi (1996), for distribution at the First World Congress Against the Commercial Sexual Exploitation of Children.
2  Lively comments that, seen positively, black people 'are more authentic and less emotionally inhibited than Europeans. Seen negatively, they are closer to some inherent evil, some heart of darkness, in human nature' (1999, p. 55). Likewise, the model of the child as empty, vacant and untouched by civilization has both positive and negative sides. Just as we can project onto the blank screen of the child the angelic innocence that we may like to imagine as human beings' natural state, so we can project onto the child the demonic monsters we fear we would become were we not constrained by adult rationality and civilization. (Consider, for example, representations of the child in films like *The Exorcist*, or Golding's novel *The Lord of the Flies*. See Kincaid, 1998, pp. 156–60.)

# References

Abiala, K., 2003: 'Sexual trafficking in Moldova, Estonia and Sweden: Context, actors and attitudes', paper presented to 'Gender and Power in the New Europe', 5th European Feminist Research Conference, 20–4 August.

ACPE, 2001: *Draguignan: Trial Against Sexual Tourism. Information sheet*. Association Contre la Prostitution Enfantine, 14 rue Mondetour, 75001 Paris, France.

Aggleton, P. (ed.), 1999: *Men Who Sell Sex*. London: UCL.

Aguilar, M., 1994: Alarma corrupcion de menores en Puntareas. *Sucesos*. San José, Costa Rica. 9 January.

Agustín, L., 2001: 'Mujeres inmigrantes ocupadas en servicios sexuales', in Colectivo Ioé (ed.) *Mujer, Inmigración y Trabajo*. Madrid: IMSERSO.

Agustín, L., 2004: 'Migrants in the mistress's house: Other voices in the "trafficking" debate', *Social Politics*, forthcoming.

Aldridge, A., 2003: *Consumption*. Cambridge: Polity.

Alexander, M., 1997: 'Erotic autonomy as politics of decolonization: An anatomy of the feminist and state practice on the Bahamas tourist economy', in M. Alexander and C. Mohanty (eds) *Feminist Genealogies, Colonial Legacies, Democratic Futures*. London: Routledge.

Alexander, P., 1997: 'Feminism, sex workers and human rights', in J. Nagle (ed.) *Whores and Other Feminists*. London: Routledge.

Allison, A., 1994: *Nightwork: Sexuality, pleasure and corporate masculinity in a Tokyo hostess club*. Chicago: University of Chicago Press.

AMC, 2000: *Asian Migrant Yearbook 2000: Migration facts, analysis and issues in 1999*. Hong Kong: Asian Migrant Centre.

*Ananova*, 2002: 'US court legalizes virtual paedophilia', *Ananova*, www.ananova.com/news/story/sm_568280.html

Anderson, B., 2000: *Doing the Dirty Work? The global politics of domestic labour*. London: Zed.

Anderson, B. and O'Connell Davidson, J., 2002: *Trafficking – A demand led problem?* Stockholm: Save the Children Sweden.

Anderson, B. and O'Connell Davidson, J., 2003: *Is Trafficking in Human Beings Demand Driven? A multi-country pilot study*. IOM Migration Research Series, No. 15. Geneva: International Organization for Migration.

Anderson, P. and Witter, M., 1994: 'Crisis, adjustment and social change: A case study of Jamaica', in E. Le Franc (ed.) *Consequences of Structural Adjustment: A review of the Jamaican experience*. Kingston: Canoe Press.

Andrijasevic, R., 2003: 'The difference borders make: (Il)legality, migration and "trafficking" in Italy among "eastern" European women in prostitution', in S. Ahmed, C. Castaneda, A. Fortier and M. Sheller (eds) *Uprootings/ Regroundings: Questions of home and migration*. Oxford: Berg.

Antonius-Smits, C., Altenberg, J., Burleson, T., Taitt-Codrington, T., Russel, M. van, Van der Leende, D., Hordijk, D. and Prado, R., 1999: 'Gold and commercial sex: Exploring the link between small-scale gold mining and commercial sex in the rainforest of Suriname', in K. Kempadoo (ed.) *Sun, Sex, and Gold: Tourism and sex work in the Caribbean*. Oxford: Rowman and Littlefield.

Apostolopoulos, Y., Sonmez, S., Smith, D. and Kronenfeld, J., 2003: 'Cruising America's highways – risk networks, truckers and transmission', *American Sexuality Magazine*, Vol. 1, No. 2, *www.nsrc.sfsu.edu*

Archard, D., 1993: *Children: Rights and childhood*. London: Routledge.

Archard, D., 2003: 'Children's rights and human rights', paper presented to 'Child Abuse and Exploitation: Social, Legal and Political Dilemmas Workshop', International Institute for the Sociology of Law, Onati, 29–30 May.

Archer, L. (ed.), 1988: *Slavery and Other Forms of Unfree Labour*. London: Routledge.

Ariès, P., 1962: *Centuries of Childhood*. London: Cape.

Ariyo, D., 2003: *New Dimensions in the Trafficking of Children to the UK*. AFRUCA, Unit 4S Leroy House, 436 Essex Rd, London N1 3QP, UK.

Assiter, A. and Carol, A. (eds), 1993: *Bad Girls and Dirty Pictures*. London: Pluto.

Axelsson, M., 1996: *Rosario is Dead*. Stockholm: Raben Prisma.

Bagley, C., 1999: 'Child and adolescent prostitution in Canada and the Philippines: Comparative case studies and policy proposals', in C. Bagley and M. Kanka (eds) *Child Sexual Abuse and Adult Offenders: New theory and research*. Aldershot: Ashgate.

Barnardos, 2004: 'Minimum wage not enough for all young people', *www.barnardos.org.uk*

Barrios, M., Perez Roca, A., Bravo, G., Muniz, M. and Avedano, 1892: 'Informe emitado por la seccion IV de la academia en el projecto de ordenanza sobre la prostitucion', *La Cronica Medica*, Vol. 9, p. 103.

Barry, K., 1995: *The Prostitution of Sexuality*. New York: New York University Press.

Bartley, P., 2000: *Prostitution: Prevention and reform in England, 1860–1914*. London: Routledge.

Baudrillard, J., 1990: *Fatal Strategies*. London: Pluto.

Bauer, A., 2001: *Goods, Power, History: Latin America's material culture*. Cambridge: Cambridge University Press.

BBC Monitoring Service, 2003a: 'Child trafficking charges against Moldovan diplomat said to be exaggerated', 13 November.

BBC Monitoring Service, 2003b: 'Child-smugglers sentenced in Ukraine', 13 November.

BBC News online, 2003: 'Tony Martin: Crime and controversy', Friday, 13 June.

Beare, M., 1999: 'Illegal migration: Personal tragedies, social problems, or national security threats?', in P. Williams (ed.) *Illegal Immigration and Commercial Sex: The new slave trade*. London: Frank Cass.

Beauvoir, S. de, 1972 [1949]: *The Second Sex*. Harmondsworth: Penguin.

Bebel, A., 1997 [1883]: 'Woman and socialism', in M. Ishay (ed.) *The Human Rights Reader*, London: Routledge.

Beck, U., 1992: *Risk Society: Towards a new modernity*. London: Sage.

Beddoe, C., 1998: 'Beachboys and tourists: Links in the chain of child prostitution in Sri Lanka', in M. Opperman (ed.) *Sex Tourism and Prostitution: Aspects of leisure, recreation and work*. New York: Cognizant Communications.

Bell, S., 1994: *Reading, Writing and Rewriting the Prostitute Body*. Bloomington: Indiana University Press.

Bernard, F., 1987: 'On paedophilia', *Paidika: The Journal of Paedophilia*, Vol. 1, No. 1, pp. 46–8.

Bernstein, E., 2001: 'The meaning of the purchase: Desire, demand and the commerce of sex', *Ethnography*, Vol. 2, No. 3., pp. 389–420.

Bickford, A., 2003: 'See the world, meeting interesting people, have sex with them: Tourism, sex and recruitment in the U.S. Military', *American Sexuality Magazine*, Vol. 1, No. 5, *www.nsrc.sfsu.edu*

Bindman, J., 1997: *Redefining Prostitution as Sex Work on the International Agenda*. London: Anti-Slavery International.

Bishop, R. and Robinson, I., 1998: *Night Market: Sexual cultures and the Thai economic miracle*. London: Routledge.

Black, M., 1995: *In the Twilight Zone: Child workers in the hotel, tourism and catering industry*. Geneva: International Labour Organization.

Blackburn, R., 1988: 'Slavery – its special features and social role', in L. Archer (ed.) *Slavery and Other Forms of Unfree Labour*. London: Routledge.

Blanchet, T., 1996: *Lost Innocence, Stolen Childhood*. Dhaka: University Press Limited/Radda Barnen.

Bott, E., 2004: 'Working on a working-class utopia: Marking young Britons in Tenerife on the new map of European migration', *Journal for Contemporary European Studies*, Vol. 12, No. 1, pp. 57–70.

Boushaba, A., Tawil, O., Imane, L. and Himmich, H., 1999: 'Marginalization and vulnerability: Male sex work in Morocco', in P. Aggleton (ed.) *Men Who Sell Sex*. London: UCL.

Boyden, J., 1990: 'Childhood and the policy makers: A comparative perspective on the globalisation of childhood', in A. James and A. Prout (eds) *Constructing and Reconstructing Childhood: Contemporary issues in the sociological study of childhood*. Basingstoke: Falmer.

Brace, L., 2003: 'Forcible contrasts? Self-owners, victims and hustlers', paper presented to 'Child Abuse and Exploitation: Social, Legal and Political Dilemmas Workshop', International Institute for the Sociology of Law, Onati, 29–30 May.

Brace, L., 2004: *The Politics of Property: Freedom and belonging*. Edinburgh: Edinburgh University Press.

Brace, L. and O'Connell Davidson, J., 1996: 'Desperate debtors and counterfeit love: The Hobbesian world of the sex tourist', *Contemporary Politics*, Vol. 2, No. 3, pp. 55–77.

Brown, L., 2000: *Sex Slaves: The trafficking of women in Asia*. London: Virago.

Cabezas, A., 1999: 'Women's work is never done: Sex tourism in Sosuá, the Dominican Republic', in K. Kempadoo (ed.) *Sun, Sex, and Gold: Tourism and sex work in the Caribbean*. Oxford: Rowman and Littlefield.

Calder, G., Galster, S. and Steinzor, N., 1997: *Crime and Servitude: An exposé of the traffic in women for prostitution in the Newly Independent States*. New York: Global Survival Network.

Califia, P., 1994: *Public Sex: The culture of radical sex*. San Francisco: Cleis.

Campbell, C., 2001: '"Going underground and going after women": Masculinity and HIV transmission amongst black workers on the gold mines', in R. Morrell (ed.) *Changing Men in Southern Africa*. London: Zed.

Cassirer, B., 1992: *Travel and the Single Male*. Channel Island, CA: TSM.

Castells, M., 1998: *End of Millennium*. Oxford: Blackwell.

Castles, S., 2003: 'Towards a sociology of forced migration', *Sociology*, Vol. 37, No. 1, pp. 13–34.

Caverno, A., 1992: 'Equality and sexual difference: Amnesia in political thought' in G. Bock and S. James (eds) *Beyond Equality and Difference: Citizenship, feminist politics, female subjectivity*. London: Routledge.

Chan, D., 1999: Speech to the First National Conference on Gender and Development in Cambodia, Phnom Penh, 7–9 September, *www.bigpond.com.kh/users/ngoforum/child_prostitution.htm*

Chant, S. and McIlwaine, C., 1995: *Women of a Lesser Cost*. London: Pluto.

Chapkis, W., 1997: *Live Sex Acts*. London: Cassell.

Cheng, S., 2003: '"R and R" on a "hardship tour": GIs and Filipina entertainers in South Korea', *American Sexuality Magazine*, Vol. 1, No. 5, *www.nsrc.sfsu.edu*

Chikwenya, C., Michelo, W., Lubilo, M. and Fuglesang, M., 1997: *What's Up Kafue? An assessment of the livelihood, sexual health and needs of young people in Kafue District*. Lusaka: SIDA.

Chow, R., 1999: 'The politics of admittance: Female sexual agency, miscegenation, and the formation of community in Frantz Fanon', in A. Alessandrini (ed.) *Frantz Fanon: Critical perspectives*. London: Routledge.

Clift, S. and Carter, S. (eds) 2000: *Tourism and Sex: Culture, commerce and coercion*. London: Pinter.

Cochrane, J., 1999: 'Wealthy clients demand virgins for "safe sex"', *South China Morning Post*, 6 November.

Cohen, E., 1982: 'Thai girls and farang men: The edge of ambiguity', *Annals of Tourism Research*, Vol. 9, pp. 403–28.

Connell, J., and Hart, G., 2003: *An Overview of Male Sex Work in Edinburgh and Glasgow: The male sex worker perspective*. Medical Research Council, Social and Public Health Sciences Unit. Occasional Paper No. 8, June.

Creed, G., 1994: 'Sexual subordination: Institutionalized homosexuality and social control in Melanesia', in J. Goldberg (ed.) *Reclaiming Sodom*. London: Routledge.

CSC, 2001: *Global Report on Child Soldiers*. London: Coalition to Stop the Use of Child Soldiers, available at *library.amnesty.it/cs/childsoldiers.nsf/fffdbd058ae6002426d7? Open Document*

Cusick, L., Martin, A. and May, T., 2003: *Vulnerability and Involvement in Drug Use and Sex Work*. Home Office Research Study 268. London: Home Office.

Davies, P. and Feldman, R., 1999: 'Selling sex in Cardiff and London', in P. Aggleton (ed.) *Men Who Sell Sex*. London: UCL.

Davis, N. (ed.), 1993: *Prostitution: An international handbook on trends, problems and policies*. Westport, CT: Greenwood Press.

Derks, A., 2000: *Combating Trafficking in South-East Asia: A review of policy and programme responses*. Geneva: IOM.

Dickenson, D., 1997: *Property, Women and Politics*. Cambridge: Polity.

Dodd, V., 2002: 'Law increases danger, prostitutes say', *Guardian*, 16 September.

Doezema, J., 1999: 'Loose women or lost women? The re-emergence of the myth of "white slavery" in contemporary discourses of trafficking in women', *Gender Issues*, Vol. 18, No. 1, pp. 23–50.

Doezema, J., 2001: ' "Ouch! Western feminists" "wounded attachment" to the "third world prostitute" ', *Feminist Review*, No. 67, Spring, pp. 16–38.

Doezema, J., 2002: 'Who gets to choose? Coercion, consent, and the UN Trafficking Protocol', in R. Masika (ed.) *Gender, Trafficking and Slavery*. Oxford: Oxfam.

Douglas, M., 2002: *Purity and Danger*. London: Routledge.

Dowden, R., 2002: 'Woman who was raped faces death by stoning', *The Independent*, 5 January.

DPA, 1999: Open Letter to UNESCO. Danish Pedophile Association. News. *www.danpedo.dk/english/news.shtml*

Dworkin, A., 1987: *Intercourse*. London: Secker & Warburg.

Dyer, C., 2002: 'Parents "get away with murder" ', *Guardian*, 1 November.

ECPAT, 1996: *ECPAT Newsletter*, No. 16. Bangkok: End Child Prostitution in Asian Tourism.

ECPAT, 1998: 'The street of little flowers', *ECPAT Newsletter*, No. 22. Bangkok: End Child Prostitution in Asian Tourism.

ECPAT, 1999: *A Step Forward*. Bangkok: End Child Prostitution in Asian Tourism.

ECPAT UK, 2001: *The Trafficking of Children into the UK for Sexual Purposes*. London: End Child Prostitution in Asian Tourism.

Enloe, C., 1989: *Bananas, Beaches and Bases: Making feminist sense of international politics*. Berkeley: University of California Press.

Enloe, C., 1993: *The Morning After: Sexual politics at the end of the Cold War*. Berkeley: University of California Press.

Ennew, J., 1986: *The Sexual Exploitation of Children*. Cambridge: Polity.

Esadze, L., 2003: 'Trafficking in women and children: A case study of Georgia', paper presented to the Second Preparatory Seminar for the Eleventh OSCE Economic Forum 'National and International Economic Impact of Trafficking in Human Beings', Ioannina, Greece, 17–18 February.

ESCAP, 2000: *Sexually Abused and Sexually Exploited Children and Youth in the Greater Mekong Subregion*. New York: United Nations, Economic and Social Commission for Asia and the Pacific.

Euler, C. and Welzer-Lang, D., 2000: *Developing Best Professional Practice for Reducing Sexual Abuse, Domestic Violence and Trafficking in Militarised Areas of Peacetime Europe*. The Research Centre on Violence, Abuse and Gender Relations, Leeds Metropolitan University, Calverley St, Leeds LS1 3HE, UK.

Evans, D., 1993: *Sexual Citizenship*. London: Routledge.

Faugier, J. and Sargeant, M., 1997: 'Boyfriends, pimps and clients', in G. Scambler and A. Scambler (eds) *Rethinking Prostitution*. London: Routledge.

Faulkner, W., 1961: *The Wild Palms*. Harmondsworth: Penguin.

Feingold, D., 1998: 'Sex, drugs and the IMF: Some implications of "Structural Adjustment" for the trade in heroin, girls and women in the Upper Mekong Region', *Refuge*, Vol. 17, No. 5, Special Issue.

Feingold, D., 2000: 'The hell of good intentions: Some preliminary thoughts on opium in the political ecology of the trade in girls and women', in G. Evans, C. Hutton and K. Eng (eds) *Where China Meets Southeast Asia: Social and cultural change in the border regions*. Singapore: Institute of Southeast Asian Studies.

Fenichel, O., 1954 [1935]: 'The scopophilic instinct and identification', in H. Fenichel and D. Rappaport (eds) *The Collected Papers of Otto Fenichel*, First Series, London: Routledge & Kegan Paul.

Fernandez, N., 1999: 'Back to the future? Women, race and tourism in Cuba', in K. Kempadoo (ed.) *Sun, Sex, and Gold: Tourism and sex work in the Caribbean*. Oxford: Rowman and Littlefield.

Foggo, D., 2002: 'It's like a sweet shop: If this girl's not right, get another', *Daily Telegraph*, 15 September.

Folkationen mot Pornagrafi, 1996: *Commercial Child Pornography in Sweden: Silenced knowledge and obscured oppression*. Stockholm: Folkationen mot Pornagrafi.

Ford, K. and Wirawan, D., 2000: 'Tourism and commercial sex in Indonesia', in S. Clift and S. Carter (eds) *Tourism and Sex: Culture, commerce and coercion*. London: Pinter.

FPA, HK, 2000: *Report on the Youth Sexuality Study, 1996*. Hong Kong: Family Planning Association.

Freedland, J., 1996: 'A sex lesson too far', *Guardian*, 21 February.

Friedman, M., 1962: *Capitalism and Freedom*. Chicago: University of Chicago Press.

Frith, M., 2003: 'Children given "golden goodbyes" to leave home', *The Independent*, 18 July.

Fryer, P., 1984: *Staying Power*. London: Pluto.

Gagnon, J. and Parker, R., 1995: 'Conceiving sexuality', in R. Parker and J. Gagnon (eds) *Conceiving Sexuality: Approaches to sex research in a postmodern world*. London: Routledge.

Gallagher, A., 2001: 'Human rights and the new UN protocols on trafficking and migrant smuggling: A preliminary analysis', *Human Rights Quarterly*, Vol. 23, No. 4, pp. 975–1004.

Gallagher, A., 2002: 'Trafficking, smuggling and human rights: Tricks and treaties', *Forced Migration Review*, No. 12, pp. 25–8.

Gathorne-Hardy, J., 1999: *Alfred Kinsey: A biography*. London: Pimlico.

Geary, D., 2004: 'Europe and slave protests in the Americas (1780–1850)', *Mitteilungsblatt des Instituts für Soziale Bewegungen*, Heft 31. Bochum: Ruhr University.

Geraci, J., 1997: *Dares to Speak: Historical and contemporary perspectives on boy-love*. London: Gay Men's Press.

Geras, N., 1998: *The Contract of Mutual Indifference*. London: Verso.

Gibson, B., 1995: *Male Order: Stories from boys who sell sex*. London: Cassell.

Giddens, A., 1992: *The Transformation of Intimacy: Sexuality, love and eroticism in modern societies*. Cambridge: Polity.

Gilfoyle, T., 1992: *City of Eros: New York City, prostitution and the commercialization of sex*. New York: W.W. Norton.

Gill, L., 2003: 'Consuming passions: The school of the Americas and imperial sexuality', *American Sexuality Magazine*, Vol. 1, No. 5, *www.nsrc.sfsu.edu*

Gillan, A., 2003: 'If you break your promise lightning will kill you', *Guardian*, 30 July.

Golman, A., 1996: 'Give her a piece of land to grow', in W. Wang (ed.) *Give Her a Piece of Land to Grow*. Tapei: End Child Prostitution in Asian Tourism Taiwan.

Goodall, R., 1995: *The Comfort of Sin: Prostitutes and prostitution in the 1990s*. Folkestone: Renaissance Books.

Grittner, F., 1990: *White Slavery: Myth, ideology and American law*. New York: Garland.

Günther, A., 1998: 'Sex tourism without sex tourists', in M. Opperman (ed.) *Sex Tourism and Prostitution: Aspects of leisure, recreation and work*. New York: Cognizant Communications.

Haaken, J., 1999: 'Heretical texts: *The Courage to Heal* and the incest survivor movement', in S. Lamb (ed.) *New Versions of Victims: Feminist struggle with the concept*. London: New York University Press.

Haavio-Mannila, E. and Rotkirch, A., 2000: 'Gender liberalisation and polarisation: Comparing sexuality in St Petersburg, Finland and Sweden', *The Finnish Review of East European Studies*, Vol. 7, Nos. 3–4, pp. 4–25.

Hall, C., 1994: 'Gender and economic interests in tourism prostitution: The nature, development and implications of sex tourism in South-East Asia', in V. Kinnaird and D. Hall (eds), *Tourism: A gender perspective*. London: Routledge.

Hall, C., 1998: 'The legal and political dimensions of sex tourism: The case of Australia's child sex tourism legislation', in M. Opperman (ed.) *Sex Tourism and Prostitution: Aspects of leisure, recreation and work*. New York: Cognizant Communications.

Hammer, D., 1997: *Thai Scene*. Swaffham: Gay Men's Press.

Hartman, C., Burgess, A. and Lanning, K., 1984: 'Typology of collectors', in A. Wolbert Burgess (ed.) *Child Pornography and Sex Rings*. Lexington, MA: Lexington Books.

Hartsock, N., 1985: *Money, Sex and Power*. Boston: Northeastern University Press.

Hashim, I., 2003: 'Discourse(s) of childhood', paper presented to 'Child Abuse and Exploitation: Social, Legal and Political Dilemmas Workshop', International Institute for the Sociology of Law, Onati, 29–30 May.

Hausbeck, K. and Brents, B., 2000: 'Inside Nevada's brothel industry', in R. Weitzer (ed.) *Sex for Sale*. London: Routledge.

Hawkes, S., Hart, G., Johnson, A., Shergold, C., Ross, E., Herbert, K., Mortimer, P., Parry, J. and Mabey, D., 1994: 'Risk behaviour and HIV prevalence in international travellers', *AIDS*, Vol. 8, pp. 247–52.

Herdt, G., 1982: *Rituals of Manhood: Male initiation in Papua New Guinea*. Berkeley: University of California Press.

Higate, P., 2003: 'Revealing the soldier: Peacekeeping and prostitution', *American Sexuality Magazine*, Vol. 1, No. 5, www.nsrc.sfsu.edu

Hinsliff, G., 2003: 'Children forced into UK slavery', *Observer*, 18 May.

Hobson, J. and Heung, V., 1998: 'Business travel and the emergence of the modern Chinese concubine', in M. Oppermann (ed.) *Sex Tourism and Prostitution: Aspects of leisure, recreation and work*. New York: Cognizant Communications.

Hoffman, J., 2001: 'Is victimhood compatible with contract?', paper presented to the ESRC seminar series, 'Beyond Contract: Border, Bodies and Bonds', University of Warwick, 14 December.

Hoigard, C. and Finstad, L., 1992: *Backstreets: Prostitution, money and love*. Cambridge: Polity.

Home Office, 1996: *Action against the Commercial Sexual Exploitation of Children*. London: Home Office Communication Directorate.

*Hong Kong Economic Times*, 1993: 'Sacrifice a generation of women to obtain economic development', *Hong Kong Economic Times*, 2 August.

Howard, D., 1999: *Dominican Republic*. London: Latin America Bureau.

HRW, 2002: 'Hopes betrayed: Trafficking of women and girls to post-conflict Bosnia and Herzegovina for forced prostitution', *Human Rights Watch*, Vol. 14, No. 9, November.

HRW, 2003: *Stop the Use of Child Soldiers!* New York: Human Rights Watch.

Hubbard, D. (ed.) 2002: *'Whose Body is it?' Commercial sex work and the law in Namibia*. Windhoek: Legal Assistance Centre.

Hughes, D., 2000: 'Men create the demand; women are the supply', *Feminista!*, Vol. 4, No. 3, *www.feminista.com/archives/v4n3/hughes.html*

Hyam, R., 1990: *Empire and Sexuality: The British experience*. Manchester: Manchester University Press.

IAF, 2001: Special Issue: Prostitution in the Nordic Countries. *International Abolitionist Federation Newsletter*. August.

Institute for Public Policy, Moldova, 2003: *National Report on the Phenomenon of Trafficking in Children for Sexual Exploitation and Labour in Moldova*. Moldova: Institute for Public Policy.

ILO, 1996: *Child Labour: Targeting the intolerable*. Geneva: International Labour Organization.

ILO, 2002: 'Getting at the roots: Stopping exploitation of migrant workers by organized crime'. International Labour Office. Paper presented to International Symposium on the UN Convention Against Transnational Organized Crime: Requirements for Effective Implementation. Turin, 22–3 February.

INSAF, 1995: *The Needs of Children in Goa: Towards building an adequate response. Interim report*. Panjim: Indian National Social Action Forum.

Ireland, K., 1993: *Wish You Weren't Here*. London: Save the Children.

IRIN, 2003: 'Focus on the "sugar daddy" phenomenon'. Johannesburg: Integrated Regional Information Networks, 24 July.

Itzin, C., 2000: 'Child sexual abuse and the radical feminist endeavour', in C. Itzin (ed.) *Home Truths About Child Sexual Abuse*. London: Routledge.

IUSW, 2003: 'Common arguments against prostitution', *www.iusw.org* (International Union of Sex Workers).

Jackson, S. and Scott, S., 2000: 'Childhood', in G. Payne (ed.) *Social Divisions*. Houndmills: Macmillan.

James, A. and Prout, A., 1997: 'A new paradigm for the sociology of childhood? Provenance, promise and problems', in A. James and A. Prout (eds) *Constructing and Reconstructing Childhood: Contemporary issues in the sociological study of childhood*. (second edition). London: Falmer.

James, A., Jenks, C. and Prout, A., 1998: *Theorizing Childhood*. Cambridge: Polity.

*Japan Times*, 1998: 'Survey shows friends and family influence "enjo kosai" trend'. *The Japan Times*, 23 April.

Javate de Dios, A., 2002: 'Revisiting the issue of trafficking in women: Comments on policy implications of a gender and rights framework', paper presented to ASEM Seminar, Promoting Gender Equality to Combat Trafficking in Women and Children, organized by the Swedish Ministry for Foreign Affairs, Bangkok, 7–9 October.

Jeffreys, S., 1990: *Anticlimax: A feminist perspective on the sexual revolution*. London: Women's Press.

Jeffreys, S., 1997: *The Idea of Prostitution*. Melbourne: Spinifex.

Jenks, C., 1996: *Childhood*. London: Routledge.

Johnson, K., 2000: 'Pedophile playground', *TIME Asia*, 13 November.

Jordan, J., 1997: 'User buys: Why men buy sex', *Australian and New Zealand Journal of Criminology*, Vol. 30, pp. 55–71.

Kadjar-Hamouda, E., 1996: *An End to Silence: A preliminary study on sexual violence, abuse and exploitation of children affected by armed conflict.* Geneva: NGO Group for the Convention on the Rights of the Child.

Kane, J., 1998: *Sold for Sex.* Aldershot: Arena.

Kane, S., 1993: 'Prostitution and the military in Belize: Planning AIDS intervention in Belize', *Social Science and Medicine*, Vol. 36, No. 7, pp. 965–79.

Kannabiran, K., 1996: 'Rape and the construction of communal identity', in K. Jayawardena and M. De Alwis (eds), *Embodied Violence: Communalising women's sexuality in South Asia.* London: Zed.

Karlen, H., 1996: 'Foreword' to M. Axelsson, *Rosario is Dead.* Stockholm: Raben Prisma.

Kelly, J., Gray, H., Sewankambo, N., Serwadda, D., Wabwire-Mangen, F., Lutalo, T. and Wawer, M., 2003: 'Age differences in sexual partners and risk of HIV-1 infection in rural Uganda', *Journal of Acquired Immune Deficiency Syndromes*, Vol. 32, No. 4, pp. 446–51.

Kelly, L., 1996: 'Paedophiles and the cycle of abuse', *Trouble & Strife*, No. 33, pp. 44–9.

Kelly, L. and Regan, L., 2000a: *Rhetorics and Realities: Sexual exploitation of children in Europe.* London: Child and Woman Abuse Studies Unit.

Kelly, L. and Regan, L. 2000b: 'Stopping traffic: Exploring the extent of and responses to trafficking in women for sexual exploitation in the UK', *Police Research Series*, Paper 125. London: Home Office.

Kempadoo, K., 1994: 'Prostitution, marginality and empowerment: Caribbean women in the sex trade'. *Beyond Law.* Vol. 5, No. 14, pp. 69–84.

Kempadoo, K. (ed.) 1999a: *Sun, Sex, and Gold: Tourism and sex work in the Caribbean.* Oxford: Rowman and Littlefield.

Kempadoo, K., 1999b: 'Continuities and change', in K. Kempadoo (ed.) *Sun, Sex and Gold: Tourism and sex work in the Caribbean.* Oxford: Rowman and Littlefield.

Kempadoo, K., 1999c: 'Slavery or work? Reconceptualizing Third World prostitution', *Positions*, Vol. 7, No. 1, pp. 225–37.

Kempadoo, K., 2001: 'Freelancers, temporary wives, and beach-boys: Researching sex work in the Caribbean', *Feminist Review*, No. 67, pp. 39–62.

Kempadoo, K. and Doezema, J. (eds) 1998: *Global Sex Workers: Rights, resistance and redefinition.* London: Routledge.

Kempadoo, K. and Ghuma, R., 1999: 'For the children: Trends in international policies and law on sex tourism', in K. Kempadoo (ed.) *Sun, Sex and Gold: Tourism and sex work in the Caribbean.* Oxford: Rowman and Littlefield.

Khan, S., 1999: 'Through a window darkly: Men who sell sex to men in India and Bangladesh', in P. Aggleton (ed.) *Men Who Sell Sex.* London: UCL.

Kincaid, J., 1992: *Child-Loving: The erotic child and Victorian culture.* New York: Routledge.

Kincaid, J., 1998: *Erotic Innocence: The culture of child molesting.* Durham, NC: Duke University Press.

King, R., 2002: 'Towards a new map of European migration', *International Journal of Population Geography*, Vol. 8, pp. 89–106.

Kinnell, H., 1991: *Prostitutes' Experience of Being in Care: Results of a safe project investigation.* Birmingham Community Health Trust, Safe Project.

Kinsey, A., Pomeroy, W. and Martin, C., 1948: *Sexual Behavior in the Human Male*. Philadelphia: Saunders.

Kitzinger, J., 1997: 'Who are you kidding? Children, power and the struggle against sexual abuse', in A. James and A. Prout (eds) *Constructing and Reconstructing Childhood: Contemporary issues in the sociological study of childhood* (second edition) London: Falmer.

Kleiber, D. and Wilke, M., 1995: 'AIDS and sex tourism: Conclusions drawn from a study of the social and psychological characteristics of German sex tourists', in D. Friedrich and W. Heckmann (eds) *AIDS in Europe: The behavioural aspect. Vol. 2: Risk behaviour and its determinants*. Berlin: Edition Sigma.

Krafft-Ebing, R. von, 1965 [1891]: *Psychopathia Sexualis: A medico-economic study*. New York: Putnam & Sons.

Kruhse-Mount Burton, S., 1995: 'Sex tourism and traditional Australian male identity', in M. Lafabt, J. Allcock and E. Bruner (eds) *International Tourism: Identity and change*. London: Sage.

Kvinnoforum and Kvinna till Kvinna, 2003: *IOM Regional Counter-Trafficking Programme in the Western Balkans*. Stockholm: Sida.

La Fontaine, J., 1990: *Child Sexual Abuse*. Cambridge: Polity.

Lamb, S. (ed.) 1999: *New Versions of Victims: Feminist struggle with the concept*. New York: New York University Press.

Lanning, K., 1984: 'Collectors', in A. Wolbert Burgess (ed.) *Child Pornography and Sex Rings*. Lexington, MA: Lexington Books.

Laurindo da Silva, L., 1999: 'Travestis and gigolos: Male sex work and HIV prevention in France', in P. Aggleton (ed.) *Men Who Sell Sex*. London: UCL.

Lederer, L., 1996: *National Legislation on and International Trafficking in Child Pornography*. Center on Speech, Equality and Harm, University of Minnesota Law School, Minneapolis, MN 55455, USA.

Lee-Wright, P., 1990: *Child Slaves*. London: Earthscan.

LeFranc, E. (ed.), 1994: *Consequences of Structural Adjustment: A review of the Jamaican experience*. Kingston: Canoe Press.

Leridon, H., Zesson, G. and Hubert, M., 1998: 'The Europeans and their sexual partners', in M. Hubert, N. Bajos and T. Sandfort (eds) *Sexual Behaviour and HIV/AIDS in Europe*. London: UCL.

Lever, J. and Dolnick, D., 2000: 'Clients and call girls: Seeking sex and intimacy', in R. Weitzer (ed.) *Sex for Sale*. New York: Routledge.

Lévi-Strauss, C., 1971: 'The family', in H. Shapiro (ed.) *Man, Culture and Society*. London: Oxford University Press.

Li, C., West, D. and Woodhouse, T., 1990: *Children's Sexual Encounters with Adults*. London: Duckworth.

Liberty, 2002: 'The Liberty guide to human rights', *www.YourRights.org.uk*

Lim, L., 1998: *The Sex Sector: The economic and social bases of prostitution in Southeast Asia*. Geneva: International Labour Office.

Lindgren, L., 1996: 'The World Congress – an important turning point', *Barnen Och Vi*, Special Features Issue. Stockholm: Radda Barnen.

Lister, R., 1997: *Citizenship: Feminist perspectives*. Houndmills: Macmillan.

Lively, A., 1999: *Blackness, Race and the Imagination*. London: Vintage.

Locke, J., 1993 [1689]: *The Second Treatise on Civil Government*, in *Locke's Political Writings*, ed. D. Wootton. London: Penguin.

Lott, T., 1998: *Subjection and Bondage*. Oxford: Rowman and Littlefield.

Lutzen, K., 1995: '*La mise en discours* and silences in research on the history of sexuality', in J. Gagnon and R. Parker (eds) *Conceiving Sexuality*. London: Routledge.

McClintock, A., 1995: *Imperial Leather: Race, gender and sexuality in the colonial contest*. London: Routledge.

McGill, C., 2003: *Human Traffic: Sex, slaves and immigration*. London: Vision.

MacInnes, J., 1998: *The End of Masculinity*. Buckingham: Open University Press.

McIntosh, M., 1996: 'Feminist debates on prostitution', in L. Adkins and V. Merchant (eds) *Sexualizing the Social*. London: Macmillan.

McIntyre, S., 1999: 'The youngest profession – the oldest oppression: A study of sex work', in C. Bagley and M. Kanka (eds) *Child Sexual Abuse and Adult Offenders: New theory and research*. Aldershot: Ashgate.

McKeganey, N. and Barnard, M., 1996: *Sex Work on the Streets: Prostitutes and their clients*. Buckingham: Open University Press.

MacKinnon, C., 1988: 'Desire and power: A feminist perspective', in C. Nelson and L. Grossberg (eds) *Marxism and the Interpretation of Culture*. London: Macmillan Education.

Månsson, S.-A., 2001: 'Prostitutes' clients and the image of men and masculinity in late modern society', in B. Pease and K. Pringle (eds) *A Man's World? Changing men's practices in a globalized world*. London: Zed.

Marriott, D., 2000: *On Black Men*. Edinburgh: Edinburgh University Press.

Marx, K., 1977: *Economic and Philosophic Manuscripts of 1844*. London: Lawrence & Wishart.

Masters, B., 1993: *The Shrine of Jeffrey Dahmer*. London: Hodder & Stoughton.

Matthews, R., 1997: *Prostitution in London: An audit*. London: Middlesex University.

Mayorga, L., 1998: 'Life history interviews of people living in a poor urban community in Santafé de Bogatá, 1996–1998'. Unpublished paper.

Mayorga, L. and Velasquez, P., 1999: 'Bleak pasts, bleak futures: Life paths of thirteen young prostitutes in Cartagena, Colombia', in K. Kempadoo (ed.) *Sun, Sex, and Gold: Tourism and sex work in the Caribbean*. Oxford: Rowman and Littlefield.

Meisch, L., 1995: 'Gringas and otavalenos: Changing tourist relations', *Annals of Tourism Research*, Vol. 22, No. 2, pp. 441–62.

Melrose, M., Barrett, D. and Brodie, I. 1999: *One Way Street? Retrospectives on Childhood Prostitution*. London: The Children's Society.

Mickelson, R. (ed.), 2000: *Children on the Streets of the Americas*. London: Routledge.

Midgley, C., 1998: 'Anti-slavery and the roots of "imperial feminism"', in C. Midgley (ed.) *Gender and Imperialism*. Manchester: Manchester University Press.

Miles, R., 1987: *Capitalism and Unfree Labour*. London: Tavistock.

Mill, J.S., 1910 [1859]: *On Liberty*. London: Routledge.

Miller, W., 1997: *The Anatomy of Disgust*. Cambridge, MA: Harvard University Press.

Mills, C., 1998: *The Racial Contract*. Ithaca, NY: Cornell University Press.

Mitter, S., 1986: *Common Fate, Common Bond: Women in the global economy*. London: Pluto Press.

Montgomery, H., 1998: 'Children, prostitution and identity: A case study from a tourist resort in Thailand', in K. Kempadoo and J. Doezema (eds) *Global Sex Workers: Rights, resistance and redefinition*. London: Routledge.

Montgomery, H., 2001: *Modern Babylon? Prostituting children in Thailand.* Oxford: Berghahn Books.

Monto, M., 2000: 'Why men seek out prostitutes', in R. Weitzer (ed.) *Sex for Sale.* London: Routledge.

Moon, K., 1997: *Sex Among Allies.* New York: Columbia University Press.

Morris-Jarra, M., 1996: 'No such thing as a cheap holiday', *Tourism in Focus*, No. 26, Autumn, pp. 6–7.

Morrison, J. 2000: 'The policy implications arising from the trafficking and smuggling of refugees into Europe'. Documentation of the European Conference 'Children First and Foremost – Policies towards Separated Children in Europe'. Stockholm: Save the Children Sweden.

Morse, E., Simon, P. and Burchfiel, K., 1999: 'Social environment and male sex work in the United States', in P. Aggleton (ed.) *Men Who Sell Sex.* London: UCL.

Moya, E. de and García, R., 1999: 'Three decades of male sex work in Santo Domingo', in P. Aggleton (ed.) *Men Who Sell Sex.* London: UCL.

Muntarbhorn, V., 1996: 'International perspectives and child prostitution in Asia', in US Department of Labor and Bureau of International Labor Affairs, *Forced Labor: The prostitution of children.* Washington, DC: United States Department of Labor, Bureau of International Labor Affairs.

Muntarbhorn, V., 1998: *Extraterritorial Criminal Laws Against Child Sexual Exploitation.* Geneva: UNICEF.

Muntarbhorn, V., 2001: *Report of the Second World Congress against Commercial Sexual Exploitation of Children.* Yokohama, 17–20 December.

NACLA, 1997: Report on the Americas, *North American Congress on Latin America*, Vol. 30, No. 5.

Naegele, J., 2001: 'Albania: Growth rates steady, but emigration on rise', *www.rferl.org/nca/features/2001/10/19102001094916.asp*

Nagel, Joane, 2003: *Race, Ethnicity and Sexuality.* Oxford: Oxford University Press.

Nagle, J. (ed.), 1997: *Whores and Other Feminists.* London: Routledge.

Nencel, L., 2001: *Ethnography and Prostitution in Peru.* London: Pluto.

NGO Group for the Convention on the Rights of the Child, 1996: *United Nations Mechanisms for Use by National NGOs in the Combat against the Sexual Exploitation of Children.* Geneva: NGO Group for the Convention on the Rights of the Child.

NSWP, 1999: 'Commentary on the draft Protocol to Combat International Trafficking in Women and Children supplementary to the draft Convention on Transnational Organized Crime', *www.walnet.org/nswp* (Network of Sex Work Projects).

Nzula, A., Potekhin, I. and Zusmanovich, A., 1979: *Forced Labour in Colonial Africa.* London: Zed.

O'Carroll, T., 1980: *Paedophilia: The radical case.* London: Peter Owen.

O'Connell Davidson, J., 1995: 'British sex tourists in Thailand', in M. Maynard and J. Purvis (eds) *(Hetero)Sexual Politics.* London: Taylor and Francis.

O'Connell Davidson, J., 1996: 'The sex exploiter', theme paper for the First World Congress Against the Commercial Sexual Exploitation of Children, Stockholm, August.

O'Connell Davidson, J., 1998: *Prostitution, Power and Freedom.* Cambridge: Polity.

O'Connell Davidson, J., 2001a: 'The sex exploiter', theme paper for the Second World Congress Against the Commercial Sexual Exploitation of Children, Yokohama, December.

O'Connell Davidson, J., 2001b: 'The sex tourist, the expatriate, his ex-wife and her "Other": The politics of loss, difference and desire', *Sexualities*, Vol. 4, No. 1, pp. 5–24.

O'Connell Davidson, J., 2001c: *Children in the Sex Trade in China*. Stockholm: Save the Children Sweden.

O'Connell Davidson, J., 2002: 'The rights and wrongs of prostitution', *Hypatia*, Vol. 17, No. 2, pp. 84–98.

O'Connell Davidson, J. and Sánchez Taylor, J., 1996a: 'Child prostitution: Beyond the stereotypes', in J. Pilcher and S. Wagg (eds) *Thatcher's Children? Politics, childhood and society in the 1980s and 90s*. London: Falmer.

O'Connell Davidson, J. and Sánchez Taylor, J., 1996b: *Child Prostitution and Sex Tourism in South Africa*. Research Paper. Bangkok: End Child Prostitution in Asian Tourism.

O'Connell Davidson, J. and Sánchez Taylor, J., 1996c: *Child Prostitution and Sex Tourism in Goa*. Research Paper. Bangkok: End Child Prostitution in Asian Tourism.

O'Connell Davidson, J. and Sánchez Taylor, J., 1996d: *Child Prostitution and Sex Tourism in Costa Rica*. Research Paper. Bangkok: End Child Prostitution in Asian Tourism.

O'Connell Davidson, J. and Sánchez Taylor, J., 1999: 'Fantasy islands: Exploring the demand for sex tourism', in K. Kempadoo (ed.) *Sun, Sex and Gold: Tourism and sex work in the Caribbean*. Oxford: Rowman & Littlefield.

O'Connell Davidson, J. and Sánchez Taylor, J., 2001: *Children in the Sex Trade in the Caribbean*. Stockholm: Save the Children Sweden.

O'Grady, R., 1993: *The Rape of the Innocent*. Bangkok: End Child Prostitution in Asian Tourism.

O'Grady, R., 1996: *The ECPAT Story: A personal account of the first six years in the life of ECPAT*. Bangkok: End Child Prostitution in Asian Tourism.

O'Neill, M., 1997: 'Prostitute women now', in G. Scambler and A. Scambler (eds) *Rethinking Prostitution: Purchasing sex in the 1990s*. London: Routledge.

O'Neill, M. and Barberet, R., 2000: 'Victimization and the social organization of prostitution in England and Spain', in R. Weitzer (ed.) *Sex for Sale*. London: Routledge.

Opperman, M. (ed.), 1998: *Sex Tourism and Prostitution: Aspects of leisure, recreation and work*. New York: Cognizant Communications.

Palmer, G., 1983: *British Industrial Relations*. London: George Allen & Unwin.

Pateman, C., 1988: *The Sexual Contract*. Cambridge: Polity.

Pateman, C., 1992: 'Equality, difference, subordination: The politics of motherhood and women's citizenship', in G. Bock and S. James (eds) *Beyond Equality and Difference: Citizenship, feminist politics, female subjectivity*. London: Routledge.

Parekh, B., 1995: 'Liberalism and colonialism: A critique of Locke and Mill', in J. Nederveen and B. Parekh (eds) *The Decolonization of Imagination*. London: Zed.

Patterson, O., 1982: *Slavery and Social Death*. Cambridge, MA: Harvard University Press.

Patullo, P., 1996: *Last Resorts: The cost of tourism in the Caribbean*. London: Latin America Bureau.

Pheterson, G., 1989: *A Vindication of the Rights of Whores*. Seattle: Seal Press.

Phillips, A., 2002: *Equals*. London: Faber & Faber.

Phillips, J., 1999: 'Tourist-oriented prostitution in Barbados: The case of the beach boy and the white female tourist', in K. Kempadoo (ed.) *Sun, Sex and Gold: Tourism and sex work in the Caribbean.* Oxford: Rowman and Littlefield.

Phoenix, J., 1999: *Making Sense of Prostitution.* Houndmills: Macmillan.

Phongpaichit, P., 1999: 'Trafficking in people in Thailand', in P. Williams (ed.) *Illegal Immigration and Commercial Sex: The new slave trade.* London: Frank Cass.

PIE, 1978: *Paedophilia: Some questions and answers.* London: Paedophile Information Exchange.

Pilcher, J., 1995: *Age and Generation in Modern Britain.* Oxford: Oxford University Press.

Plumridge, E., Chetwynd, J., Reed, A. and Gifford, S., 1997: 'Discourses and emotionality in commercial sex: The missing client voice', *Feminism and Psychology*, Vol. 7, No. 2, pp. 165–81.

Potts, L., 1990: *The World Market for Labour.* London: Zed.

*Pravda*, 2003: 'Human trafficking practiced all over the world', *Pravda*, 15 May, *english.pravda.ru/main/18/90/361/9989trafficking.html*

Prokhovnic, R., 1999: *Rational Woman: A feminist critique of dichotomy.* London: Routledge.

Prosser, D., 1999: *A World for Children.* Series broadcast 18 September–23 October, BBC World Service.

Psimmenos, I., 2000: 'The making of periphractic spaces: The case of Albanian undocumented female migrants in the sex industry of Athens', in F. Anthias and G. Lazaridis (eds) *Gender and Migration in Southern Europe.* Oxford: Berg.

Puwar, N., 2004: *Space Invaders: Race, gender and bodies out of place.* Oxford: Berg.

Pyne, H.H., 1995: 'AIDS and gender violence: The enslavement of Burmese women in the Thai sex industry', in J. Peters and A. Wolper (eds) *Women's Rights, Human Rights: International feminist perspectives.* New York: Routledge.

Radda Barnen, 1996: *Barnen Och Vi*, Special Feature Issue.

Ramdin, R., 1994: *The Other Middle Passage.* London: Hansib.

Ratnapala, N., 1999: 'Male sex work in Sri Lanka', in P. Aggleton (ed.) *Men Who Sell Sex.* London: UCL.

Raymond, J., 2001: *Guide to the New UN Trafficking Protocol.* North Amherst, MA: Coalition Against Trafficking in Women.

Ren, X., 1993: 'China', in N. Davis (ed.) *Prostitution.* Westport, CT: Greenwood Press.

Ribbens McCarthy, J., Edwards, R. and Gillies, V., 2000: 'Moral tales of the child and the adult: Narratives of contemporary family lives under changing circumstances', *Sociology*, Vol. 34, No. 4, pp. 785–803.

Ritzer, G., 2001: *Explorations in the Sociology of Consumption.* London: Sage.

Rodriguez, L., Guven-Lisaniler, F. and Ugural, S., 2001: 'Sex work and state regulations in North Cyprus', paper presented to the International Political Economy Association annual conference, Florence, 8–11 November.

Ross, E. and Rapp, R., 1981: 'Sex and society: A research note from social history and anthropology', *Comparative Studies in Society and History*, No. 23, pp. 51–72.

Roujanavong, W., 1994: 'Thailand's image attracts the wrong people', *ECPAT Newsletter*, No. 11, December.

Rozzi, E., 2002: *The Evaluation of the Best Interests of the Child in the Choice between Remaining in the Host Country and Repatriation: A reflection based on the Convention on the Rights of the Child*. Rome: Save the Children Italy.

Rubin, G., 1993: 'Misguided, dangerous and wrong: An analysis of anti-pornography politics', in A. Assiter and A. Carol (eds) *Bad Girls and Dirty Pictures*. London: Pluto.

Rubin, G., 1997: 'The traffic in women: Notes on the "political economy" of sex', in L. Nicholson (ed.) *The Second Wave: A reader in feminist theory*. London: Routledge.

Rubin, G., 1999: 'Thinking sex: Notes for a radical theory of the politics of sexuality', in R. Parker and P. Aggleton (eds) *Culture, Society and Sexuality: A reader*. London: UCL.

Rusakova, M., 2001: *The Commercial Sexual Exploitation of Children in St Petersburg and North West Russia*. Stockholm: Save the Children Sweden.

Ryan, C., 2000: 'Sex tourism: Paradigms of confusion', in S. Carter and S. Clift (eds) *Tourism and Sex: Culture, commerce and coercion*. London: Pinter.

Ryan, C. and Hall, M., 2001: *Sex Tourism: Marginal People and Liminalities*. London: Routledge.

SACCS, 1999: *Invisible Slaves*. New Delhi: South Asian Coalition on Child Servitude.

Saeed, F., 2002: *Taboo! The hidden culture of a red light area*. Oxford: Oxford University Press.

Safa, H., 1997: 'Where the big fish eat the little fish: Women's work in the Free Trade Zones', Report on the Americas, *North American Congress on Latin America*, Vol. 30, No. 5, pp. 31–6.

Sánchez Taylor, J., 2000: 'Tourism and "embodied" commodities: Sex tourism in the Caribbean', in S. Clift and S. Carter (eds) *Tourism and Sex: Culture, commerce and coercion*. London: Pinter.

Sánchez Taylor, J., 2001a: *A Fine Romance? Tourist women and local men's sexual economic exchanges in the Caribbean*. Ph.D. thesis, Department of Sociology, University of Leicester.

Sánchez Taylor, J., 2001b: 'Dollars are a girl's best friend? Female tourists' sexual behaviour in the Caribbean', *Sociology*, Vol. 35, No. 3, pp. 749–64.

Sanghera, J., 2002: 'Enabling and empowering mobile women and girls: Strategy paper on the safe migration and citizenship rights of women and adolescent girls', paper presented to Swedish Ministry for Foreign Affairs and United Nations Development Fund for Women Seminar on Promoting Gender Equality to Combat Trafficking in Women and Children, Bangkok, Thailand, 7–9 October.

Sayer, D., 1991: *Capitalism and Modernity: An excursus on Marx and Weber*. London: Routledge.

Scambler, G. and Scambler, A. (eds), 1997: *Rethinking Prostitution: Purchasing sex in the 1990s*. London: Routledge.

Scheper-Hughes, N., 1992: *Death without Weeping: The violence of everyday life in Brazil*. Berkeley: University of California Press.

Seabrook, J., 1996: *Travels in the Skin Trade: Tourism and the sex industry*. London: Pluto.

Seabrook, J., 2000: *No Hiding Place: Child sex tourism and the role of extraterritorial legislation*. London: Zed.

Seabrook, J., 2001: *Children of Other Worlds: Exploitation in the global market*. London: Pluto.

Shelley, L., 2003: 'Trafficking in women: The business model approach', paper presented to Organization for Security and Cooperation in Europe Second Preparatory Seminar for the Eleventh OSCE Economic Forum 'National and International Economic impact of Trafficking in Human Beings', Ioannina, Greece, 17–18 February.

Siden, A., 2002: *Warte Mal! Prostitution after the Velvet Revolution.* London: Hayward Gallery.

Silbert, M. and Pines, A., 1981: 'Sexual abuse as an antecedent to prostitution', *Child Abuse and Neglect*, Vol. 5, pp. 407–11.

Silvestre, E., Rijo, J. and Bogaert, H., 1994: *La Neo-prostitucion Infantil en Republica Dominicana.* Santa Domingo: UNICEF.

Simpson, A., 2001: *The Measure of a Man: Boys, young men and dangerous ideologies of masculinity in the time of HIV/AIDS.* Report for Save The Children Sweden.

Sklair, L., 2002: *Globalization: Capitalism and its alternatives.* Oxford: Oxford University Press.

Skrobanek, S., Boonpakdi, N. and Janthankeero, C., 1997: *The Traffic in Women.* London: Zed.

Smith, A., 2000: 'Beyond the hysteria', *Screaming Hyena*, e-journal of Queer Writing and Review, Issue 13–14.

Social Care Group, 1999: *UN Convention on the Rights of the Child, 1989: Second UK report.* London: Department of Health.

*South China Sunday Morning Post*, 1994: 'Question of sex raised in survey', *South China Sunday Morning Post*, 6 February.

Steele-Perkins, C., 2003: 'The last resort', *Observer Magazine*, 29 June.

Stenvoll, D., 2002: 'From Russia with love? Newspaper coverage of cross-border prostitution in Northern Norway 1990–2001', *The European Journal of Women's Studies*, Vol. 9, No. 2, pp. 143–62.

Stoler, A., 1997: 'Carnal knowledge and imperial power', in R. Lancaster and M. di Leonardo (eds) *The Gender Sexuality Reader.* London: Routledge.

Stoller, R., 1975: *Perversion: The erotic form of hatred.* New York: Karnac.

*Straits Times*, 2000: 'Virgin ruse', *Straits Times* (Singapore) Interactive, 16 July, available from *www.bigpond.com.khluserslngoforum/child_prostitution.htm*

Sturdevant, S. and Stoltzfus, B., 1992: *Let the Good Times Roll: Prostitution and the US military in Asia.* New York: New Press.

Sutton, A., 1994: *Slavery in Brazil: A link in the chain of modernization.* London: Anti-Slavery International.

Svensson, B., 2000: *Victims and Perpetrators: On sexual abuse and treatment.* Stockholm: Save the Children Sweden.

Tanaka, Y., 2002: *Japan's Comfort Women: Sexual slavery and prostitution during World War II and the US occupation.* London: Routledge.

Task Force on Trafficking in Human Beings, 2003: Regional Clearing Point, First Annual Report on Victims of Trafficking in South Eastern Europe. Vienna: Stability Pact for South Eastern Europe – Task Force on Trafficking in Human Beings.

Tronto, J., 1989: 'Women and caring: What can feminists learn about morality from caring?', in A. Jaggar and S. Bordo (eds) *Gender/Body/Knowledge: Feminist reconstructions of being and knowing.* London: Rutgers University Press.

Truong, T., 1990: *Sex, Money and Morality: Prostitution and tourism in Southeast Asia.* London: Zed.

Turley, D., 2000: *Slavery*. Oxford: Blackwell.

Turshen, M., 2001: 'The political economy of rape: An analysis of systematic rape and sexual abuse of women during armed conflict in Africa', in C. Moser and F. Clark (eds) *Victims, Perpetrators or Actors? Gender, armed conflict and political violence*. London: Zed.

Uddin, F., Sultana, M. and Mahmud, S. (revised by M. Black and H. Goodman), 2001: *Growing up in the Brothel: Children in the Daulotdia and Kandapara brothel communities of Bangladesh*. Save the Children Australia.

UNHCR, 2000: Refugee Children and Adolescents: A progress report. Executive Committee of the High Commissioner's programme. Geneva: United Nations High Commission for Refugees.

UNHCR, 2001: *How to Guide: Sexual and gender-based violence programme in Liberia*. Geneva: United Nations High Commission for Refugees, Health and Community Development Section.

UNICEF, 2001: *The Situation of Children and Families in the Republic of Moldova, 2000–2001: Assessment and analysis*. Moldova: UNICEF Moldova.

UNICEF, 2003: 'Landmines – a deadly inheritance', *www.unicef.org/graca/mines.html*

UNICEF, ECPAT, NGO Group for the Convention on the Rights of the Child, 1996: *Background Document*. World Congress against Commercial Sexual Exploitation of Children, Stockholm, Sweden, 27–31 August.

United Nations, 1995: Promotion and protection of the rights of children: Sale of children, child prostitution and child pornography. Note by the Secretary-General. Doc. A/50/456. New York, United Nations, General Assembly.

UNRISD, 2000: *Visible Hands: Taking responsibility for social development*. Geneva: United Nations Research Institute for Social Development.

USAID, 2000: *Children on the Brink*. Washington: United States Agency for International Development.

Veblen, T., 1994 [1899]: *Theory of the Leisure Class*. London: Penguin.

Visram, R., 2002: *Asians in Britain: 400 years of history*. London: Pluto.

Vogel, U., 2000: 'Private contract and public institution: The peculiar case of marriage', in M. Passerin d'Entreves and U. Vogel (eds) *Public and Private: Legal, political and philosophical perspectives*. London: Routledge.

Warburton, J. and Camacho de la Cruz, C. 1996: 'A right to happiness', *www.focalpointngo.org*

Webster, P., 1999: 'Teacher free after sex with pupil', *Guardian*, 12 November.

Weeks, J., 1985: *Sexuality and its Discontents*. London: Routledge.

Weeks, J., 1991: *Against Nature: Essays on history, sexuality and identity*. London: Rivers Oram.

Weitzer, R. (ed.), 2000: *Sex for Sale*. London: Routledge.

Wellings, K., Field, J., Johnson, A., Wadworth, J. with Bradshaw, S., 1993: *Sexual Behaviour in Britain: The National Survey of Sexual Attitudes and Lifestyles*. Harmondsworth: Penguin.

West, D., 1992: *Male Prostitution*. London: Duckworth.

WHO, 2003: *Healthy Environments for Children: Facts and figures*, Fact Sheet No. 272. Geneva: World Health Organization, April.

Williams, P.J., 1997: *Seeing a Colour-Blind Future: The paradox of race*. London: Virago.

Williams, S., 1999: *Commercial Sexual Exploitation of Children in Jamaica*. Unpublished report, Caribbean Child Development Centre, School of Continuing Studies, University of the West Indies, Mona, Kingston.

Wilson, W., 1998: *Fantasy Islands: A man's guide to exotic women and international travel*. Alameda, CA: Roam Publishing.

Witter, M. and Kirton, C., 1990: *The Informal Economy in Jamaica: Some empirical exercises*. Working Paper No. 36. Institute of Social and Economic Research, University of the West Indies, Mona, Kingston.

Wolthius, A., 2002: 'Child trafficking from Eastern to Western Europe: the position of the victim', paper presented to the International Congress on Child Trafficking: Young Slaves without Borders, Rome, 11–12 July.

Wood, G., 2001: 'Sex and the city', *The Observer Magazine*, 1 April, pp. 21–3.

Wood, K. and Jewkes, R., 2001: ' "Dangerous" love: Reflections on violence among Xhosa Township youth', in R. Morrell (ed.) *Changing Men in Southern Africa*. London: Zed.

Xie Guangmao, 2000: 'Women and social change along the Vietnam–Guangxi border', in G. Evans, C. Hutton and K. Eng (eds) *Where China Meets Southeast Asia: Social and cultural change in the border regions*. Singapore: Institute of Southeast Asian Studies.

Yavetz, Z., 1988: *Slaves and Slavery in Ancient Rome*. Oxford: Transaction.

Yuval-Davis, N., 1997: *Gender and Nation*. London: Sage.

Zalduondo, B. de and Bernard, J., 1995: 'Meanings and consequences of sexual-economic exchange: Gender, poverty and sexual risk behavior in urban Haiti', in R. Parker and J. Gagnon (eds) *Conceiving Sexuality*. London: Routledge.

Zelalem, Y., 1998: *Clients of Girl Child Prostitutes: Realities from some selected areas of Addis Ababa*. MA thesis, School of Graduate Studies, Addis Ababa University.

Zi Teng, 2000: Report on Conference for Sex Workers in East and South-East Asia, January 4–6. Hong Kong: Zi Teng and Asia Monitor Resource Centre.

# Index